RESEARCHING THE ACCOUNTING CURRICULUM: STRATEGIES FOR CHANGE

RESEARCHING THE ACCOUNTING CURRICULUM: STRATEGIES FOR CHANGE

Editor:
WILLIAM L. FERRARA
Pennsylvania State University

Associate Editors:
JAMES B. BOWER
University of Wisconsin
HAROLD Q. LANGENDERFER
University of North Carolina
MILTON F. USRY
Oklahoma State University
DOYLE Z. WILLIAMS
Texas Tech University

AMERICAN ACCOUNTING ASSOCIATION
1975

*Copyright, American Accounting Association, 1975. All rights reserved
Library of Congress Catalog Card Number 74-25242
Printed in the United States of America*

CONTENTS

FOREWORD.. ix
SYMPOSIUM PARTICIPANTS xii

SYMPOSIUM PROGRAM

SUNDAY EVENING, MAY 19, 1974

Panel Discussion
    The Future of the Accounting Curriculum in a College of Business Administration

Panelists
    Gerald L. Cleveland, Seattle University................... 1
    James Don Edwards, University of Georgia.............. 7
    Charles W. Lamden, Peat, Marwick, Mitchell & Company 11
    Vernon K. Zimmerman, University of Illinois............. 17

MONDAY, MAY 20, 1974

MORNING SESSIONS: ADVANCED FINANCIAL ACCOUNTING

    The Advanced Financial Accounting Curriculum—Recent Developments and the Need to Reconsider Content, Sequence and the Blending of Theory and Practice in Courses Beyond the Introductory Level

Paper:
    Jay M. Smith, Brigham Young University............... 23
Critique:
    Kenneth W. Perry, University of Illinois................ 45

    The Advanced Financial Accounting Curriculum—Interaction with other Disciplines: Quantitative, Behavioral, the Business Administration Core

Paper:
    John A. Tracy, University of Colorado 49
Critique:
    Thomas F. Keller, Duke University..................... 61

AFTERNOON SESSIONS: ADVANCED MANAGERIAL ACCOUNTING

The Advanced Managerial Accounting Curriculum—Recent Developments and the Need to Reconsider Content, Sequence and the Blending of Theory and Practice in Courses Beyond the Introductory Level

Paper:
    Edward L. Summers, University of Texas at Austin 67
Critique:
    Alfred Rappaport, Northwestern University 81

The Advanced Managerial Accounting Curriculum—Interaction with other Disciplines: Quantitative, Behavioral, the Business Administration Core

Paper:
    Edwin H. Caplan, University of New Mexico 83
Critique:
    Don T. DeCoster, University of Washington 97

MONDAY EVENING, MAY 20, 1974

Models for Financial Accounting vs. Models for Management Accounting: Can (Should) They Be Different?

Paper:
    Nicholas Dopuch, University of Chicago 103
Critique:
    Robert N. Anthony, Harvard University 123

TUESDAY, MAY 21, 1974

MORNING SESSIONS: AUDITING AND TAXATION

The Auditing Curriculum—Is There a Need for Change?

Paper:
    Robert L. Grinaker, University of Houston 127
Critique:
    Alvin A. Arens, Michigan State University 147

The Taxation Curriculum—Is There a
Need for Change?

Paper:
 Ray M. Sommerfeld, University of Texas at Austin........159
Critique:
 Donald H. Skadden, University of Michigan.............171

AFTERNOON SESSIONS: NOT-FOR-PROFIT
ORGANIZATIONS AND SOCIAL MEASUREMENT

Not-for-Profit Organizations in the Accounting
Curriculum—Where and How?

Paper:
 Robert J. Freeman, University of Alabama.............175
Critique:
 Lennis M. Knighton, Brigham Young University........ 195

Social Measurement in the Accounting Curriculum—
Where and How?

Paper:
 Ralph Estes, Wichita State University.................. 203
Critique:
 R. Lee Brummet, University of North Carolina.......... 219

SUMMATION: THE STEERING COMMITTEE 223

Foreword

As in the past, when there is a need for a substantial research effort in accounting education, the Price Waterhouse Foundation is ready and willing with its generous financial support. For this support, which is more adequately described on the next page, all members of the American Accounting Association are most appreciative, especially those who had the opportunity to participate in this symposium designed to identify problem areas and procedures to resolve them.

It was obvious to all participants that the papers and critiques presented at the symposium were of such import that they should be made available at cost to all interested in accounting education. Thus, a request was made of Robert N. Anthony, 1973-74 President of the American Accounting Association, to approve making available all papers and critiques. He did approve, and we now have available many facets of the curriculum and educational thinking of one of the most outstanding groups of accounting educators ever brought together to consider curriculum issues.

As can be seen from the table of contents, which is a summarized version of the symposium program, each paper presented during the morning and afternoon sessions was followed by a critique. A typical morning or afternoon session revolved around a schedule similar to the following: presentation of papers and critiques—one and one-half hours, small group discussion sessions—one hour, and summarizations—one-half hour. Members of the steering committee served as discussion leaders for the small group discussions and also took the lead in the summarization sessions. To offset the heavy morning and afternoon schedules, the evening programs revolved around more general issues which educators are always ready to take on.

As for the ultimate impact of the symposium only time will tell. The papers and critiques in this volume will undoubtedly have a wide ranging impact on accounting education. The consensus recommendation, of the symposium participants, concerning how the American Accounting Association should utilize remaining Price Waterhouse Foundation funds should also fundamentally affect accounting education for many years to come. The "consensus recommendation" is reviewed in the "summation" section of this volume as is a brief history of the origins of the symposium and the Price Waterhouse Foundation grant.

This foreword would not be complete without some mention of the outstanding group of men who were so generous in helping me every step of the way from the inception to the successful culmination of the symposium. James B. Bower, Harold Q. Langenderfer, Milton F. Usry and Doyle Z. Williams were just great people to work with as was Doug Starr, my super assistant, who will soon join the staff of the University of Houston. Paul L. Gerhardt, Administrative Secretary of the American Accounting Association also rendered much in the way of valuable assistance for which I am truly grateful.

William L. Ferrara

AAA Receives $100,000 Grant

(as reported in Accounting Education News,
Vol. 1, No. 1, October, 1973)

The Price Waterhouse Foundation has announced a Research Grant to the American Accounting Association in the amount of $100,000 to support research in accounting education. The grant is intended as support for a major effort to raise the level of accounting education with *particular emphasis on revising the accounting curricula for advanced courses* in Financial and Managerial Accounting.

The Grant by The Price Waterhouse Foundation is the outgrowth of a realization that the extraordinary potential of the Association as an instrument for advancing accounting education cannot be utilized effectively by continuing to function solely on a committee basis and with a meager commitment of financial resources. The grant will make possible the selection of primary researchers and assistants who can be compensated on the basis of their academic salary so that they can be released of teaching responsibilities to devote full time to selected research projects. The unique human resources available in the Association also will be utilized in an advisory capacity, first to select the projects and the researchers and then in consulting on the projects as the research progresses. The expectation is that the research will culminate in one or more publications in the educational research series of the Association.

This grant by The Price Waterhouse Foundation is, in a sense, a promising extension to the important work sponsored and published by the Foundation, *A New Introduction to Accounting*. The grant will provide continued and expanded impetus to the American Accounting Association's involvement in accounting education and clearly demonstrates the viable partnership between practitioners and academicians in the furtherance of the accounting profession. The initial stages of the grant will be under the guidance of the new standing Committee on Accounting Education, chaired by Harold Q. Langenderfer, who until recently was Director of Education for the American Accounting Association.

SYMPOSIUM PARTICIPANTS

Robert N. Anthony
Ross Graham Walker Professor of
   Management Control
Harvard University

Alvin A. Arens
Associate Professor of Accounting
Michigan State University

James B. Bower
Professor of Business
University of Wisconsin

R. Lee Brummet
Willard J. Graham Professor of
   Business Administration
University of North Carolina

James Bulloch
Director
Institute of Management Accounting

Edwin H. Caplan
Professor of Accounting
University of New Mexico

Gerald L. Cleveland
Dean, School of Business
Professor of Accounting
Seattle University

Don T. DeCoster
Professor of Accounting
University of Washington

Nicholas Dopuch
Professor of Accounting
University of Chicago

James Don Edwards
Research Professor of Accounting
University of Georgia

Ralph W. Estes
Elmer Fox Professor of Accounting
Wichita State University

William L. Ferrara
Professor of Accounting
Pennsylvania State University

Robert J. Freeman
Professor of Accounting
University of Alabama

William R. Gifford
Price Waterhouse & Company

Robert L. Grinaker
Professor of Accounting
University of Houston

Thomas F. Keller
Professor of Business Administration
Duke University

Lennis M. Knighton
Professor of Accounting and
  Public Administration
Brigham Young University

Charles W. Lamden
Peat, Marwick, Mitchell and Co.
Chairman of the Committee on
  Education
National Association of State Boards
  of Accountancy
Formerly Dean of the School of
  Business Administration
San Diego State College

Harold Q. Langenderfer
Professor of Accounting
University of North Carolina

James A. McFadden
Chairman of the Board
Transportation Data Communications, Inc.
Chairman of the Committee on Professional
    Development
Financial Executives Institute

Lawrence Olewine
Special Assistant for Education
Offtce of the Assistant Secretary of
    Defense (Controller)
Member of the Education and Training
    Committee
Federal Government Accountants
    Association

Kenneth W. Perry
Professor of Accountancy
University of Illinois

Alfred Rappaport
Professor of Accounting and
    Information Systems
Director of the Center for Advanced
    Study in Accounting and
    Information Systems
Northwestern University

Donald H. Skadden
Arthur Young Professor of Accounting
University of Michigan

Jay M. Smith
Professor of Accounting
Brigham Young University

Ray M. Sommerfeld
Arthur Young Professor of Accounting
University of Texas at Austin

Edward L. Summers
Professor of Accounting
University of Texas at Austin

Daniel L. Sweeney
Director, Relations with Educators
American Institute of Certified
    Public Accountants

John A. Tracy
Professor of Accounting
Head of Accounting Division
University of Colorado

Milton F. Usry
Regents Professor of Accounting
Oklahoma State University

Doyle Z. Williams
Professor of Accounting
Coordinator, Area of Accounting
Texas Tech University

Vernon K. Zimmerman
Dean, College of Commerce and
    Business Administration
Professor of Accountancy
University of Illinois

The Future of the Accounting Curriculum in a College of Business Administration

Gerald L. Cleveland

The topic of this panel should not lead to apprehension that the place of accounting education in the curricula of business schools is being questioned. In the first few years of the 1970's, accounting has largely regained its position of eminence in business schools. The currently strong status of accounting is partly attributable to the effect of factors related to dampened economic conditions and business adjustments which began to appear in 1969 and 1970 in most parts of the United States. Subsequently, the attention directed to financial management and reporting has led to renewed demand for accounting education, particularly in undergraduate programs.

With the resurgence of accounting, new methods and content are coming into courses. These are natural developments; accounting education, like the art of accountancy, always will be adapting to change and factors that trigger change. Students must be prepared to cope with change. In accounting education, theory should serve at least two purposes. One objective of theory is to explain or articulate the rationale of concepts. Theory should also be useful in making predictions or in providing vision to deal with new, unresolved problems. The latter goal of theory is especially important in developing graduates who will be able to adjust to future needs.

Generally, most accountants now must have broader perspective and vision than in the past. Behavioral, environmental, and quantitative courses have become part of accounting education as well as other collegiate education for business. In some instances in the last decade, accounting was deemphasized as other disciplines became popular; in some colleges and universities accounting education lost status. Some of this was brought about by accounting professors failing to let others in the business school know what they were doing. Accounting educators, like other academicians, have sometimes been guilty of writing and talking among themselves for their own professional needs. This has deprived others of knowing about developments in accounting and, accordingly, has caused others to underestimate the efforts of accounting educators. Accounting professors need to share viewpoints and also learn what other business educators are doing if mutual respect and good results are to be achieved.

The Image of the Accounting Curriculum

The future of the accounting curriculum in a business school depends, in part, upon the image of accounting education held by educators in other fields represented in the business school. At the present time in 1974, it appears that the future of accounting in the business school is very bright. Various market forces are creating favorable attitudes toward accounting on the part of students, faculty members, deans, and others in universities. Likewise, external constituents of universities seem to be looking favorably upon the position and nature of accounting in the business school.

Some accounting educators, as well as some practitioners, seem to believe that the reduction in the required hours for an accounting major in many business bachelor's degree programs has weakened the position of accounting education. The broad curriculum standards of the American Assembly of Collegiate Schools of Business have also been cited as contributing to the deemphasis of accounting in undergraduate business programs accredited by AACSB. These beliefs seem to be ill-founded apprehensions based upon the misconception that the eminence of accounting depends on the amount of units and courses available in the curricula of the business school.

In past decades, many successful accountants completed their accounting studies in programs which emphasized procedural aspects and detailed applications in problems. The "lock-step" process of development emphasized lengthy drills and/or practical exercises. These time-consuming educational methods have gradually been replaced, at least in part, by more efficient processes.

Rigorous, high-quality accounting programs do not depend for success upon a certain amount of credit hours or number of courses. Recent changes in the quality of accounting education are attributable to many factors, including improvements in educational materials and the increase in the supply of well-prepared accounting professors. The latter development particularly has contributed to the advancement of more conceptual, analytical education in the classroom.

Identifying Intentions and Objectives

In the next few years, perhaps the biggest concern of accounting educators should be the predictable demand for vocational education. This emphasis could affect the nature and quality of accounting education in universities. Professors, as well as deans, will have to resist the pressures to develop courses which represent training as opposed to education. Universities generally are not well equipped to provide vocational training.

Universities, however, need not shy away from practical education. There is no conflict between practical education and liberal education. Likewise, it is possible to develop excellence at different levels of education. But universities should avoid creeping or drifting into types of vocational training that can best be supplied by other institutions.

In the years ahead, many types of accounting services will be needed. Universities must be careful to identify their intentions and the objectives of their accounting programs. Other institutions exist to serve other needs, and at this time it appears that vocational programs offered by others will be well financed. Nevertheless, universities will continually have to resist the financial "bait" offered for development of vocational education.

Accounting educators, like others, will have to continue to avoid placing undue emphasis upon the departmentalization of faculties in business schools and within universities. When a department becomes isolated and autonomous, there is a tendency for professors within the department to start to teach things which are or should be provided by other departments. Within a business school, departments must cooperate if a "management by programs" approach is to be efficiently used in developing and delivering the curricula for the bachelor's degree.

Accounting and the Business School

Accounting is part of business and business schools could not fulfill their missions without some education in accounting. Similarly, accounting programs and students need studies in the other functional fields in business, the management sciences, and the behavioral, environmental and quantitative areas. Accountants probably can quickly learn highly technical, professional aspects on the job if they have been broadly educated in business while acquiring their accounting education.

Creation of separate professional schools of accountancy would tend to produce graduates who would be narrower. Although a place exists for narrowly prepared and highly specialized accountants, the status of accountancy will be enhanced if accountants are prepared to become business leaders. Leadership, of course, depends upon many attributes; but much of the curricula of business schools is devoted to the belief that managerial talents can be improved through education. Accountants should not be denied that part of education designed to develop leadership. In addition to the possibility that professional schools of accountancy might not offer education designed to develop leadership attributes, they also might fail to emphasize the "business approach" to accounting and auditing. In other words, professional schools might emphasize accounting for accounting's sake. The utilitarian nature of accountancy could become obscure, as could the awareness that accounting is part of the management function in business.

Accounting in Private Universities in Metropolitan Areas

In most private universities in metropolitan areas, the conventional accounting specialization in a business degree program will continue to be popular. Many business students choose the accounting concentration because it tends to offer excellent placement opportunities following graduation. Students in private universities ordinarily pay (through tuition) for a large part of the costs of their education. They usually look upon their investment in education as one that should yield returns. Most private schools are pleased, indeed anxious, to serve the demand for utilitarian education in accounting.

Although the future of the accounting curriculum appears to be bright in business schools in small private metropolitan universities, it does not seem likely that major innovations in accounting education will come from this source. In most of these universities, teaching loads are heavy and professors find little time for research concerning curriculum development. These schools are, therefore, likely to continue to provide accounting education (1) as wanted by the students, and (2) in accordance with the needs of the accounting profession, business firms, and other organizations in the private and public sectors of activity. In other words, the small private schools will continue to be responsive to demands based on current needs.

If the period for a college education is eventually reduced from four to three years as recommended by a Carnegie Commission report, small private universities are likely to attempt to supply an accounting education in a business degree program within the reduced time. The financial condition of many of these schools requires that students be accommodated in the patterns which they request. Currently, for example, enrollments in accounting courses are being significantly increased by students with degrees who have returned to school to study accounting.

Accounting education in the United States has a tradition of being rigorous and demanding. This is likely to continue as attempts are made to cover more material and topics in the same or a lesser number of credit or contact hours. Similarly, it seems likely that both conceptual and methodological aspects will continue to receive emphasis in accounting education.

Most schools will attempt to offer a broad program which provides some opportunities for studies in auditing and income tax as well as the usual advanced financial and managerial topics. Small private universities ordinarily should avoid proliferation of courses and/or high degrees of specialization. On the other hand, most schools in metropolitan areas will continue to provide accounting education designed to assist students preparing for professional examinations. The education will be part of the curricula of the business school and will be designed to accommodate the student who seeks a bachelor's degree in business with an accounting concentration.

Conclusion

In summary, it seems reasonable to predict gradual and continuous evolution of the design, content, and methods of accounting education within business schools in the United States. Small private universities in metropolitan areas are not likely to be leaders in introducing radical changes. However, these schools will be responsive to their constituents and will change as mainstreams of thought change.

This symposium, designed to identify curricula problems in advanced financial and managerial courses, is a significant step in providing the foundation for improvements in accounting education. All accounting educators should be interested in the recommendations to be made concerning researching the accounting curriculum and strategies for change.

The Future of the Accounting Curriculum in a College of Business Administration

James Don Edwards

Academic Environment

The future of the accounting curriculum in a College of Business Administration depends upon the environment within which the program is functioning. There are several questions which seem appropriate when we consider the academic environment in which the accounting curriculum is functioning. For the last several years it has been apparent in many institutions that the accounting curriculum has been functioning basically in a hostile environment—one in which the faculty of the College of Business Administration has had a desire to educate the generalist who was concerned with the management function, the decision-making process, rather than in preparing professional accountants for careers in business, public accounting, and government. Other institutions have found that the professional accounting program has been functioning in an environment in which the faculties of the various academic disciplines in Business Administration and Economics have been supportive of the professional programs in accountancy and have supported the faculties in developing professional programs which would be meaningful to individuals entering public accounting, business or government.

The impact of the setting within which the accountancy program finds itself substantially influences the nature of the accounting program. Some faculties, with the assistance of outside recommendations such as the Ford and Carnegie Reports, have downgraded accounting in the professional aspect of the program to such an extent that it is difficult to determine whether or not some accounting courses have any accounting content. If this is the kind of environment in which an accounting program finds itself, it may be appropriate to determine whether or not accounting is located in an organizational structure in which professional programs may be offered to students entering the accounting profession.

The Accounting Program's Place in the Organizational Structure

It would seem to me if the accounting program finds itself in a hostile organizational environment, the accounting faculty should set in motion a new organizational structure which would be more conducive to the educational objectives of a professional accounting program. The location of the accounting program therefore has substantial impact on the content and the direction of the curriculum itself. The content of the curriculum and the control of the curriculum is a deciding factor in locating the accounting program. It is appropriate that the accounting courses be truly professional courses which contain both theoretical and conceptual materials, but also recognize the practicality within which accounting functions. Accounting functions within the practical world of business in which decisions are quantified and the financial impact of those decisions are reported to users of financial statements. The environment is such that if professionals can be educated and provided the opportunity to attain a meaningful education within this environment, then a College of Business Administration may be an appropriate place for the professional accounting program.

Accounting As A Professional School

It may be appropriate, however, to look at the three traditional professions and determine how they have handled the problems of providing educational opportunity for professionals entering their fields. These would be (1) Schools of Law, (2) Schools of Medicine and (3) Schools of Theology. Each of these disciplines has seen fit to establish independent schools outside of Arts and Sciences or outside of the natural sciences to obtain their educational objectives for their students.

Each of these segments of the University is headed by a Dean or Director who reports directly to the chief administrative adademic officer within the University community. This gives the faculties of these schools the freedom to develop truly professional programs and provide a maximum educational opportunity for their students. It is true that all three of these professional schools are graduate schools, and the students entering them generally have Bachelor Degrees in some other academic discipline. However, accounting is growing at such a rate and has such great social responsibility that it seems appropriate that the curriculum content of our program be such that we provide the maximum educational opportunity for the students.

The way to do this is to establish an organizational structure that will give the faculties of a professional program in accounting the following kinds of areas within their control: (1) Curriculum—Course content—both as it relates to accounting and as it relates to other required courses beyond the accounting curriculum. The intent here would not be to require more and more accounting but rather to provide the basic educational materials in such areas as communication skills, quantitative methods, the social sciences and the behavorial sciences that would be most appropriate to a professional entering accounting. (2) The organizational structure should provide the opportunity for the administrative officer of the unit to control the budget as it related to the faculty. This would give substantial autonomy to the faculty and the administration of that faculty in determining the direction and priorities as it related to the professional program in accounting. It would also provide a focus for alumni and for individuals outside the educational institution to provide financial resources to support that particular unit. The financial resources provided through a College of Business Administration could erode through a dean establishing priorities which would, in effect, level the allocation of resources internally and externally in such a way that the resources or monies given to the accounting faculty would not in fact be additional money, but in effect would provide a leveling effect through the college.

The major challenge which will face the accounting faculties themselves in such an organizational structure will be the development of an appropriate academic program to provide the maximum educational opportunity for the student, and this will involve a major structural reassessment of the content of all of our accounting courses along the lines of providing both a theoretical framework and a practical application, if you like, in each of the cases. Now this has been true in the three professional programs mentioned previously—law, medicine and theology. In Law schools, for example, individuals have experience in terms of preparing briefs, they have mock court trials in which the individuals have experience or simulated experience in courtroom experience. In case of theology, the individuals not only have the background of studying the Bible and other related theological material but also have experience in terms of providing sermons, instruction and related feedback. In Medical school there is the study of the basic sciences and then its application in terms of the knowledge acquired in the basic sciences in laboratories. Then the practicing of medicine is begun within the hospitals. Hence, medicine is a practical field. This kind of activity is a requirement in each of these kinds of academic programs. We in accounting should learn from these experiences in developing an accounting curriculum for individuals who are going to enter professional accounting as a career.

Effects of Professional School of Accounting

The one fear that an old experienced administrator might have in terms of developing schools of accounting is that "the domino theory" would be put into effect. The domino theory here would mean that once a major state university with an outstanding accounting faculty established a professional school of accounting, with a dean or director outside the College of Business, then all of the other institutions in the country offering accounting programs would feel the need to develop such schools. Again we should learn from the experiences of law, medicine and theology that the development of these professional programs were slow in parallel with the development of the universities as it related to quality instruction. In accounting we should have, in my opinion, a very small number of professional schools initially so that the major curriculum changes, necessary both in accounting and in related subject matter, could take place and could be meaningfully structured and useful to other educational institutions. It is not a question of who will be first and who will have the largest program, but rather whether or not academic programs in accounting can be developed in such a way that they will be accepted within the University community and also within the practice of public accounting, government and industry.

Acceptance of the Organizational Structure

It is important for us as accounting educators to remember that the acceptance of our organizational structure is important within the academic community because that is where we are going to be functioning as educators. It must have respectability and quality, and it must have the support of the administration in terms of resources and physical facilities. It is also important for the product of the educational institutions to have acceptability in terms of the market place. The five-year student, the individual who completes a totally professional program, is going to be in great demand in this market in which we find ourselves and in which supply does not yet meet the demand. So looking down the road, it is important that we embark upon a new experimental program which would provide professionals the means to meet some of the needs of accounting education of the future. The challenge is ours, the question is whether or not we will be able to muster the resources to accomplish these objectives in the 1970's.

The Future of the Accounting Curriculum in a College of Business Administration

Charles W. Lamden

The opportunity to participate in this symposium on researching the accounting curriculum is indeed an exciting one. This is particularly so since the challenge is to develop strategies for change.

The proposed investigations involve a determination of what is to be anticipated for the future of the accounting profession and what the appropriate accounting curriculum should be. An intriguing aspect of anticipating the future and developing procedures to meet the anticipated needs is that the investigators also have the opportunity to influence the future developments.

During the course of this symposium a great deal of emphasis will be placed on the identification of specific future curricular problems in financial accounting, managerial accounting, auditing and taxation, and in accounting for not-for-profit organizations and for social measurement. The procedures that will be recommended will necessarily be based upon certain assumptions about the future.

As I understand my function on this evening's introductory panel, I am to discuss the future milieu for the accounting curriculum from the viewpoint of the accounting profession. Accordingly, I should like to discuss the following questions:

1. What is the future of the accounting profession?
2. What should the future accountant be expected to learn at the University and what should he learn "on-the-job?" In other words, what is the "cut-off" between education and firm training?
3. What is the most effective organization for accounting education in the future?

The Future of the Accounting Profession

While there is general consensus today that accounting is a profession, it is anticipated that some of the confusion in the minds of the general public as to who is a member of the "accounting profession" will be clarified. Today the terms "accounting" and "profession" have different meanings to different people. A wide variety of persons in various callings, vocations and employments are often designated as "professionals" or "members of a profession." Also, a variety of persons including those who keep records, do bookkeeping, prepare financial statements, develop or maintain financial information systems, prepare tax returns, engage in internal and external auditing and a myriad of related activities are often designated as "accountants" or in the "field of accounting."

It is anticipated that the standards and requirements for recognition as a "professional accountant" will be raised to the point where the public can clearly distinguish between professional accountants and non-professional bookkeepers and tax preparers. It is also anticipated that the professional status of management accountants, internal auditors and governmental accountants will be clarified. Today, for the most part, members of these groups achieve professional status by obtaining the CPA certificate, even though they are not engaged in public accounting. It is anticipated that the professional examinations for these groups (e.g., the CMA and CIA examinations) will demonstrate the knowledge and expertise required for professionals.

It is also anticipated that the "professional status" of accountants, which requires the respect and trust of the general public, will be greatly enhanced in the future. Today, the accounting profession is subject to conflicting pressures. The standards and practices are being severely questioned as manifested by public criticism and legal actions. The public is demanding more candid disclosure and higher standards of accountability. It is anticipated that the profession will respond affirmatively to these demands.

It is also anticipated that the profession will assume greatly increased responsibility in the services it renders to the public. Today there is a tendency for the profession to limit its services, to be very cautious and to be deeply concerned about legal liability. To the extent that such caution results in a limitation of the work done in order to limit responsibility, it appears to be counter-productive. Criticism and legal liability result from what the public feels should be done. It is anticipated that the profession will realize that the only effective defenses against such criticisms will be top quality performance, true independence, and the presentation of reliable information in the areas where service is required by the public. Accordingly, it is anticipated that professional services will be provided for forecasts, social measurements, interim statements, performance audits, management audits and other extensions of the attest function.

Finally it is anticipated that the state of the art will be greatly enhanced based on overall agreement as to fundamentals underlying accounting principles and standards. The state of the art today leaves much to be desired.

Not only are there many knowledge frontiers yet to be conquered, but there are large and obvious gaps in the body of knowledge. The Financial Accounting Standards Board (FASB) has just started to study a few of them. But even more fundamental, there is not even agreement on some of the basic aspects of financial accounting.

Marshall Armstrong, chairman of the FASB, has stated the problem as follows:

> "... it seems clear to me ... that without agreement on the objectives of financial accounting, without some notion of the kinds of information which users of financial statements need, without specification of the basic concepts which underlie accounting, and without some guidelines for application of the basic concepts to specific situations, neither the Financial Accounting Standards Board, nor those who prepare financial statements, nor those who audit them, will have anything but an intuitive basis for assessing the merits of various accounting alternatives. Without agreement on fundamentals, logical inconsistencies can easily develop between one accounting standard and another..."*

While the establishment of the FASB is an important step in the right direction, one such organization cannot produce all of the basic knowledge and concepts that will be required. A true profession must be based on appropriate academic training and research. In the recognized "professions" today, this is centered in the University. The anticipation is that some day this will also become true in accounting.

If the accounting profession achieves the various goals that I anticipate, then the accounting curriculum of the future must be designed to implement those anticipations. In any event, it is hoped the various accounting curricula discussed during the next two days will reflect the procedures required to implement the profession of the future.

"Cut-Off" Between Education and Firm Training

Both accounting practitioners and accounting students have expressed concern about the "relevance" of a number of aspects of

---

*Status Report No. 6, Financial Accounting Standards Board, November 28, 1973.

current accounting curricula. Yet it has been my experience that the objective of accounting educators in designing curricula has been to provide the accounting education required by their graduates. This is particularly true of the areas covered in this symposium.

At least one reason for current criticism is that the coordination between educators and the accounting profession (practitioners) has been assumed, but in many instances there has been no mechanism being implemented on a continuous basis to be certain that such coordination existed in fact.

A factor in obtaining good coordination is to understand what is meant by relevant. The question is: relevant to what? This depends upon the objectives of the users because what is relevant to one objective is not relevant to another. There also are questions of perspective and timing. A student's perspective changes about courses in foreign languages, for example, when he finds himself in an overseas assignment later in his career.

Almost every practicing CPA knows of a course which he took in college that seemed the least relevant (and sometimes the least interesting) at the time, and yet it proved to be most helpful later in his career. On the other hand, some courses that had the appeal of "reality" in the college milieu proved to be of little value subsequently. Attempts to bring the business world into the classroom generally have not been successful. For the most part, attempts to teach experience have proved to be ineffective and often the experiences taught (or described) are not the ones the students find in their future professional practice. Because of this, the better university programs in accounting are emphasizing conceptual understanding rather than procedural skills.

Current trends in university education for accounting thus place responsibility for obtaining experience with the individual and with the accounting firm he joins. This experience must, of course, be based on a body of background knowledge which includes studies in the humanities, economics and behavioral sciences, mathematics (including statistics and probability), business administration (including finance, production, marketing, personnel management and organization and management theory), the legal environment of business and the basic concepts of accounting and auditing.

The philosopher, Josiah Royce, has said, "Education is learning to use the tools the race has found indispensable." For the professional accountant these "tools" include (1) the broad general knowledge of disciplines that will give him an understanding of the present and future political, economic and social environment, (2) the semitechnical knowledge that will make available to him such tools as mathematics, statistics, communications skills, economics and finance, and (3) the technical knowledge of the expert accountant.

At the present time it appears to be generally understood that the professional accountant will obtain most of his semitechnical knowledge as well as his background of broad general knowledge at the university. His major responsibility after he begins practice, and that of the training program of his firm, is to expand his technical knowledge as an expert accountant.

While this "cut-off" between education and practice is generally understood, specific implementation for curriculum development apparently gives rise to questions. The distinction between conceptual knowledge and the technical knowledge of the expert is not always easy to determine. Thus, the general guideline is not sufficient when the accounting educator is attempting to make the decision whether or not specific subject matter should be included in his course. Also, concepts can be quite sterile when presented without the benefit of examples drawn from experience. And to complicate the matter even more, the greater the depth of study of a given concept, the more likely it is to overlap with technical knowledge.

Even though different practitioners will identify the "cut-off" at different points, it would seem to be essential that an authoritative body of practitioners coordinate closely with a representative group of educators to agree on the approximate "cut-off." This will be especially important as the "state of the art" advances and as the relative importance of "education" and "experience" change in the basic requirements for a "professional accountant." The nature and organization of the accounting educational institution will also have a bearing on the "cut-off."

Effective Organization of Accounting Education in the Future

While the overall charge for the symposium involves strategies for change based on researching the accounting curriculum and no specific reference is made to the structure of the organization in which the courses will be taught, the assumption seems to be that the courses will be taught in Departments of Accounting in Schools of Business. This is made more explicit in the subject assigned to this evening's panel—"The Future of the Accounting Curriculum in a College of Business Administration."

In anticipating the future of the accounting profession and accounting education, however, it is quite probable that the current organization structure in which accounting is taught will not be the most significant structure in the future. To clarify this point it may be helpful to separate the discussion between the short range and long range futures.

For the short run, it is probably appropriate to consider the proposals for curriculum research for the courses which will be given in the currently structured Department of Accounting. Even for the short run, however, I think we would be remiss if consideration is not given to the possibility that the subject areas (financial accounting, management accounting, auditing, tax, etc.) are not necessarily fixed. I strongly feel that there should be a reorganization of the way advanced accounting material is presented.

It is quite possible that the basic concepts of accounting and auditing should be included in one unit rather than in discrete units. The same may be true for financial accounting and management accounting. In other words, I would like to see a grid made of the basic concepts that a graduate of an accounting program should have. Then one of the research studies could be directed to an analysis and evaluation of how the various parts could best be assembled into courses or study units.

While I would visualize that the emphasis in this research project would be directed to the undergraduate curriculum, the project (or a follow-up project) could also consider the segments that fit best into a graduate program and the interaction between undergraduate and graduate curricula. Possibly, for the short run, two models could be developed. In one, the basic concepts would be covered primarily in the undergraduate program. In the other, they would be covered almost exclusively in a graduate program based on a Liberal Arts undergraduate degree.

For the long run, I anticipate that professional schools of accountancy must be considered. In my opinion, this will be the most effective organization of accounting education for the future accounting profession. I strongly urge that the curriculum researchers keep this in mind as they develop their proposals.

The Future of the Accounting Curriculum in a College of Business Administration

Vernon K. Zimmerman

The invitation to participate as a panelist to discuss the future accounting curriculum in a college of business administration is a welcome one. It is encouraging to note that the American Accounting Association is sponsoring such a symposium. The topic is indeed timely and the joint inputs of accountants and their leading academic association are vital.

Perspective on the Contemporary Accounting Curriculum

While preparing these comments, I could not help but note a certain contemporary irony hidden in the title relating to the present discussion of professional schools of accountancy. I thought I might simply assert to you that the professional school of accountancy is the wave of the future and, therefore, the present college of business administration would have no involvement in the future accounting curriculum. That particular organizational development may still occur but if I am an accurate assessor of the speed of curricular and organizational change in the contemporary American university scene, I suggest that our topic is still very relevant. We will be involved with curricular problems within the structure of the modern business administration school for some time.

I do not wish to digress too widely on the topic of a professional school of accountancy, but I do note it is an important topic. It is slowly receiving the attention it deserves. The academic community is more thoughtfully considering the impact of the establishment of a professional school on the total educational structure for accounting. The majority of the members of the public accounting profession seem to have already determined in favor of such a school. I submit that this well-intentioned endorsement, if too agressively sought and attempted to be implemented, could hinder what might be a very logical and sound development. Specifically, the officers of the American Assembly of Collegiate Schools of Business are reacting apprehensively to the school of accountancy concept, apparently because of what they preceive to be undue and hasty pressure from partisans of that concept. Detailed and comprehensive discussions are needed to insure that the proposal has a fair hearing.

I do not believe that if accounting were taught in a school of accountancy we would lessen our interest in considering the possible changes in our present accounting curriculum. The need for continuous review of our instructional offerings parallels the changes in the accounting environment upon which accounting rests as well as new developments in learning theory and pedgogical techniques. One area of vital concern to me should the independent school approach be adopted is the ability of accountants to maintain effective relationships with neighboring disciplines, both on the teaching and research levels.

The Present Attraction of the Study of Accounting to Students

Very relevant to our overall discussion of an appropriate accounting curriculum for tomorrow's accountants is the matter of the present acceptance of the accounting curriculum by new students. Student response to date is quite positive. We are finding a strong demand nationally to enroll in accounting programs. This has just been corroborated by our projected enrollment statistics of this fall. There has been a significant shift to the study of business on our campus relative to other years. Our undergraduate business enrollment has increased 40% in two years and the accounting area has shared proportionately in this increase.

We have attempted to determine the reason for this renewed interest in business generally and specifically accounting. Some of the answers are very direct. Honor students in Liberal Arts and Sciences have told us that they simply saw no reasonable hope of livelihood as a "psych" or history major. This may not be the most flattering of reasons to learn that accounting was selected but as individuals who believe in the efficiency of the market place, I am sure we understand it.

In summary, there is an increased demand, both absolute and relative, for study in accounting. This will have an impact upon our proposed future curriculum, as an adequate supply of academic staff would permit specialization in instruction whereas a shortage would not.

I also wish to note an important new educational development which I consider to be very important in our curricular planning. It involves the significant number of students of community and junior colleges who are concluding two years of baccalaureate-oriented study and now seek admission to four-year accounting programs. I do not want to digress into the ever-present bureaucratic and jurisdictional problems that are involved in the meshing of two separate educational systems—the two and four year colleges. This type of work is not intrinsically interesting, but it is essential and, as Dean, I have spent perhaps the greatest single portion of my time on the effort called "the articulation between the junior and senior colleges."

The impact of the junior college system is just now becoming significant. Last year, approximately 200 students entered our College at the junior level. This was more than triple the number of the year before and I look for a significant increase during the next several years. We can expect to plan for a curriculum in senior schools of business for students who will enroll for advanced accounting courses. I believe the implications on our present programs are clear.

The Profile of the Undergraduate Accounting Student

We should be aware of the expected background and capability of our future accounting students. As noted above, there is a strong trend presently for increased enrollment in the study of business and specifically accounting. On many campuses this has resulted in the closing of enrollments in the colleges of business administration. The students allowed to enroll in many of these colleges tend to be of a higher quality as measured by the standard aptitude tests and high school performance records. For example, our College in Urbana this fall has an increase in the average high school percentile ranking of its new freshmen from the 76th to the 85th percentile. In addition, there was a marked improvement in the ACT scores of our freshman applicants. I think this experience has been realized in a number of other schools and has some long-run implications concerning the increase in campus prestige for accountants similar to that which the law and engineering students have enjoyed.

The Accounting Curriculum in a College of Business Administration

Our attention is focused on the future of the accounting curriculum in a college of business administration. Certainly accounting is one of the disciplinary cornerstones of any modern college of business administration, whether it is viewed as those courses necessary for a capable accounting major or as a sequence of courses essential to the appropriate educational program of majors in other business disciplines. In the latter case, we can all agree, I believe, that finance majors have many areas of intellectual overlap with accountants and that certain central aspects of accounting are essential to the preparation and analysis of the data studied by students of finance. In addition, we can recognize the importance of appropriate accounting courses for marketing, organizational behavior, and economics majors in a school of business administration.

Thus, there are really two future concerns of the accounting curriculum in the college of business administration. The one injor in that
curriculum and the other involves the identification of those appropriate courses taught for the non-accounting major or of new courses specifically designed for the non-accounting business student.

To translate the two areas of curricular concern identified above into a more meaningful manner, I suggest the following considerations. These will be important, I believe, in determining the future of the accounting curriculum in a college of business administration:

1. The impact of the changing American educational pattern (particularly the junior college—senior college relationship).

2. The role of accounting in public administration activities (particularly in such areas as the state and federal governmental units, hospitals, universities, and other not-for-profit institutions).

3. The academic and professional relationship of information science and accounting areas.

4. The recognition of the professional, academic, and managerial aspects of accounting with particular emphasis upon the basic core of courses considered essential for an accounting curriculum.

5. Possible innovation in accounting courses.

6. The intensive and realistic development of macro-accounting (or social accounting) in both methodology and theory and its incorporation into the future accounting curriculum.

One of the ways in which the curriculum would change in light of the changing student body is a necessary experimentation in both course content and type of instruction. In this way, we can attempt to determine what the contemporary accounting student can effectively assimilate. The experimentation will lead, in my opinion, to more challenging and expanded work in accounting.

I also believe that the successful integration of the computer into the accounting curriculum will occur in the next decade. Much experimentation in this area has occurred. We need to be careful that the new computer-based class material does not simply evolve into a system of "electronic page-turning," but rather that the new instructional techniques will enable the utilization of computers to permit our students to develop more quickly and more effectively in their accounting competence. I do not believe that the necessary pedagogical developments have yet been achieved to allow us to use the computer in this instructional way effectively. But progress is apparent, and the future accounting curriculum will be greatly influenced by this new technique.

The Master of Business Administration and Its Influence on Accounting Education

An interesting and important development of the last decade has been the impact of the MBA degree upon educational programs for accounting. In many ways this is an interesting phenomenon because by definition the MBA graduate is a generalist. In theory, the entering MBA candidate does not have a business background, does not have an undergraduate business education but will, in two years, be exposed to all of the business disciplines with the idea of being able to be a successful manager upon graduation. The bachelor's, master's, and doctoral degrees in accounting, on the other hand, are by definition and design, programs in specialized education. Accounting is the admitted and desired focal point.

How did this interrelationship of the MBA educational program and the accounting educational program come about? The primary factor, in my opinion, is the widespread acceptance of the MBA graduate as a potentially superior graduate. Perhaps this condition is attributable more to public relations than academic but the conclusion seems generally accepted. You have probably read, as I have, in *The Wall Street Journal* and other publications, of the MBA graduates and their widespread acceptance and success.

Based upon my personal experience I found that accounting firms in the early '60's began to hire more MBA graduates possessing a minimum amount of accounting for their professional practice. Sometimes these graduates were placed in the managerial advisory service area. On many other occasions, they were given additional technical accounting training through a continuing education program. In this way the firms assumed the responsibility for the additional technical training necessary to convert the generalist to an individual with the essential level of specialized training in accounting.

In one of my discussions with a partner of a large public accounting firm, I was amused to hear him complain:

1. That some of the University of Illinois graduates could not do such audit steps as proof of cash, and
2. That they paid a premium to hire MBA's.

We determined that the MBA's were the ones who had not previously been exposed to the proof of cash type of procedure and thus were unfamiliar with this particular technique. I suggested that if he wished a technically qualified person he should hire the bachelor's and master's graduates in accounting and that it was unfair to expect a generalist to have the specialist training of the other type of graduate. The partner viewed me quizzically and, as I recall, gave no reply.

The present general acceptance of the MBA type of educational program in business does have some important implications for accounting as well as other business disciplines. The focus centers on the existence of two contrasting avenues of study of the business disciplines, one at the undergraduate level and the other at the graduate level.

In my opinion, the undergraduate accounting will continue to be an important avenue of education for the profession of accounting although the MBA type of graduate program will expand in absolute and relative measures. The accounting educator must assume the responsibility to devise programs suited for both the undergraduate and graduate aspirants with appropriate pedagogical recognition of the differing maturities and motivations that exist.

A number of MBA programs have developed sub-programs identified as "the accounting option." It is here that real educational concern is necessary to avoid an undesirable blurring between two legitimate separate educational programs—the MBA and the Master of Science in Accounting. Accounting faculties are obliged to accept the need to cooperate within the larger structure of the contemporary organic university but they also must insist on their prerogatives to design and teach the accounting courses in that university and to determine to the best of their ability the optimum content of the academic program for accounting majors.

In conclusion, we are fortunate to be debating the difficult but interesting question of how best to structure a modern accounting curriculum. We are part of a lively and accepted profession and the accounting academician does not need to seek arguments of socially intrinsic values to justify his continued presence in the contemporary American educational scene as the humanities and others seem personally obliged to do. Our challenges are ones generated by our operation in an active society in which new and often conflicting ideas are advanced and attempted. We need constantly to seek that elusive balance in our academic work that gives our students the essential, general as well as the specialized discipline background.

The Advanced Financial Accounting Curriculum—Recent Developments and the Need to Reconsider Content, Sequence and the Blending of Theory and Practice in Courses Beyond the Introductory Level

Jay M. Smith

I was extremely pleased last fall to read of the second Price Waterhouse and Co. grant for the improvement of the accounting curriculum; this one for the accounting courses beyond the introductory level. The initial grant that was directed to the Introductory Accounting courses has resulted in recommendations that will move these first courses toward a more user-oriented approach. Text materials are in advanced stages of preparation to implement these recommendations.

While I have in the past observed considerable research and innovation in introductory accounting, accounting professors have apparently assumed that innovation and experimentation in the financial accounting courses beyond the Introductory was less important or even unnecessary. We can observe many innovations in curriculum development in cost and managerial accounting, some in auditing and taxes, but very little in the advanced financial accounting sequence.

One of the principal outlets to describe such innovations in the past has been the Education section of the *Accounting Review*. A review of articles in this section since 1960 revealed only three that involved suggestions for the Intermediate or Advanced Accounting courses. Another outlet has been South-Western Publishing Co.'s monthly publication, *Collegiate News and Views*. A similar analysis of this publication since 1960 disclosed only one article dealing with Intermediate Accounting. A third source has been the *Accounting Trends* series edited by Tom Burns and published by McGraw-Hill Book Co. each year. Course syllabi from many colleges and universities are gathered for this publication. Seven issues have been published since its first issue in 1967. Analysis of these syllabi show that most of them included under the financial accounting title are graduate theory courses. Again, very little innovative material at the undergraduate level was noted in my review. Clearly Price Waterhouse & Co. has identified an area in which much work is needed.

For purposes of this paper, the advanced financial accounting sequence is defined as the traditional Intermediate and Advanced Accounting courses plus a course in Accounting Theory. It is recognized that some schools have broken from this sequence, at least in course title. In my experience, Intermediate Accounting has generally been a full year required accounting course taught at the junior level. Advanced Accounting has been a one-term course that has increasingly become an elective course in the curriculum. Accounting Theory, generally taught at the senior level, has not been included as widely in the curriculum. Sometimes it is used as a capstone required course in accounting similar to the management policy course for all business students. In other cases, it is one of several accounting electives for seniors.

South-Western Publishing Company recently conducted a college catalog survey dealing with these courses. The results of this survey are summarized as follows:

	Undergraduate	Junior and Community Colleges
Total colleges surveyed	2,169	1,187
Intermediate accounting-2 terms	769	410
Intermediate accounting-1 term	206	183
Advanced accounting-2 terms	332	19
Advanced accounting-1 term	380	60
Advanced accounting-problems	130	10
Accounting theory	161	2

This paper will not include discussions concerning auditing, taxes, or accounting for non-profit organizations because of their separate treatment in the seminar. There could be, however, some argument for including material from these areas in the advanced financial accounting as defined in this paper in lieu of offering separate courses in the curriculum.

It will be the objective of this paper to identify areas in which research and materials are needed to improve the advanced financial accounting curriculum. Much of our present structure seems to be an historical accident created largely by patterns established by early text book authors and perpetuated in succeeding editions of the texts. Some of these patterns continue to be useful and should be retained. Others are questionable, and perhaps should be eliminated. In order to better analyze the needs in this area, a brief historical review of the pertinent texts and courses will be made. This will be followed by an analysis of the content and sequencing problems inherent in the advanced financial accounting curriculum, including recent attempts to innovate in these areas.

A related problem to content and sequencing is the amount of blending of theory and technique that is desirable and/or possible within the elements of the sequence. Because it is considered significant, it will be treated separately. Although particular teaching methodologies can be used throughout any curriculum, and thus are not necessarily a part of the charge for this paper, I will include a discussion of those methodologies that seem to hold special promise for the advanced financial accounting curriculum. However, the interaction of financial accounting with other disciplines such as quantitative, behavioral, and business administration core is to be discussed as a separate topic at the seminar.

Historical Development

The great increase in the number of students majoring in accounting that has occurred since World War II has resulted in a relatively young accounting faculty for the country as a whole. This means that for many of us, present curriculum patterns are looked at from the more narrow viewpoint of our own experience as undergraduates in post-World War II education and our teaching within that same structure. To understand our present position more fully, a broader historical perspective seems important.

Courses within Colleges and Universities

A summary of instruction in accounting from 1900 to 1926 was prepared by C.E. Allen and published in the June, 1927, *Accounting Review*.[1] From this source we learn that accounting instruction in the United States started slowly in the late 19th Century. By 1900, there were only 13 colleges and universities giving college credit for accounting subjects. The largest number of courses given by an institution was four. Included in the four courses was a Principles of Accounting course and an Advanced Accounting course. Five of the thirteen schools offered the advanced course. The number of schools offering accounting expanded greatly during the next few years, and the offerings within each school also expanded. By 1910, there were 52 schools teaching accounting; by 1926, 335 schools. The pattern of a principles course followed by an advanced course became the norm.

Textbook Development

A review of book reviews and text advertisements in early editions of the *Accounting Review* indicates that early textbooks followed this same pattern. Perhaps the first accounting textbook series was written by Roy B. Kester and published by Ronald Press in 1918 and 1921. The series contained three volumes, all entitled Accounting Theory and Practice. Volume II included treatment of the balance sheet items, extensive treatment of depreciation (six chapters), consolidations, trust and fiduciary accounting, and liquidation accounting. Volume III included chapters on accounting for specific businesses such as banks, insurance companies, and railroads.

In 1924, Professor H.A. Finney published his two volume *Principles of Accounting* that would prove to be so popular in the classroom. These volumes assumed that the student had already taken one year of accounting. It was intended that they would be used over a two-year period if all of the problem material was fully explored, or over a one-year period if the problem material was only sampled. The volumes were revised in 1928 with the same basic format. The sequence of topics in the volumes didn't follow the pattern that is common today. For example, consolidations were treated in the middle of Volume I rather than in the last volume as is true in the current series.

Although the pattern of an introductory principles course followed by one or more advanced courses was the norm, 20 of the 335 schools teaching accounting in the colleges in 1926 offered a second course that was labeled "Intermediate Accounting." The first textbook I found that carried this title was written by Harry Allschuler in 1932. It was edited for Ronald Press by David Himmenblau, a noted professor in the early days of accounting education. This was followed in 1933 by an Intermediate Accounting textbook written by Jacob B. Taylor and Herman Miller. But the major textbook contribution to the concept of an Intermediate-Advanced accounting sequence to the Principles course was Professor Finney who, in 1934, published his revised and restructured Principles volumes in a two volume series, *Principles of Accounting, Volume I, Intermediate* and *Principles of Accounting, Volume II, Advanced*. He also added an Introductory text to complete the three part sequence that is still typical in the accounting curriculum of most universities and colleges.

All authors didn't immediately follow this departure to an intermediate concept. In 1941, for example, both the Noble, Karrenbrock and Simons text and the Paton second level text were published and labeled *Advanced Accounting*. In the Preface to the Noble text, the authors state that:

> Throughout the country a second year of Accounting study is at the present time the normal requirement for students in collegiate schools of business. University educators feel that these students need to follow the first year course in principles with a year of advanced problems showing application in various business situations....The problems of actuarial science and its application to advanced accounting are reserved for the last three chapters of the book. Instructors may assign these chapters with earlier related chapters in the book, may postpone their consideration until the end of the course, may insert them at any time, or may omit them altogether.[2]

Interestingly, even the authors of these early editions wrestled with the placement problem of actuarial science material.

By 1949, the Finney series was in its third edition and the Noble *Advanced* text was replaced by a two volume series by Karrenbrock and Simons, *Intermediate* and *Advanced Accounting*. The pattern now seemed to be firmly established. The sequencing of topics selected by Professor Finney in his 1934 texts continues to exert considerable influence on the current editions as can be seen in Exhibits A and B. There have been attempts made to break away from this early sequencing, but the accounting professors have effectively suppressed these innovations on any wide-spread scale at the most effective place—the adoption list at University bookstores. Even the noted accounting educator, William Paton, was unsuccessful in attempting to stem the movement to the Finney three part series. In 1952, he published with his son a volume entitled *Asset Accounting*. In the preface to this work, the authors comment on the sequencing and content problem as follows:

> With all these possibilities at hand (courses that could be taken after introductory accounting) there is not much to be said for the use of the nondescript headings "intermediate accounting" and "advanced accounting" for courses and text books designed for students who have completed the year's work in principles. Such labels encourage hit and miss bundling together of assorted topics as opposed to careful selection of related materials.[3]

Although adopted at some leading schools, this text was unsuccessful in changing the pattern. It is unfortunate that the accepted labels imply that the intermediate material is at a lower level of difficulty than that contained in the so called advanced course. I admire the Patons for their attempt and agree with their preface statement. Perhaps this current emphasis upon the advanced financial accounting curriculum can encourage relabeling that will better describe the true nature of the course's content.

The influence of the textbooks on the content and sequencing of courses cannot be over-emphasized. As the number of schools offering accounting expanded, more instructors were recruited with limited background in academic work. Many of these were teaching part time. Faculty loads for full-time instructors were heavy, frequently with multiple preparations. It was too difficult for an instructor to strike out on his own with a realignment of material. "Teach the text" seemed to become the norm. Innovations outside of textbooks were often left to the more affluent universities that stressed graduate education or whose student enrollment was small enough to lend itself to more intimate teaching. Innovations within the textbooks have been limited by the realization by authors that moving too fast from the established and accepted pattern could cause a severe loss in adoptions.

This pattern has not been as noticeable in the "Theory" course because of the flexibility usually found in this course. Currently, the most widely accepted theory text is one authored by Eldon Hendricksen. This text, now in its revised edition, has been widely adopted as a basis for the content of the theory course. Usually it is accompanied by considerable supplemental material.

AAA Curriculum Committees

Some attempts at curriculum guidance have been made by committees of the American Accounting Association. These committee reports, however, have not always been published. When they were published, they did not have sufficient follow-up by the profession to have any great impact on curriculum development.[4] The most recent report by a committee dealing with courses in financial accounting was published in the *1972 Committee Reports Supplement*.[5] It is a well written report and deserves the attention of all who teach and develop curriculum in advanced financial accounting courses. This Committee rejects the course content approach to curriculum development because it feels that such an approach destroys the dynamic character of accounting. They stress that each University should do its packaging according to its market and its faculty resources. The report identifies four levels of accounting knowledge, and maintains that the curriculum should be geared to the appropriate level. The four levels identified by the Committee are as follows:

Level I - Basic course. User oriented.
Level II - Heavy user oriented. Analysis of financial statements. Development of data and restructuring for specific use.
Level III - Providers of economic information. Future professional accountants. In depth analysis.
Level IV - Research. New knowledge exploration. Theory emphasis.[6]

Levels II and III pertain to this paper. Both the heavy user and the provider must be accommodated in advanced financial accounting curriculum.

Recent Developments in Content and Sequencing— Intermediate and Advanced Accounting

As demonstrated in Exhibits A and B, there has not been significant change in the structure of the more popular textbooks in the Intermediate-Advanced courses in the past forty years. Movements of a chapter or two back and forth between the Intermediate and the Advanced texts and the addition, or deletion, of a few chapters as accounting has become more complex constitute the major innovations. Unfortunately, innovations by specific teachers are not well documented. Thus, my discussion of recent developments will be drawn primarily from my own personal observations and experience.

I tend to agree with the 1972 AAA Committee report referred to earlier. It is probably fruitless to try to establish "the" correct content and sequencing for Intermediate and Advanced Accounting. If such an attempt were successful, it would probably do more damage by the rigidity it would introduce than it would do good by the improvement in present textbook sequencing. The curriculum for a course should be dynamic; changing to meet new conditions with fresh input continually coming from the instructors. For many educators, the challenge of developing innovative curricula is a major outlet for creative effort. Faculties in today's universities generally have their terminal doctorate degrees, and thus have received more advanced academic training than their counterparts of twenty years ago. Teaching loads have been reduced. There seems to be less need today to rely on the textbook to structure a course than was true in years past.

The Integrated Approach

While I was at Minnesota, several of us on the faculty in accounting felt that we were artificially dividing financial and managerial accounting by separating them in the class catalog and placing different labels on them. Although the users were different, the principles and procedures followed in both areas seemed to be directly related. This relationship was often obscured by course separation.

With these thoughts in mind, we developed a three quarter sequence of Intermediate and Cost/Managerial Accounting for our students. When we discussed cash and its reporting problems for the external financial statements, we also discussed cash budgeting and forecasting. When we discussed the reporting problems of leases, we also examined the lease-buy decision and examined in depth the true nature of leases as a method of financing acquisitions. We were hampered, as can be imagined, by a lack of integrated textual material and by the extra effort that such integration required of the participating faculty. Some faculty members who were asked to teach the sequence felt that these two areas were too specialized for one teacher to present. After one or two years of experimentation, the problems overcame the enthusiasm of the faculty and we separated the managerial accounting elements and again placed them together in the third quarter of the sequence. Our conclusion at that time was that the resource limitations made it very difficult to continue with the integrated approach.

A fair measure of student attitude and ability to integrate was never made because of the resources required to create a proper experimental environment. Most of us participating in the project felt that there was merit to the integrated approach. But how was such merit to be quantified? Perhaps this is one of the greatest needs of the academic world, financial assistance to better evaluate the ideas that are generated by individual faculties and later implemented within the curriculum.

The Modularized Approach

A possible answer to the need for flexibility in course content and sequencing may be found in the work Professor Dale Taylor and I have been doing at Brigham Young University for the past two years. We are convinced that there is nothing magical about the ten week quarter or the fifteen week semester. Education has placed artificial bounds around the learning process. Too often we as teachers seem to feel that the main curriculum challenge is how to fit twenty-eight chapters of an Intermediate Accounting textbook into two fifteen week semesters of school. We tend to lose sight of the major goal that we as educators should have, that of helping each individual student to master those concepts that will help him reach his own goals. Students come into Intermediate Accounting with a variety of backgrounds and with somewhat different end objectives. The problem then is how to put these students into one course that will meet these different needs. The Elementary and Secondary schools have recognized this problem and have widely adopted various forms of modularized, self-paced, competency based instruction. This is what we have experimented with at BYU for Intermediate Accounting, and I would suggest that this is one of the best ways to break away from the textbook content and sequencing straight jacket.

I'll be the first to maintain that a well written text is an essential ingredient to a course. A student receives much comfort, sometimes too much, from a well written and well defined text. However, a text should not be the course. A teacher should never abdicate his responsibility by accepting the text as any more than an aid to teaching. If teaching loads and the variety of preparations are too burdensome to permit this attitude, a re-allocation of University resources seems essential. At BYU we divided our Intermediate Accounting course into ten modules. Concept objectives were written for each module, and reading, problem and case material was selected that would best complement the classroom experience. The teacher was looked upon as a tool to learning. The student received the major responsibility for mastering the objectives.

A more complete description of our experience, including a description of our competency based examinations and team teaching experiment, is included in the Education section of the April, 1974 *Accounting Review*. Such methodologies can be and are being applied to a variety of courses at the University level. Accounting need not be an exception. The greatest benefit that we found with our approach was that for the first time, we felt free from the restrictions of a single text. The module objectives were independent of the text. The reading references could be altered as either the adopted text changed or as additional supplemental material became available. The modules themselves could be prepared to utilize that teaching methodology best adapted to a particular concept area. Thus, for a review of accounting procedures, programmed learning materials could be used. For analysis of financial statements, actual case studies of published financial statements could be prepared. The content and sequencing of the adopted text becomes less important than the quality of th textual presentation and the relevance of the problem material. This approach opens the door for using more than one text through the reserve library facilities. If a particular treatment of a topic seems to be treated more clearly in another text, a professor could easily include this in the reading assignment in place of the treatment presented by the authors of the adopted text. We considered at BYU the extension of this philosophy to requiring no text as we might do in a graduate seminar, but then rejected this approach as not being feasible with undergraduate students at this level of their education.

Some portability of modules developed at a particular school to other schools is possible, and would be especially desirable if extensive visual and other aids were developed. However, to me the most exciting aspect of this approach is the freshness that individual faculties can bring to their courses. No packaging can retain the currency that is required in our fast-moving profession. Indeed this is one of the more serious problems that authors of textbooks face; the long publication lead time that makes material written at least one year old as the brand new edition comes into print.

Perhaps an even greater advantage to the modular approach is an extension that we are still working on; that of permitting students to select those modules that best fit their needs. In other words, to permit students, within some definable limits, to structure their own course. Thus, for the heavy user of financial statements, maybe one-half of the Intermediate and Advanced Accounting modules would be appropriate. Instead of registering for two or three Intermediate or Advanced courses, he could register for one or two courses and select particular topics to study. Such flexibility requires a flexibility on the part of the faculty and the school. Experimentation is now going on in various academic fields at BYU for registering for and receiving unit or even ½ unit credit for modules passed in a given course. The use of such a concept would make it possible to teach heavy users and preparers of financial statements in the same module and avoid separate financial accounting courses for non-accounting (non-preparer) students. Faculty loads would have to be measured by the presentations given, and lectures or discussion sessions could be scheduled several times throughout the term to accommodate different students and their schedules.

Our BYU experience has shown that students are not always ready to assume the responsibility that such modularization permits. If all courses in the curriculum were scheduled in this way, the student would be better able to schedule his own time. But until such happens, the student still tends to lean heavily upon the faculty for specific direction and to spend time on the traditional courses with imposed time schedules. This has forced us to a schedule that the majority of students tend to follow. Such polarization does not necessarily mean the failure of the modularized system. Flexibility of the modules is still present. New subjects can be easily introduced with new or revised modules. Modules presenting concepts of auditing, not-for-profit accounting, and systems can be included in the set of those available. An atmosphere of studying a module to obtain mastery is present. Perhaps in time and with additional experimentation, complete flexibility as discussed previously can be attained.

Both experiences that I have had, therefore, at Minnesota and at BYU, tend to support the view that the content and sequencing of Intermediate and Advanced Accounting can be determined independent of textbook presentations. I believe that the modular approach might make the integrated approach that we tried at Minnesota feasible. Materials could be developed with this philosophy that could lead to a unified package of relevant material for the student.

Need For Content and Sequencing Guidelines

Some guidelines for content and sequencing are undoubtedly necessary, even under a modularized approach. If the curriculum structure at a given school restricts the number of courses a student may take in accounting, the professor will be asked to place priority judgments on the various topics that are available. The faculty at Minnesota and BYU tried to get at this problem by asking the question, "What concepts and abilities do you think a student should have mastered before he or she should be classified as an 'accounting major'?" Those things that are considered essential should be included in a required part of the accounting curriculum. Those things that are judged to be of less importance or of a specialized nature could be delegated to the elective courses or modules. As might be suspected, the most interesting aspect of both of these experiences in polling the faculty was the wide divergence of views on some topics. We did, however, after considerable faculty discussion, finally attain some consensus in both cases. Perhaps some research on a wider representation of faculty could help determine a consensus on this question from the entire academic profession.

Need For Research

I hope that other schools will experiment with different forms of modularized instruction or other techniques that will encourage the teachers to keep the financial accounting curriculum dynamic and alive. The second level financial accounting instruction should be the most exciting of the curriculum. Regardless of the specialization that follows, this area contains the core, the essence of accounting. The more documented experimentation that we have, the better our chances are for truly affecting a change in curriculum that will extend across specific school boundaries.

Blending of Theory and Technique

One of the most important questions that can be asked concerning course content is the degree to which the traditional Intermediate and Advanced courses should stress procedures as opposed to theory. At the extremes, one instructional philosophy argues that these courses should stress the procedural aspects of the material. How are various transactions recorded in debit and credit terms? What is a generally accepted procedure and what is not, and how do these transactions affect the amounts that are shown in the financial statements? No attempt is made in this extreme to ask "why" or to examine the economic or business foundation for the procedure. These questions, it is argued, can be best taught in a separate theory class after the student has mastered "what is" to a higher degree. At the other extreme, little attention is paid to the recording phase. Attention is given to the economic support for valuation methods, to various arguments as to the alternative bases of asset and income measurement, and to historical analyses of changes in these views by responsive associations of the profession. Procedures, it is argued, are taught in Introductory Accounting and repetition is a waste of time. Of course, there are many positions in between these extremes.

Rather than trying to present arguments pro and con for the extremes, at which points very few would admit to be standing, I will present my feelings and supplement them with some of the developments reported in the literature. I have long maintained that the teaching of technique without a fairly heavy dose of theory is a disservice to the student and makes legitimate the charge heard often early in accounting education that accounting is not really an academic discipline. Indeed, it is hard for me to imagine teaching Intermediate Accounting without some theory.

In a recent article appearing in the *Journal of Accountancy*, Professor Robert Sterling argues that educators have contributed to the resistance to improvements within the profession by teaching only what is acceptable without presenting research evidence that might contradict the established practice. He summarizes his article by stating, "If accounting educators teach research results as the desired state of the art, and accepted practice as the current state, the resistance to reform within the accounting profession might be somewhat lessened."[7] An insight into how Professor Sterling would implement this philosophy in accounting courses is provided by a description of his Advanced Accounting Theory class at the University of Kansas.[8] Two goals are specified in the course description: (1) To discover what is present accounting theory, and (2) To compare the present theory with the objectives of accounting. The discovery of present accounting theory was facilitated by having the students prepare decision tables that precisely described the framework for determining how transactions should be recorded. For example, the students prepared a decision table for revenue realization, and then tested it against actual transactions common to business.

While care must be exercised to distinguish between current practice and possible reformed practice, this blending of theory and practice can make accounting come alive to the students and better prepare them to cope with the complex, diverse problems they will face after they leave school.

The 1971-1972 AAA Committee on Courses in Financial Accounting stressed the importance of this blending by identifying six objectives of the financial accounting curriculum:

1. Provide a basic understanding of the conceptual framework underlying the measurement and communication of economic data.
2. Provide the future accountant with the technical competence for effectively measuring, assimilating, and communicating economic data, primarily for external use.
3. Provide an understanding of alternative models for measuring and communicating economic data, primarily for external use.
4. Be relevant to current problems and adaptive to changing social and economic conditions.
5. Cultivate a keen, analytical, inquiring mind.
6. Provide the student the incentive to grow and keep pace with ever-changing issues, conditions, forces, and ideas.[9]

In my opinion, these objectives can be reached only by a careful blending of theory and techniques.

While my experience has indicated that such blending of theory and procedures is possible and desirable, I am keenly aware of at least one real danger in this approach; that the procedures and techniques of accounting will be de-emphasized to the point that students will be able to argue and debate issues, but never be able to make a complex adjusting entry or to perform an analysis of complex transactions. This difficulty will be compounded even more if the Price Waterhouse recommendations for Introductory Accounting are implemented. In earlier years, the Intermediate course tended to repeat both in format and content that which was included in the Introductory course. Repetition was accepted as a desirable teaching method for the complex subject of accounting. Procedures were stressed in one, two or more practice sets spaced throughout the first two years of financial accounting. The 1971-1972 AAA Committee on Courses in Financial Accounting rejected the repetition philosophy and strongly urged a move away from it.[10] The recommended Price Waterhouse Introductory Accounting course stresses the use of accounting information rather than its preparation. While some introduction to the accounting cycle is intended, it is purposefully kept minimal. This course is directed to the Level I user. Thus, if the Intermediate Accounting course combines theory with procedures, the emphasis on techniques is again minimized with the possible undesirable results of a graduating accountant who is missing essential skills to be fully successful.

This is exactly the situation we felt that we had at BYU in 1971. We had changed our curriculum so that accounting majors were coming into Intermediate Accounting with only one term of Introductory Accounting. Although the Introductory course had not gone as far as that recommended by the Price Waterhouse study group, it still covered a broad range of topics with a definite de-emphasis on procedural abilities. As the faculty worked with accounting majors in advanced financial and managerial accounting classes, the lack of ability to handle routine accounting system transactions and analyses made us stop and question what was wrong. Our review of the problem revealed a basic lack of background in the fundamental steps of the accounting process. Many of the senior students in accounting were still struggling with the debit-credit framework. The lack of ability in this essential tool area was getting in the way of our desire to delve more deeply into the theoretical impact of alternative methods upon the financial statements. It was somewhat like trying to teach students calculus when they had only a limited knowledge of algebra. After reviewing the situation and discussing the problem with students and recruiters, we decided to reinstate a friend long ago discarded on the scrap pile of accounting education progress—the practice set. We selected a set from those available that we felt would both challenge the student in a limited time and give him the training he needed in the basics of the accounting system. We placed it in the first module of Intermediate Accounting, a review module.[11]

This module stressed the accrual concept, and provided drill for

students in the mastery of the recording and adjusting procedures. Students took a pre-test to see if they needed the module. Some transfer students, for example, came from schools that still taught a procedural introductory course and could by-pass the review module. Students were permitted to go on to the second module after passing a competency test and completing the practice st.
Although there has not been enough time to measure the results of this experiment, the faculty working with this project were generally pleased with the resulting increase in interest and abilities for th balance of the course. Rather than being "turned-off" by the details of a practice set, most students were appreciative of seeing for the first time how an accounting system fits together.

Practice sets apparently fell into disrepute because large numbers of introductory students were forced to spend time making accounting entries when they never intended to become a preparer of the accounting records. So much emphasis was placed on procedures that students could not see how the results could be useful in business decision making. So, as the introductory emphasis changed to reach the majority of the students, the non-accounting major, the practice set was discarded. But in so doing, in my opinion, we discarded an important teaching aid for our accounting majors. Research and experimentation is needed to determine if we would not benefit our accounting majors by its reinstatement. Our yet limited experience at BYU suggests that we would.

Some might question placing such a module in a second level course. We certainly have at BYU. Our preference would be to include this material in a second semester course following the general introductory course and to be directed to the Level II and Level III users. This course could include computerized practice sets and thus introduce modern systems concepts that have changed the recording and summarizing phases of the accounting process. It could be taught largely with a programmed learning approach. If this were done, the Intermediate course could be started at a truly advanced level. It appears that such modification will be possible at BYU beginning this fall.

This discussion of the review module might seem to be somewhat diversionary; however, in my experience, the ability to satisfactorily blend theory and techniques requires a better procedural foundation than many students obtain in their introductory courses. In examining the curriculum innovations reported in the literature, it is apparent that there is a movement to a blending of theory and techniques. The theory material included in the leading Intermediate Accounting texts has been expanded, and a separate theory chapter is now included in the majority of them. In the only

Intermediate Accounting article appearing in the *Collegiate News and Views* over the last decade, Mary Burnet of the Rochester Institute of Technology suggests deviating from the problem-oriented approach by requiring written reports on accounting topics; by analyzing actual annual financial statements as contained either in Moody's Industrial Manual, in microfiche records, or in annual stockholder's reports; and by including broad reading assignments from the literature of both the AICPA and the AAA.[12] The use of guest lecturers to supplement the procedural aspects of the course is used at both Ohio State University[13] and Boston University.[14]

Need For a Separate Theory Course

If the Intermediate and Advanced curriculum blend theory with practice, is there still a place for the Theory course in the curriculum? I feel that there is, and that it is in this course that teacher innovation is critical. Most business schools now offer a Business Policy course which is designed as a capstone course for the entire business curriculum. Such a capstone course is also needed in accounting. I do not believe it should be an isolated course where for the first time a student is introduced to the literature of accounting and challenged to evaluate the arguments presented. A student should have some of these experiences much earlier in his academic experience. The content of this last course might not be as important as the environment that is created for it.

Many objectives could be enumerated for such a course. It should create a desire in each student to continue his learning experience after graduation. It should provide an atmosphere where the fragmentation of courses and modules can be replaced by a unifying concept of accounting; where the relationships between the specialties of accounting such as auditing, financial accounting, managerial accounting, and systems can be explored and understood. It should provide an exciting experience in exploring contemporary problems involving accounting issues within the profession and within the economy. It should relate information from other disciplines such as economics, statistics, and behavioral science to the problems of accounting. Of all the courses in the curriculum for accounting majors, it should be the most dynamic and innovative.

The University of Iowa conducts a senior seminar that not only includes accounting, but also finance. A team approach is used, and an emphasis is placed upon analysis of articles from the current literature.[15] Marvin Carlson suggests introducing hypothetical problems to students that were previously unfamiliar to them, and then requiring them to formulate a method of accounting that applies those concepts of accounting that seem applicable in the circumstances.16 Lee Seidler, professor at New York University, argues for using international accounting in the theory course:

> This approach has become a laboratory for the practical demonstration of unresolved theoretical questions that exist in American accounting. What is only discussed, pro and con, in the United States has often been tried in other parts of the World. As a matter of fact, practical responses have at least been attempted for virtually every major theoretical disputation in American accounting.17

These references give some insight into the wide variety of approaches that can be taken in this capstone course. Perhaps what is needed most is a better medium for reporting the experiences of individual professors with such a course. I realize that all schools do not have a broad enough accounting program to include a separate theory course in their structure. As pointed out by Patrick Kemp, it is even more important in those circumstances to weave theory into existing financial accounting courses.18

Summary and Conclusions

The goal of this paper and the others presented at this Symposium is to provide information that will help to develop a program to improve accounting instruction beyond Introductory Accounting. A historical review of the financial accounting curriculum reveals that much of what we are doing today is influenced by a pattern that developed forty years ago. Some parts of the pattern are still useful. Other parts can and should be questioned and perhaps abandoned. Innovative work in the Advanced Financial Accounting curriculum is either largely lacking or has never been documented for the use of others teaching in this area. Perhaps a better mechanism for reporting on innovations is needed, although the *Accounting Review, Trends,* and *Collegiate News and Views* all apparently are looking for good contributions in this and other areas. Perhaps a standing Education Committee of the American Accounting Association is needed with sub-committees formed to encourage experimentation and its reporting.

Based upon my own personal experience, I feel that a modularized approach to Intermediate and Advanced Accounting should be seriously explored within the academic world and the results shared among experimenting schools and other interested parties. Consideration should be given by the AAA to developing a means for arriving at a consensus among academicians as to the concepts and techniques that an accounting major should have upon his graduation. Modules developed in these areas could be labeled as "required", and materials developed within the modules could be shared among schools, perhaps on a publication basis. This approach could also lead to a uniform classification of modules and their general content that would permit more ready interchange between participating schools. Experimentation should continue with the senior seminar capstone course, and encouragement given to the development of materials that could be broadly used in such seminars.

Most importantly, the spirit of educational research that has been fostered by the Price Waterhouse grants should not be left to slip into history. Recognition for innovative educational research at department, college, university, and profession levels is necessary. The apparent lack of research in the past can be attributed partly to a lack of recognition for such efforts. Universities and their faculties have justly been criticized in some cases by legislators, boards of trustees, students, and alumni for their unwillingness to keep current or ahead of innovative teaching techniques and concepts. It is my hope that the American Accounting Association can more effectively foster this spirit in the years ahead.

FOOTNOTES

1. C. E. Allen, "The Growth of Accounting Instruction Since 1900," *Accounting Review* (June 1927), pp. 150-66.

2. H. Noble, W. Karrenbrock and H. Simons, *Advanced Accounting* (South-Western Publishing Co., 1941), preface.

3. William Paton and William Paton, Jr., *Asset Accounting* (Macmillan Co., 1952).

4. For example, the 1961-62 Committee on Courses and Curricula, Accounting Courses for Accounting Majors published their report in the July, 1963, issue of the *Accounting Review*. The 1964-1967 Committee to Compile a Revised Statement of Educational Policy included in its report, published in the *1968 Committee Reports,* material from the 1963 Committee on Advanced Accounting Instruction that had not been previously reported. As far as I can tell, neither of these publications received much attention academically.

5. "Report of the Committee on Courses in Financial Accounting," Supplement to *Accounting Review* (1972), pp. 295-316.

6. Ibid, p. 302.

7. Robert R. Sterling, "Accounting Research Education, and Practice," *Journal of Accountancy* (September 1973), pp. 44-52.

8. Thomas L. Burns, ed., *Accounting Trends II* (McGraw-Hill Book Co.), pp. 37-8.

9. "Report of the Committee on Courses . . . ," Supplement to *Accounting Review* (1972), p. 299.

10. Ibid, p. 312.

11. Similar suggestion was made by Donald Emblen in January 1963 *Accounting Review* "When Should Techniques Be Presented," pp. 159-60.

12. Mary Burnet, "Enriching the Intermediate Accounting Course," *Collegiate News and Views* (December 1969), pp. 25-7.

13. Thomas L. Burns, ed., *Accounting Trends VII* (McGraw-Hill Book Co.), p.22.

14. Thomas L. Burns, ed., *Accounting Trends VI* (McGraw-Hill Book Co.), p. 7.

15. *Accounting Trends VII*, p. 20.

16. Marvin L. Carlson, "An Application of Concepts in the Theory Course," *Accounting Review* (July 1967), pp. 596-8.

17. Lee Seidler, "International Accounting—the Ultimate Theory Course," *Accounting Review* (October 1967), pp. 775-81.

18. Patrick S. Kemp, "A Current Topics' Course in the Accounting Curriculum," *Accounting Review* (April 1963), pp. 398-400.

EXHIBIT A
Chapter Content of Intermediate Accounting Textbooks
(Number of chapters for each subject)

Subject	Finney 1934	Gentry & Johnson 7th ed. 1974	Simons 5th ed. 1972	Meigs Mosich, etc. 3rd ed. 1974	Welsch Zlatkovich etc. 3rd ed. 1972
Fundamental processes	2	2	2	1	1
Financial statements	1	2	2	2	2
Corporations-equity	4	4	4	4	4
Cash	½	1	1	1	1
Receivables	1½	1	1	1	1
Inventories	1	3	3	3	3
Tangible fixed assets	3	3	3	2	2
Intangible fixed assets	1	1	1	1	1
Funds and investments	4	1	2	1	2
Current liabilities	½	½	1	1	1
Long-term liabilities	½	1	1	1	1
Analysis of financial state	4		2	1	2
Actuarial	2	1			1
Analysis of work. cap. (Funds statement)	2	1	1	1	1
Correction of errors	1	½	1		½
Theory		1	1	1	1
Single entry records		½	1	½	
Price level statements		1	1	1	
Pensions and leases		1½		1	1
Consignments	1				1
Accounting-income taxes		1		1	
Installment sales	1				1
Accounting changes				½	½
Total chapters	30	27	28	25	28

Jay M. Smith

EXHIBIT B
Chapter Content of Advanced Accounting Textbooks
(Number of chapters for each subject)

Subject	Finney 1934	Gentry & Johnson 6th ed. 1971	Simons & Karrenbrock 4th ed. 1966	Meigs Johnson etc. 1966	Griffin, William etc. 1971
Partnerships	5	3	4	4	3
Venture accounting	2		1		
Insurance	1				
Sick business	4		3	3	1
Branch accounting	1	1	2	1	1
Consolidations	9	8	8	6	12
Capital budgeting	1			1	
Foreign exchange	1	1	1	1	1
Estates and trusts	1	1	2	2	1
Actuarial		2	3	2	
Governmental	1	1	2	2	1
Bank accounting	1				
Stock brokerage acctg.	1				
National income					2
Installment sales		½	1	1	
Consignments		½	1	1	
Accounting measurement					1
Price level statements				1	
Replacement cost				1	
Total chapters	28	18	28	26	23

The Advanced Financial Accounting Curriculum—Recent Developments and the Need to Reconsider Content, Sequence and the Blending of Theory and Practice in Courses Beyond the Introductory Level

A Critique
Kenneth W. Perry

Needless to say, I am honored to participate in this symposium along with such a distinguished group of accounting educators. This is particularly true since the main thrust of the program is directed toward something that is very dear to my heart—the undergraduate accounting curriculum.

In our original conversation regarding the symposium, Bill indicated that he wanted me to be a discussant and to critique Professor Smith's paper on "The Advanced Financial Accounting Curriculum." Since a "discussant," by dictionary definition, is a person who participates in a formal discussion or symposium and a "critique" is an article or essay criticizing a literary or other work, I perceive my assignment to be twofold: first, to critique Professor Smith's paper and second, to participate in the subsequent discussion with the members of the symposium. At this time I shall address myself to the first part of the assignment—that of critiquing Professor Smith's paper.

While the word "critique" in its narrow sense connotes only criticism, I intend to use it not only in that sense but at times in a somewhat broader way to include a certain degree of supportive commentary and/or elaboration. Obviously, when critiquing someone else's written work there is often a great temptation to indicate how one would have written the paper in the first place. While I shall try to minimize this type of response, there is the possibility that I may think caution is necessary in a given situation or recommendation, in which case I shall so indicate.

Historical Development

To set the appropriate background for his paper, Professor Smith initially gives an overview of the historical development of accounting education in the United States with major emphasis being placed on textbook development, because he concludes, and perhaps rightly so, that this is his best source of information regarding what traditionally has been taught in the various colleges and universities. According to Professor Smith, much of our present educational structure, as it relates to accounting, seems to be an historical accident created largely by patterns established by early textbook writers and perpetuated in succeeding editions and in new textbooks written by other authors.

While I tend to agree with Professor Smith's conclusions regarding the effect of textbooks on the curriculum, I would hasten to add that we are looking at a two-sided animal in this instance, and we cannot ignore the other side. We have on the one hand the author of the textbook and on the other, those educators who adopt the text, thus establishing the market. This, of course, is nothing more than the practicable application of two basic concepts with which we as accounting educators are familiar, namely: (1) the so-called user-oriented approach, and (2) the EMH (efficient market hypothesis) approach.

To be successful (I am assuming success to mean that the book sells), the author of a textbook must give the user—the teacher in this instance—what he wants. Furthermore, it must be packaged in the way the teacher wants it packaged. Another text which may be equally as well-written and packaged will not suffice. For example, users of advanced financial accounting textbooks appear to want partnership material packaged in one neat section of 3-5 chapters and *not* integrated throughout the text. As a matter of fact, the market literally demands that the neat little package be inserted in a particular spot in the text. While we as educators may not necessarily agree with this, if we as authors want the book to sell we cannot ignore the professor who adopts the book, because it is he who establishes the market.

Professor Smith concludes the section on the historical development of accounting education in the United States by referring to and tending to agree with the 1972 report of the American Accounting Association's Committee on Courses in Financial Accounting, a report which rejects the course-content approach to curriculum development because it was felt that the use of such an approach would destroy the dynamic character of accounting education. According to the report, each college or university should do its own packaging according to the needs of its particular faculty and market. I, too, basically agree with this conclusion. I do, however, disagree with Professor Smith's concluding remark in this section that both the heavy user and the provider of economic information must be accommodated in the advanced financial accounting curriculum.

When Professor Smith first employed the term "heavy user," I thought that it was perhaps a matter of loose verbiage and that he actually was referring to the so-called "user-oriented approach." However, since he uses the same term, and in the same vein, throughout the remainder of his paper, I am forced to take issue with him. For example, in his section on *The Modularized Approach* he refers to the heavy user of financial statements being in the intermediate course and to the teaching of the heavy user of financial statements. While many of the students enrolled in the advanced accounting curriculum may eventually become heavy users of financial statements, I think the AAA Committee had in mind the orientation of the financial statements toward the user, not the teaching of the ultimate user.

Recent Developments

Since there has been little change in the structure of advanced financial accounting textbooks in recent years and since there is an absence of any substantial amount of well-documented information relating to recent innovations by specific teachers, in the section on recent developments Professor Smith drew heavily from his own experience.

Although he discusses what he terms "the integrated approach" briefly, most of this section deals with the so-called "modularized approach." Regarding the integrated approach, he points out that he and some of his colleagues at the University of Minnesota came to the conclusion that they were artificially dividing financial and managerial accounting by separating them in the class catalog and placing different labels on them. As a result they tried to integrate the two areas. While I tend to agree with Professor Smith's position that the integrated approach is best, I think his criticism of the nonintegrated approach at Minnesota applies equally as well to the artificial, if not arbitrary, compartmentalization of accounting material into modules. I am of the opinion that to do our best job, we as educators cannot segregate accounting from the social whole. Likewise, I am of the opinion that for best results accounting cannot be taught in isolated bits and pieces.

Regarding Professor Smith's discussion on the modular approach, I specifically disagree on the following points: Professor Smith contends that the modularized approach would free the student from the textbook content and sequency straightjacket. He implies that the modular approach would tend to make the curriculum more dynamic and alive. I would argue that the modular approach in and of itself would tend to do just the opposite, since it has been my observation that students (perhaps unconsciously, perhaps consciously) almost automatically erect a wall against the dull, the useless, and the fragmentary.

Taken as a whole, I basically agree with Professor Smith's excellent presentation in this section. However, I do think a word of caution is in order, not to Professor Smith in particular but rather to all involved in the educational process. With regard to accounting, the educational matrix centers on an area of specialization. It needs stimulation. It best thrives in a climate which permits at least a certain degree of serendipity, something that an isolated, compartmentalized, fragmented curriculum based on the modularized approach may miss completely.

Conclusion

As indicated in the 1973 Trueblood report, "The fundamental function of financial accounting has been unchanged almost from its inception. Its purpose is to provide users of financial statements with information that will help them make decisions." Of course, there have been substantial changes in the types of users and the kinds of information they have sought and such undoubtedly will continue to be the case in the future. As accounting educators our responsibility, it seems to me, is clear. We *must* respond in a meaningful way to such changes, or we do a disservice to our students and to the profession as well.

Finally, we as educators must make every effort to see the situation as it is—not necessarily what we as individuals might wish it were or think it ought to be. We must realize that accounting does not exist in a vacuum, it cannot be compartmentalized into neat little packages, nor can it be isolated or segregated from the social whole. While the Trueblood study appears to have been a step in the right direction, it must be noted that it sought ends, not means. Although the Trueblood Committee and the Study Group sponsored by the Price Waterhouse Foundation both recognized the supremacy of the user, even the Trueblood Committee had to base its study on assumptions rather than facts regarding the user. According to the Committee's report, users' needs for information are not known with any degree of certainty, because the specific role financial statements play in the economic decision-making process has not been identified. Needless to say, I hope that we who are gathered here today do not concentrate all of our efforts on the means without having an end in mind. If so, we are nothing more than a group of characters running around looking for a play.

The Advanced Financial Accounting Curriculum—Interaction with other Disciplines: Quantitative, Behavioral, the Business Administration Core

John A. Tracy

Interdisciplinary Teaching: A Curse or a Blessing?

Every serious teacher of financial accounting should think about the relevance of other disciplines and research activity to our own. Personally I am committed to an interdisciplinary approach in teaching financial accounting, especially in the advanced courses. At the very least, we should make an occasional aside in the classroom that provokes the students into looking beyond the conventional boundaries of financial accounting and to relate financial accounting to other courses both in the Business School and outside. However, a serious attempt at interdisciplinary teaching of financial accounting requires much more than this.

It is tempting to take a "wine tasting" approach—just a little sip from each discipline is enough to get the flavor, aroma, and fundamentals. To continue the metaphor, we could hold wine tasting parties or serve wine in our courses. This would give the students some exposure and perhaps even an exuberance for other disciplines, which may not be a bad way to start. This may be adequate for students. For the teacher, however, my experience suggests that a "mountain climbing" approach is needed. Mastering another discipline well enough to introduce it to students in our accounting courses, even on a wine tasting basis, is a hard climb, requiring learning how to use many new tools. And, there are so many relevant disciplines.

Accounting is frequently defined as a measurement and communication system. Therefore, I have done a fair amount of reading in the communication disciplines, in preference I must admit to reading in the measurement disciplines. But one article and book has lead to another, and to another, and to another. It is very difficult to read in the general field of communication without also digging into closely allied fields, such as social psychology or any discipline which pays particular attention to language, image, and symbolic systems (such as anthropology, sociology, and religion).

For a reverse comparison, assume that a chemistry professor wanted to learn about financial accounting so that he could extract the most relevant aspects to incorporate into this teaching of the applied economic aspects of chemistry. Or better yet, assume that a theology student wanted to study the "world of business" to make his future ministry more relevant. What plan of study would we suggest to him? Quite a broad one I suspect, including economics, finance, organizational behavior, and so on. So, as we seriously approach interdisciplinary teaching of financial accounting we should be prepared for a long and meandering journey, not just a quick sight-seeing trip.

What is the "Priority of Relevance" of Other Disciplines?

Give me a week to dig into almost any other discipline, whether it be epistemology, ethology, or physical education for that matter, and I dare say that I could find many relevant points to financial accounting. Maybe it would work just as well to select another discipline at random, read up on it, and then "relevize" it to financial accounting. Of course this is a facetious remark. I mean it only to draw attention to the first problem of an interdisciplinary approach to financial accounting: Which "outside" disciplines are the *most* relevant, the *most* promising, and probably will have the *most* payoff to financial accounting? Obviously we have always considered economics and finance close relatives, even blood brothers and sisters. More recently, the polyglot behavioral sciences and the mathematical-quantitative sciences have gotten much attention. Are we optimizing our scarce resources (to borrow from our "mother" discipline Economics)? Are these the *most* relevant, that is, are these the disciplines and research areas which will have the *most* benefit to financial accounting?

"Leibnitz, it has sometimes been said, was the last man to know everything."[1] If so, it's too bad that Gottfried is not alive today; he could, perhaps, prepare a relevance priority list of other disciplines for us to study. I'm confident he would put the behavioral sciences quite high on the list for management accounting. Would he also put the behavioral sciences high on the list for financial accounting? I think he would. Political science and sociology have much to offer, it seems, especially regarding conflict resolution and the working out of disagreements among different pressure or special interest groups, and how the institutional structure of divergent groups determines and affects the "bargaining" process.

Much of the recent history (another relevant discipline?) of the APB and thence the FASB certainly is characterized by conflicts and confrontations between the accounting profession's authoritative body and other power blocks, groups, and agencies with different values and objectives. The developments within and around the accounting profession during the last decade can be explained in terms of the models and theories that political science and sociology have to offer, and these explanations may provide valuable clues for what the future holds if the institutional structure remains unchanged.

Even when we identify what seems to be highly relevant theory and research, the implications to financial accounting may not be very obvious. The abundant research on the "efficient market hypothesis" is a case in point. The research has convinced me of the weak form of this hypothesis (the random walk behavior of security prices), and the research also seems very persuasive regarding the semi-strong form (regarding the statistical correlation of returns relative to publicly available information). The strong-form (market reaction to inside information) does not seem all that well tested yet. In any case, even if we accept these research findings, does this lead us to agree with, for example, Beaver in his recent article [2] regarding the policies that the FASB should follow based on these research findings? I doubt it. I suspect that once the efficient market hypothesis research gains wider recognition among accounting teachers, the diversity of reaction and opinion will match the diversity of our generally accepted accounting principles.

The Integration Reason for Searching Other Disciplines

My basic starting point, even before trying to identify the most relevant outside disciplines to financial accounting, was to ask: What is the main reason for an interdisciplinary approach in the first place? The main reason evidently is to integrate the relevant aspects from these other disciplines into the teaching of financial accounting. Thus, I focused on the concept of *integration*. Integration means to make whole and complete. As the *American Heritage Dictionary* puts it: "to make into a whole by bringing all parts together; to unify; to join with something else; to unite." Thus, the main reason for an interdisciplinary approach is to bring something into financial accounting that should not be left out, or to desegregate financial accounting if you would.

Given my perception and understanding of how the teaching of financial accounting is organized and carried out, the basic theme of integration is divided into two quite different aspects in my mind — (1) the *external* integration of outside disciplines into the fabric of and thinking about financial accounting; and, (2) the *internal* integration of financial accounting with other branches of accounting. In other words, before we jump into the ambitious *inter*disciplinary teaching of accounting perhaps we should first consider the *intra*disciplinary aspects of teaching accounting. Clearly the general field of accounting has been subdivided into specialized branches. The more I thought about this the more I became disturbed about the lack of integration among these specialized branches of accounting. But first let me explore a few points regarding the integration of financial accounting with external diciplines.

In our search of external disciplines it seems clear to me that most of us have been too unilateral, I mean too inner directed. We look for what the outside disciplines can bring to accounting, not what accounting can take to or do for outside disciplines. Let me illustrate with just one example from the external discipline of decision making—though some of you may prefer not to call decision making a discipline. Indeed, this field of study and research has many different academic addresses. In any case, I take my cue from the book by *Thompson and Van Houten*,[3] in particular Chapter 9 "Making Decisions." This brief analysis of decision making makes several observations essential for both the teaching and the practice (the "doing") of financial accounting.

Clearly financial accounting is itself a decision making process; many decisions have to be made by those who prepare and those who audit financial reports of an entity, including both profit and non profit enterprises—any entity having external financial accountability. This chapter in *Thompson and Van Houten* brings into sharp focus, or at least made me more accutely aware of, how poorly the accounting profession has so far been able to specify and to articulate the objectives of financial reporting, the Trueblood and previous studies to the contrary. Their chapter does not use the term objectives but instead "perceived possible outcomes," a broader concept that I find more challenging to begin with. These two authors distinguish decision making objectives on a scale which on one end is called crystallized (very sharply specified, very definite) and which on the opposite end is called ambiguous (fuzzy and indefinite). I would put our attempts to delineate financial reporting objectives more towards the ambiguous end of their scale, which leaves us rather like a ship without a rudder.

Can we judge between different accounting methods, or between uniformity versus flexibility of accounting principles without a "crystallized" set of objectives for financial reporting? I doubt it. Rhetoric instead of persuasion will continue without a common reference of crystallized objectives. Rather than devoting our energies to finding the "best" accounting principles (which must be judged against well defined objectives of financial reporting), perhaps we should change direction to the more modest task of better communicating the *effects* of the accounting methods that have been decided upon. For instance, the financial report perhaps should disclose how much different the total depreciation charge-off is this year compared to last year due to the use of an accelerated method.

Also, *Thompson and Van Houten* deal with conflicts between incompatible or partly inconsistent objectives, and this seems to have much relevance to the multi-objectives nature of financial reporting. And they make a keen observation in discussion of the "bounded rationality" approach of the decision maker in complex and risky decision situations, which certainly seems to characterize financial accounting decisions: "Persons who are overwhelmed by complexity and uncertainty may welcome authoritarian figures as providing solutions."[4] This strikes me as a feasible explanation or contributing reason for the increasing authoritarian rule making power of the APB and the FASB over the last 15 years.

Whether you agree with the above line of argument or not, my main point is simply to illustrate how an external discipline can provide many insights and concepts, as well as empirically tested research findings that help to understand the practice and development of financial accounting. Someplace in the accounting curriculum the most relevant of these ideas and research conclusions should be studied by the serious student of financial accounting.

In summary, searching the behavioral and social disciplines provides many valuable insights and concepts for teaching and researching financial accounting. But as we break financial accounting out of its isolation through the interdisciplinary approach, new problems may emerge that were not even thought of before. One such "new" problem caused by my interdisciplinary search of external disciplines—I should say "new" to me at least—was raised when I turned the direction of the interdisciplinary search around and took an inside-out approach by projecting financial accounting to external disciplines.

How Well is Financial Accounting Integrated into the Disciplines It Serves?

I've come to one rather radical conclusion from my personal interdisciplinary search. When I admit this opinion, I'm sure many of you will accuse me of jumping ship. Nevertheless, by reading in the user disciplines of financial reports, especially the management and the investment/finance disciplines, it has become clear to me that the main function of accounting is to integrate itself into larger and higher order systems of decision making. As often said, accounting is an information service function; the main implication of this to me is that accounting therefore is *subservient* to the decision needs of users. It seems to me that the accounting profession, including the teaching members, has consciously or unconsciously attempted to autonomize accounting, that is, to institutionalize the financial accounting discipline outside of and separate from the decision making systems that financial accounting is trying to serve. In other words, accountants want to make accounting decisions—such as what information should be reported, how best to communicate such information, how to measure profit or some other performance characteristic, etc.

I would argue that the final stages of policy level accounting decision making is more properly the function of management and investors. The two groups (that is, management and investors) must work out some sort of agreement, or "contract," or modus operandi governing the rules of the game regarding financial reporting disclosure and accounting methods. It looks good in theory to have the public auditing profession play the role of an independent arbiter between the two groups. But as many of us believe I think, the CPA auditor is subject to far more pressure from management than can be brought to bear by investors, except through the vicissitudes of the SEC and the NYSE. Decision making by independent auditors, especially in matters of disclosure, obviously has fallen too far on the side of management. Public accountants need to design a process that gives investors more practical pressure and influence in financial accounting decision making. The so-called third party responsibility of the public accountant is more like second party behavior in actual practice.

To go to the extreme here, assume that the FASB put the basic net income measurement questions to some sort of national referendum that all 30 million investors could vote on, and it turned out that a large majority of investors decide that net income should stay as close as possible to a cash flow basis, and that they express strong disapproval of deferred income tax accounting and the deferral of intangible costs for instance. In my opinion this would settle the issue. I can imagine the reaction of some of my colleagues to this statement, which probably will be that "the function of the accounting profession is to educate the users of the financial report." But I would respond that it is also our responsibility to let the users educate us regarding what they want and what accounting decisions they want us to implement. The question turns on who should make accounting policy decisions—the accountants or the users of the financial reports?

A Valuable Lesson From Other Disciplines: The Danger of Over-generalization of Principles

Another basic observation from my reading in outside disciplines, reinforced very frequently, is the danger of over-generalization of principles. In our quest for generally acceptable accounting principles we seem to forget that generalizations have limits. Other disciplines, at least the ones I have read in, have a much broader tolerance for ambiguity and lack of closure; most writers seem very leery of overly broad generalities.

In other disciplines there is far less concern with the development of generally accepted principles in an "all pervasive" or "in every case" sense of this term. For instance, Peter Drucker in his latest magnum opus on management [5] does not push for generally accepted principles of management. Rather he stresses the themes of "tasks," "responsibilities," and "practices." To cite one specific instance of how he guards against over-generalization consider how he discusses the principle of decentralization:[6] (emphasis in the original)

> Decentralization is the best principle of organization design *where it fits*. But the specifications for its application are fairly stringent. It fits the business for which it was originally designed: manufacturing, with distinct markets for distinct product lines. It fits few nonmanufacturing businesses perfectly or even adequately. And it does not fit manufacturing businesses such as the process industries (e.g., aluminum or steel), where the same process produces a variety of products with an infinity of overlapping markets.
>
> Decentralization, we have further learned, is the best principle for the task of operating an ongoing business. It does not answer the organizational demands of the innovating task. And it is not enough, by itself, to organize the top-management task.

In short, other disciplines appear to adopt much more of an "if . . . then . . ." approach regarding generalizations. Other fields look to find the key *conditions precedent* that must be present to lead to a certain result or behavioral response. In our never ending attempt to formulate GAAP I think we all too often are over reaching—the conditions precedent are not as generally prevailing as we seem to assume. We have ignored Anthony's excellent discussion of "What Is A Valid Generalization?".[7] I have argued elsewhere[8] that our generalizations of accounting principles contain many operationally meaningless terms and concepts—our language of accounting principles lacks enough real world touchstones. I need only to mention such terms as "fairness," "usefulness," and "materiality" to make my point here I think.

In summing up the value of an *inter*disciplinary approach to financial accounting, there is little doubt that from the "outside-in" direction many other disciplines (probably too many for us to handle) have much to offer. Our problem is to optimize the search and selection of which fields to explore and in how much depth. From the "inside-out" direction, that is, projecting financial accounting to other decision making disciplines, my fundamental perception of the financial accounting task has been altered substantially. The most basic underlying function of financial accounting is to integrate its theory and practices into the higher order decision systems that it serves. Last, other disciplines teach me that we should constantly be on guard against over-generalization. Over-generalized principles cannot and will not lead to uniformity of accounting decisions given the diversity of decision situations encountered in actual practice.

The Intra*disciplinary Approach: The Need To Integrate Financial Accounting with the Other Branches of Accounting*

Finally, let me say a few words about the *intra*disciplinary aspect of teaching financial accounting that I referred to earlier. We have done very little to integrate the different branches or specializations within the general accounting curriculum. Accounting courses at the undergraduate level can be sub-divided into basic groups: the financial statement accounting series (introductory, intermediate, and advanced); the management accounting series (introductory, cost, and EPD-Data Processing-Systems); tax accounting, and auditing. (I realize I'm leaving out certain other accounting courses that may be offered.) Student learning behavior, the content of the textbooks used in these courses, and observing the lack of interaction of professors teaching these courses lead me to the inescapable conclusion that the different courses are very little integrated. Seldom is the content in one course area related to the content in the other areas.

The most serious non-integration or de facto segregation in my opinion is the cleavage between management accounting and (external) financial statement accounting. Most management accounting textbooks do not build on the foundation of financial statement accounting methods and practices. Indeed, there is almost a leprosy attitude towards the historical cost based financial statements, as if these sources of information are "obviously" misleading to intelligent management decision making. This attitude is self defeating. We know that in practice historical cost based accounting measurements are the guts of the management control accounting reporting system. The connecting links between management accounting and financial accounting should be coupled together in teaching these courses. However, my concern with the need for better integration between management accounting and financial accounting goes a little deeper than this.

Management accounting models and methods seem almost totally isolated and separate from financial accounting models and methods. I'm overstating the case here somewhat, to be sure, since one could point to certain valuation models, such as the present value paradigm, as being equally applicable both for management decision making and financial statement reporting. I should distinguish between models and methods which have practical application value, as opposed to those that do not. To be more precise therefore, the "working" models and methods of management accounting are not integrated with the "working" models and methods of financial accounting.

For instance, inventory models and methods for management decision making (the EOQ models at the most simple level) are seldom integrated or even juxtaposed with the FIFO/LIFO/Average Cost decision in financial accounting. Or to put this example in other terms, the LIFO/FIFO/Average Cost inventory decision in financial accounting does not consider what method may be best for management decision making. Likewise regarding depreciation decisions. Long-term capital investment models and methods in management accounting avoid any discussion of how to integrate the capital recovery pattern inherent in this analysis with the depreciation decision problem in financial accounting. How often do you see a discussion of depreciation in a financial accounting textbook or article that considers what is known about the capital recovery pattern from the fixed assets being depreciated?

Like most of my colleagues, in my financial classes I usually set up an inventory decision example for the students to debate and argue out. I suspect my student reaction is typical of yours. What I'd like to ask you is how often your students think to ask: What is management's sales pricing behavior? For instance, what if management clearly follows a FIFO sales pricing policy which is triggered by increases (or decreases) in the purchase or manufacturing cost of the inventory? Should the inventory cost method be consistent with management's sales pricing method?

Generally accepted accounting principles of periodic net income measurement obviously are based on the theory of matching costs and revenue. This premise in turn assumes that management decision making, especially sales pricing behavior, is also based on a "matching" process that considers the relationships and connections between costs and revenue. But if the recent *Business Week* article[9] is any indication of the state of generally accepted management principles of sales pricing behavior, then we are building on a very shaky base of assumptions for net income accounting. I do not see how accounting theory, principles, and practices can be divorced or isolated from the management decision making behavior that produces the financial results that accountants try to measure.

Management accounting, in my opinion, has as its first priority the design and implementation of "information/measurement/communication" systems that deal primarily with the "critical success factors" of the business entity. Such factors include product image, percent of customers making repeat purchases, employee morale, changes in the inventory positions of the company's customers, new product development, governmental relations, utilization of resources, the mix of processes being performed by the company—the list is long and varied to say the least. Some of these factors probably fall outside the generally accepted range of reporting responsibility of management accounting. But obviously many of these factors are the primary responsibility of management accounting.

Let me focus on one key aspect: the management accounting system should identify each significant source of profit, and measure and report the profit performance of each source relative to past periods, as well as current budgets and goals. In particular, any significant changes of profit performance between periods or between actual and budget should be highlighted in management reports, and the reasons for such changes should be explained. Should the *external* financial statements of the company also be presented on this basis?

Implications for Financial Reporting Disclosure

From my reading of *Forbes, Fortune, Business Week,* etc., it seems clear that these financial publications seek out the critical success factors of a business entity and try to get behind the published financial reports to find out the "real story." Also, note for example *Lorie and Hamilton's* book,[10] Chapter 6 in particular, for further evidence of this "let's get down to basic factors approach." And, even the New York Stock Exchange in its recent *White Paper*[11] argues for disclosure of an interperiod comparison of why the company's operating profit increased or decreased.

Financial accounting, as currently taught, is almost barren of this "management accounting" approach to disclosure. Financial accounting courses do not attempt to use the critical success factors of the business entity as the basic touchstone for developing the information content and communication format of external financial reports. Shouldn't we at least raise the question with our students: Should the external financial reports *explain* why the financial condition and performance of the company is better or worse or about the same? I ask my students to think of themselves as the non-management stockholders of a closely held corporation who sit on its board of directors. I tell them to ask themselves what they would want included in the periodic financial reports from management. Are stockholders of publicly owned corporations entitled to any less?

FOOTNOTES

1. Colin Cherry, *On Human Communication* (M.I.T. Press, 2nd ed., 1966), p. 1.

2. William H. Beaver, "What Should Be the FASB's Objectives?", *Journal of Accountancy* (August 1973), pp. 49-56.

3. James D. Thompson and Donald R. Van Houten, *The Behavioral Sciences: An Interpretation* (Addison-Wesley, 1970), pp. 160-81.

4. Thompson and Van Houten, p. 167.

5. Peter F. Drucker, *Management* (Harper Row, 1974).

6. Drucker, p. 29.

7. Robert N. Anthony, *Planning and Control Systems: A Framework For Analysis* (Division of Research, Graduate School of Business Administration, Harvard University, 1965), Appendix C, pp. 157-67.

8. John A. Tracy, "Are We Accountants Communicating With Anyone Else Than Ourselves: In Fact Are We Even Communicating With Each Other?" *DR Scott Memorial Lectures In Accountancy,* Volume V (Department of Accountancy, College of Administration and Public Affairs, University of Missouri-Columbia, 1973), pp. 101-27.

9. "Pricing Strategy In An Inflation Economy," *Business Week* (April 6, 1974), pp. 42-9.

FOOTNOTES

10. James H. Lorie and Mary T. Hamilton, *The Stock Market* (Irwin, 1973).

11. New York Stock Exchange, *Recommendations And Comments On Financial Reporting To Shareholders And Related Matters* (NYSE, December 1973), pp. 12-13.

The Advanced Financial Accounting Curriculum—Interaction with other Disciplines: Quantitative, Behavioral, the Business Administration Core

A Critique
Thomas F. Keller

The interaction of the accounting curriculum with other disciplines is the billing for this session. Why should there be an interaction? If there is an interaction, what is the nature and extent of the interaction?

John states at the very beginning that he is committed to an interdisciplinary approach in teaching financial accounting. That is wonderful, but what does it mean? He tells us that "at the very least, we should make an occasional aside . . . that provokes the students into looking beyond the conventional boundaries of financial accounting and to relate financial accounting to other courses . . ." He does admit that "a serious attempt at interdisciplinary teaching requires much more than this." Much more than an aside? Much more than relating subject matter in courses? Both? Something else? The answer is, yes. Does this statement ignore the law of diminishing returns? I can still remember as a small boy that upon being taken to the medic with a very bad upset stomach, he advised my grandmother, with whom I was staying, to give me only bananas as solid food until I gained some stability. After one banana, I suppose I seemed somewhat better, but I still find bananas rather offensive because my grandmother's philosophy was if one helps, 100 will surely provide a complete cure.

In order to address this question of interaction with any sense of perspective, I think we need to consider the discipline with which we are primarily concerned. John refers to communication. One of the principal reasons for the existence of accounting is the need for communication. While I have not studied communication theory, I would guess that if communication is to take place the signal transmitted by the sender must be subject to correct interpretation by the receiver. If this process is to be successful, the sender and receiver must have a common understanding of the code. In accounting terms this implies that the parties share a common jargon and that the translation process to the descriptors for the various attributes about which communication is necessary be understood by both the sender and the receiver. Without such a base of knowledge, precise communication is unlikely to occur.

In my opinion, accounting as a discipline should focus on developing a rather precise translation process and code which permits precise communication between the sender and the receiver. A message received should communicate specifically, information about a particular attribute.

If one accepts my opinion as at least a basis for discussion, then the implications for accounting education are:

> to develop a basis for understanding the process by which measurement rules, as processes for obtaining surrogates for attributes, are developed. The student should learn how the discipline has evolved to the present and should develop a base for continuing the development process.

> to develop a working knowledge of the communication system in use including an understanding of its logic. The student should become very proficient in the use of the communication system and also develop the required understanding to contribute to the orderly extension of the system.

Again in my opinion these so-called objectives of accounting education have implications for the education process. Frequently in an advanced society we find ourselves attempting to impart the state of the art to our students and hopefully in the process they obtain an understanding of the process. The efficient way to get the job done frequently appears to be to teach what is or to teach the state of the art. Based on my experience of meeting with students the more effective process is to help the students understand the process of how we got to the present state (mess) that we are in. This does not mean recreation of all knowledge but rather a careful consideration of some of the main themes of development.

A jump to a conclusion is in order here in the spirit of brevity. This argument does not imply to me at least that the accountant should engage in teaching related disciplines. The argument does imply, however, that the teacher have some knowledge of these disciplines and that through a system of carefully specified prerequisite course materials the student should be expected to have developed a basic knowledge of the related disciplines.

How does one decide which disciplines are relevant? I do not think that there is any set that anyone can presently set forth as the relevant set forever. Economics is obviously relevant because accounting as it has developed is principally concerned with communication about economic events. The behavioral sciences are probably relevant if one is concerned with the process of communication. Perhaps the science of politics is relevant if one is concerned with the process of the establishment of authority for the translation process and the development of a general set of communication signals. These disciplines are relevant to accounting because accounting is a communication discipline. Accounting is not a basic science founded on certain immutable facts to be discovered. Accounting is a discipline in which the basic processes probably remain rather stable but the inputs and outputs of those processes change in response to changes in the environment in which communication is necessary.

The decision maker at a variety of levels constitutes the market for the accounting product. As the process of decision making becomes more "scientific" the need for information changes. As the environment about which communication is desired becomes more complex the translation procedures require modification. This lack of stability, in the output from the accounting system and in the processes being measured, requires that accounting education at the advanced levels focus more on the process and the impact of the environment than on the state of the art. In my opinion this is the reason that accounting education must include a foundation in the behavioral sciences, which in my judgment, includes the traditional fields of economics, political science, psychology and sociology. The endorsement of these disciplines does not include the assumption that any course in these disciplines will serve the accountant equally well. Courses in these areas should focus on an explanation of the behavior of people.

An important factor to consider in this discussion is that, while accounting may not be a discipline with well-defined boundaries there are limits as to what accountants measure and there are limits as to the information reported. These limits are and should be flexible. The limits are established on the basis of need for information and the ability of accountants to develop translation methods which accurately describe attributes about which information is desired.

John is critical of the accounting profession for not stating the objectives of financial reporting. Much improvement could undoubtedly be made in this area of communication as well; however, a substantial amount of the criticism derives from users who have not attempted to listen to the statements about objectives that have been made and who have attempted to use statistical data for purposes for which it was not intended. The statement that financial statements are general purpose statements does not imply that the data contained therein can be used for any purpose whatsoever. The user should be charged with learning the code so that when he receives a message he can translate the signal accurately. If this part of the communication process were functioning efficiently, there would undoubtedly be demands for change in the present state of the art. The demands would be focused, however. They would not consist of arm waving and shouting about the failure of accounting reports to satisfy all unspecified needs.

John argues that "the accounting profession . . . has . . . attempted to autonomize accounting." This argument can be deduced from the evidence that we see around us. I would argue that the education provided accountants has contributed to this result. Accounting education has been too concerned with teaching the state of the art. The objective has been to teach the procedures for measuring various attributes. There has been little concern for helping the student who becomes the professional to understand the process of communication. There has been a misconception of the objective of accounting education. The stress has been on developing a skill rather than on developing an inquiring mind.

John throws the baby out with the bath water, however, in his section on *How Well is Financial Accounting Integrated into the Disciplines it Serves?*, when he gives the final stages of policy level accounting decision making to management and investors. This charge of course is based on my bias as to what the appropriate accounting decisions are. These decisions relate to how to translate and how to code the information to facilitate decoding by receivers. Then decisions should be made by accountants who are responsive to the needs of users. A national referendum on how to measure net income is a total abdication of responsibility and will lead to total chaos. John, would you also recommend that the steel industry hold a national referendum on pricing policy?

If one is convinced that democratic principles require a national referendum, then the referendum should be on the question of the appropriate decision model to be used in the selection, from among many alternatives, of the best equity security to provide $1,000 of income from an investment of $10,000 for a period of at least 25 years.

In my opinion, while I stated earlier accounting is not a discipline based on immutable laws of nature, accounting is more of a discipline than mere data processing. I have to believe that there is some logic to accounting and there are boundaries to the discipline. Suppose the referendum shows that the masses want a measure of cash flow. Then the question would have to be put—for what periods? If a future period is involved, then what is the method for forecasting? Such an approach is pure foolishness. Accountants must inevitably make accounting policy decisions and the education system should provide them with the training to do this in a changing world. The decision maker must specify the decision model he uses and the education system should provide him the training to do this. The accountant must be responsive to changing needs and the decision maker responsive to limitations of the translation and communication processes. There must be communication! Perhaps we should have some persons from related disciplines at this seminar.

In his section on *A Valuable Lesson From Other Disciplines: The Danger of Overgeneralization of Principles,* John hits on a symptom that something is wrong with accounting education. He argues that in accounting there is an over-generalization of principles. This may not be restricted to accounting; nevertheless, the problem probably does exist. Earlier I have indicated a concern with the stress of efficiency in teaching the state of the art as opposed to the effectiveness of helping the student to understand the discipline. The symptom John has pointed out probably derives from the problem I seem to detect in the education system. In practice there is the additional problem of justifying accounting applications on the basis of the impact on the users of the message communicated rather than on the basis of the accuracy of the message.

In his section on *The Intradisciplinary Approach: The Need to Integrate Financial Accounting With The Other Branches of Accounting,* John is guilty. I conducted a trial in Durham on May 16, 1974, of assuming that accountants are attempting to provide information for the pricing decision when net income is measured based on the theory of matching cost and revenue. I would argue that any management which uses such a measure is guilty of not properly selecting the right information for his decision model or of having no decision model or of not understanding the message that is being communicated. Accountants are too quick to accept the blame for the deficiencies of other members of the management team and too slow to recognize that the environment in which they function is changing and the needs for information are expanding and changing.

In concluding I must state that in my opinion accounting is not a discipline which can survive in isolation. Accounting is a discipline in a constant state of change, it is a discipline which will forever be the whipping post of the user of information and the focus of his complaints as the user looks for the extremes and the producer attempts to obscure the adverse and overemphasize the favorable. The accountant is the judge. In such a role the accountant must have a deep and clear understanding of the environment and the role of accounting therein. The accounting educator must try to insure that the proper framework is laid in the education process, but he must never assume that all knowledge can be provided through the accounting courses taught by accountants.

The Advanced Managerial Accounting Curriculum—Recent Developments and the Need to Reconsider Content, Sequence and the Blending of Theory and Practice in Courses Beyond the Introductory Level

Edward L. Summers

Introduction

Let us at once pay our respects to information processing. Communication has never been so important, so intensive, and so difficult as it is today. Our consideration of the curriculum dimension of management accounting presupposes that management accounting is a field within information processing and affected more by events outside its boundaries than it is able to affect those same events.

Management accounting processes and originates information for operating an organization controlling economic assets. Information reduces uncertainty, which makes it desirable to decision makers who prefer to operate in the presence of no more uncertainty than is unavoidable.

Figure I: Development of Management Accounting shows how the original record keeping functions were expanded through infusions of financial management, mechanical accounting systems, planning and control, behavioral science, microeconomics, quantitative modeling and computer science until contemporary managerial accounting not only emerged but appears to be momentarily about to transform itself into a super-discipline, integrating and enhancing all knowledge and information relating to management and capable of funneling such knowledge to decision makers for optimum decisions throughout any economic entity!

Recent Developments Bearing on Management Accounting Education

Any assessment of management accounting education should take into account five specific recent developments—two of them technological, three of them institutional—which have affected the

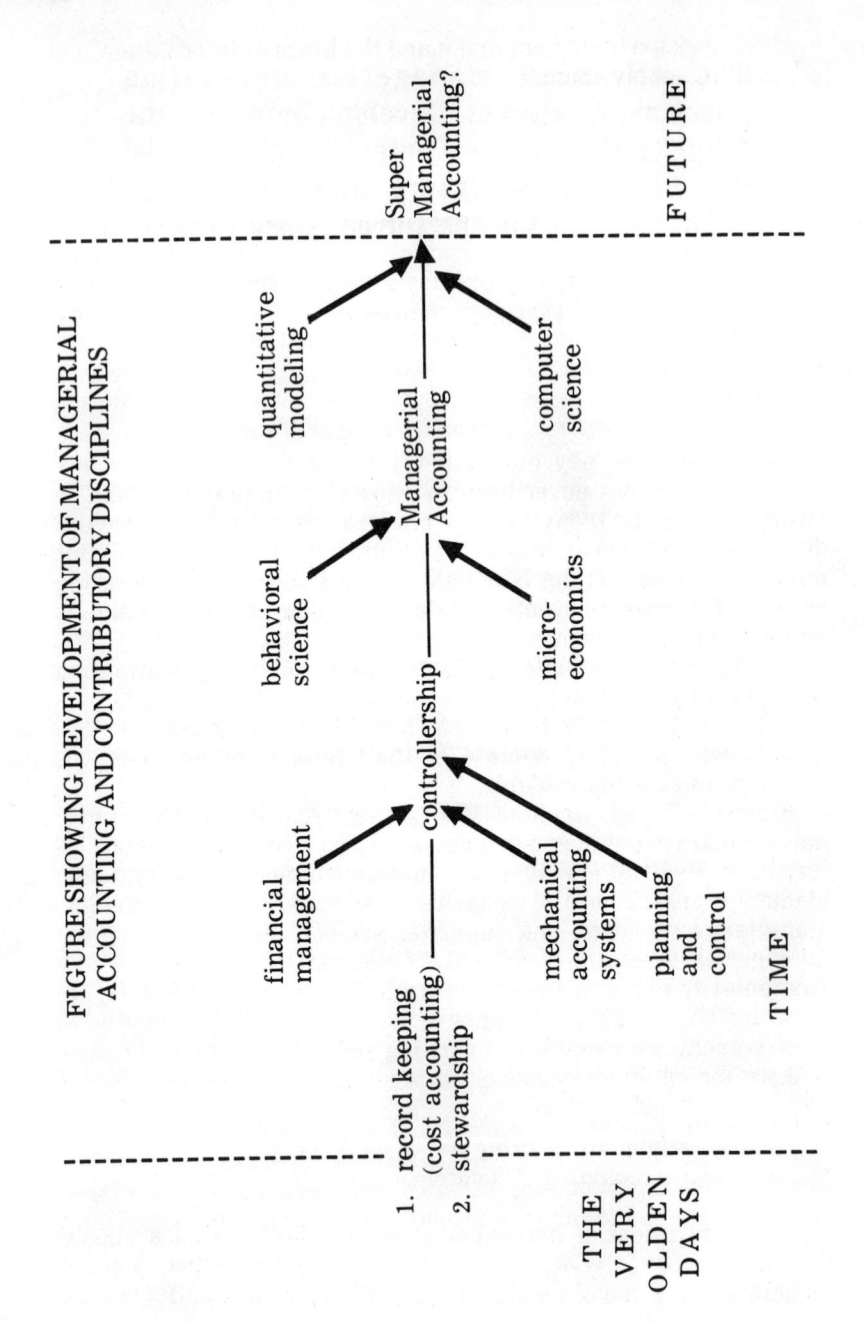

FIGURE SHOWING DEVELOPMENT OF MANAGERIAL ACCOUNTING AND CONTRIBUTORY DISCIPLINES

FUTURE

Super Managerial Accounting?

↑ ↑

quantitative modeling — computer science

Managerial Accounting

↑ ↑

behavioral science — micro-economics

controllership

↑ ↑

financial management — mechanical accounting systems — planning and control

1. record keeping (cost accounting)
2. stewardship

THE VERY OLDEN DAYS

TIME

kinds of decision managers make and the kinds of information it is possible to supply them.

The use of models to analyze specific decision information requirements.

Very few decisions are made using models. The inventory control, linear programming, capital budgeting, and critical path models we teach so proudly are operationally applicable to one or two percent of all managerial decisions, and not always to the most important or significant decisions, either. And behavioral science has illuminated an even smaller fraction of the totality of human behavior. Despite these apparent inadequacies, modeling is responsible for a systematic, non-intuitive approach to information management. The reasoning is that: If a model can be made of a decision, and within the model certain information can be identified as necessary, then *whatever* process is used to make corresponding real-world decisions, it is safe to assume that the same information will be necessary in the real-world decision process. Thus, an information system's capabilities may be appraised against the information requirements of decisions made in reliance upon it, and deficiencies systematically identified.

The computer has made information more plentiful and accessible without necessarily improving communication.

If management's inclination is to see today's high rates of social and cultural change as causing more uncertainty—the cure for which is more information—then management must be disappointed at the results of applying the supposed cure. Each information source has its own priors and there are hundreds of independent sources with access to the manager and providing much information which is contradictory or irrelevant or both. All that information makes *any* operational management information processing system appear inadequate to make sense of the inflows. The inevitable overall impression is that management accounting has fallen behind the demands made on it. Further, information is not an ordinary economic quantity. It is true that more resources may produce more information, but the rule of decreasing marginal returns does not hold—the last fact acquired may be the most relevant and uncertainty-reducing. This cannot be anticipated except by clairvoyance.

The roles of manufacturing in the private sector, and of the private sector in economic activity, are diminishing.

This change in the institutions through which accounting became important to management is continuing. The extent of governmental control over money supply and market processes is not, of course, unprecedented, but it is greater than for several generations and appears to be increasing. Relatively more of the managerial positions and information requirements are therefore in the public sector, where decision making conditions are not the same as in the private sector—though the nature of the implications for information needs is not satisfactorily clear.

There is a diminishing of rewards for initiative and risk taking by individuals. At the same time, large private sector organizations are receiving disincentives for certain kinds of "success." Increasingly, large organizations are characterized by inflexibility, risk avoidance, and mediocrity in both public and private sectors.

These trends are alarming at best. Do they foretell the ultimate collapse of competitive, risk-taking capitalism? Such a forecast would be imprudent, and it is improper for a faculty to convince itself that a curriculum of some particular character might oppose or delay such trends. But the executive is less a lone operator than before, his rewards are more in the form of job security than in upward mobility, and the sources of his motivation to excel are obscure. If there is *any* implication here for management information it is that entrepreneurial goals have changed, and information needs may have changed with them.

Inflation, apparently a permanent and unwelcome fixture in the economy, reflects scarcity of resources including food and energy and worldwide declining living standards.

Present managerial styles developed when inflation was not as important as it is now. The advent of inflation is in its own way as important and significant as is that of the computer. Inflation is a sign that normal economic decision making processes which occur between segments of society have broken down. Clearly accounting cannot repair these processes alone, and may even have contributed to the breakdown. For example, many accounting principles have assumed indefinite continuing increases in real consumption—an assumption we'd now recognize as unrealistic, but which may have hastened the onset of the decline in real consumption. What other false assumptions are now affecting information systems? Our discipline shares a responsibility to identify them.

Conditions Affecting Managerial Accounting Options in Education

The purposes of education are to provide for immediate on the job competence, for ability to learn while pursuing a career, and for a life as a responsible member of society. Managerial accounting education seeks to accomplish these purposes by conveying to an individual some ability to furnish information to decision makers on an economical basis.

The managerial interest in information processing has created a mission for accounting education: to prepare persons for careers in managerial accounting. A serious effort to perform this mission is complicated by these four observed conditions:

There is no generally recognized or articulate management accounting profession.

There is, in many university curriculum areas, strong influence and support from well-organized groups such as lawyers, doctors, clergy, architects, librarians, and accountants. Managerial accounting has no articulate voice. One may distinguish many preprofessional groups such as internal auditors, cost accountants, and data processors. Some day these groups may meld into a managerial accounting profession; until then, faculties are deprived of the strong guidance a profession can offer in curriculum structuring. Meanwhile, to whom do the managerial accounting faculties address their efforts? The only reasonable answer is—to those applied specializations which look to accounting faculties as a source of educated new entrants to their profession.

The knowledge that may be relevant to information processing is taught in many university areas.

Among these are computer science, psychology, sociology, philosophy, mathematics, economics, management, finance, statistics, engineering, and even library science. The different programs in these areas are free-standing and have little impact on each other. Should there be a unified information management responsibility center in the university? If there were, all of the areas listed above (which are represented by schools, colleges, and departments) would have to sacrifice some portion of their programs. In change-shy, non-innovative modern universities, it is questionable whether such a change with its major budgetary, administrative, and curricular alterations could be achieved—certainly not without organized popular support. Such popular support usually originates in a profession—yet managerial accounting is not a profession. It would appear that for the indefinite future information processing will be taught in competitive, even duplicative, ways in many university areas.

A university curriculum area, in order to be successful, must have extensive opportunities for research as well as teaching.

The general problems of information processing are very attractive to researchers. The appeal of these problems to so many already established disciplines has caused information processing to be researched and taught all over the campus. The problems are those of information's economy, capture, historical validity, decision relevance, predictive power, and motivating potential. Accounting brings the research of these problems its intimate knowledge of the double entry system of recording, classifying, and reporting information. Is this enough? It may be that other disciplines also have inherent advantages in the research of important information processing problems, and that neither they nor accounting alone can successfully sustain a comprehensive information management curriculum.

There is no agreed body of knowledge or way of achieving a body of knowledge for managerial accounting.

Perhaps this is for lack of trying. No reproducible research can identify a *defined* body of knowledge. The AICPA's CBOK study does not appear to be more than the subjective opinions of a few persons. Each of us may have an idea or two, or more, as to a managerial accounting body of knowledge that should be covered in a managerial accounting curriculum. These ideas are related to research and experience, but not demonstrably so in the logical sense. If a workable body of knowledge in managerial accounting is ever defined, it will not be through research but through market processes in the business environment that receive recognition in the university.

To date, research has failed to give anything like a complete answer to the faculty questions about topics comprising managerial accounting knowledge and emphasis to place on them in a curriculum. Some research has been useful primarily because it punctured old prejudices and expectations about managerial accounting—for example, the low importance in managerial practice of quantitative analysis and cost accounting—and showed how large the need for curriculum planning information really is.

Appraisal of Present Managerial Accounting Curricula

Our impression is that managerial accounting programs have upgraded at a rate less rapid than programs in computer science, financial accounting, and behavioral science. The principal development in the past decade in managerial accounting itself has been the introduction of economic analysis based on accounting information into such courses as "principles of managerial accounting" and "cost accounting." Other less dramatic developments have been teaching of "quantitative methods" as a separate subject within an accounting curriculum and selective introduction of computer material into the accounting systems part of the curriculum.

In my opinion, the following factors have limited more rapid changes in managerial accounting programs:

Relatively low mathematical sophistication of business administration students and instructors in mathematics.

Many students, even at better universities, cannot take a square root, find a logarithm, differentiate or integrate simple functions, plot linear equations, or understand the practical relevance of matrix operations. Under these circumstances, the professor who attempts to teach learning theory, linear programming, or least squares regression must first address the underlying mathematical deficiency, then secondarily (if time permits) the information significance of each technique. Many instructors, facing large classes and short of time for individual consultation with students, cannot make the extra effort. The basic business math requirement is usually a 3-6 hour course covering the most elementary topics and intended to be passed easily by most all persons taking it.

Teaching materials that are widely available do not provide for coverage of advanced materials.

Although the textbook publishers are beginning to sense the need for advanced materials, there is still, in my opinion, an unmet demand for higher level textbooks in all areas of managerial accounting. While no good purpose is served by overwhelming and confusing a student with advanced concepts he is not ready for, the impressive learning achievements of students in engineering, science, and some professional schools is convincing evidence that accounting students can learn more too. Our faculties should press their students to perform as students are pressed in other disciplines.

The large demand for accounting program graduates which has extended over two decades without subsiding.

This demand does not seem to be related to the quality of the graduates, especially since many times the amount spent on accounting ebucation in universities is spent by accounting firms and by businesses to provide further (remedial?) education for their employees. The demand derives from society's need for or desire for information. Accounting faculties have not had economic reasons to give serious thought to improvement of their programs as a necessary factor in making their graduates more desirable in the business world.

The general lack of idea exchange between managerial accounting faculty and the managerial accounting practitioners.

The natural field for research in managerial accounting is the problems encountered by managerial accountants. With a few exceptions, these problems have not been addressed by managerial accounting faculty. Some of the problems, such as computer configuration selection, have actually been belittled as lacking the relevance or sophistication necessary for serious consideration in accounting research. Yet, few more significant problems are proposed as alternatives. Certainly a greater interest in business information processing should improve our collective grasp of the body of knowledge our students should be receiving. We run the risk, without this business contact, of becoming overly reliant on textbooks and articles by our equally naive associates in the journals for definition of the curriculum.

In summary then, the present management accounting curriculum is not developing as rapidly as are competing professional and information-related curricula because the faculty and students are mathematically unsophisticated, advanced teaching materials are not widely available, accounting faculty and students have not had to compete in the market place, and managerial accounting faculty are largely isolated from the business functions for which they prepare their students.

Real change in managerial accounting probably will not occur until these four conditions are relieved. Their relief is not exclusively a curriculum matter.

There are good reasons to think that efforts to upgrade managerial accounting programs will be successful. Here are a few of them:

The information management function is becoming more professionalized.

The import of this is that more pressure from this emerging profession on universities would require faculties to re-examine their programs.

Decision makers must have an independent, unbiased source of relevant information; i.e., it is inherently unnatural and inefficient that they develop and operate information systems dependent on one or two managerial functions only.

The obvious analogy here is to the auditor, who is independent and provides information to a second party about the activities of a first party. The information manager must provide information about the activities of A to A and also to B and C. A cannot provide the information to B or C, for neither of them would attribute much credibility to it. There cannot be a blending of information management and decision making in management.

A very high level of competence is required to operate as a successful managerial accountant.

The implication is that this competence is largely dependent on a university education. The competition among disciplines for a part of the information management curricula package assures that improvement, whether in or out of accounting programs, will take place. Management accounting, if it overcomes the disadvantages enumerated earlier in this section, should improve and compete as well as any other discipline.

Accounting doctoral programs are turning out more Ph.D.'s with managerial accounting interests than at any past time.

Possible Future Trends In Managerial Accounting Curricula

The present managerial accounting curriculum may be said to begin with a limited exposure to economic analysis of traditional accounting information, then proceed to a descriptive study of cost accounting, accounting information processing systems, and quantitative and behavioral decision models. In a "typical" five year accounting program as much as 12-15 hours of accounting would be devoted to managerial accounting. If a "major" in managerial accounting is available an additional 6 to 9 hours is added to this.

To see what future trends will be, one might examine the information systems research being done in and out of accounting. Such an examination will reveal, among others, that the following topics are receiving attention:
Information economics
Computer configuration
Information storage and retrieval systems based on computers
Decision maker planning, control, and motivation
In what form might these topics appear in a future managerial accounting curriculum?

In the future, the introductory managerial accounting course will no doubt be upgraded, or followed by an upgraded course, to become a rigorous introduction to the decision-worthiness of information. Essential information about computer science, psychology, sociology, economics, finance, organization theory, mathematics, and statistics would be presented, preferably by faculty teaching courses intended for majors in those areas. The utilization of the computer science faculty to teach assembly languages and data base systems should increase.

In courses taught as accounting courses, students would learn the application in managerial accounting of the basic knowledge from these other disciplines. Such application will follow the functions managerial accountants are expected to perform, such as facilitating planning and control, maintaining standard costs, operating data precessing centers, appraising the decision-relevance of information, and so on. I would expect all the subjects which have lingered on the fringes of managerial accounting curricula for the past decade to now be integrated with the remainder of the curriculum. The future managerial accounting curriculum will be a strong area of specialization in schools of accounting and schools of business. It will be a highly quantitative area, relying more on statistics, computer science, and decision modeling than at present. Much more behavioral science will be taught earlier in the curriculum. The students and faculty alike will have more contact with the practicing managerial accountant. And there will be some kind of professional recognition for the competent managerial accountant.

APPENDIX: A Curriculum Revision Process

Curriculum development is not a new problem in education nor is it even unique to management accounting. In developing a curriculum, otherwise unrelated elements have to be brought together to work in a coordinated fashion to educate a person to acceptable standards. Some of these elements are facts—others are teaching and research resources and financial support and administrative structures. The process presented here is one which attempts to show all of these elements under consideration. The steps in such a process are as follows:

1. Identify all the specializations or functions in society which look to managerial accounting faculties for educational services.
Let these specializations be S1, S2, S3... etc.

2. Identify the set of knowledge development and transmission areas—or disciplines—which are available as educational resources and possibly relevant to some or all of S.
Let these disciplines be D1, D2, D3... etc.

3. Experts in each discipline should divide the established knowledge therein into component modules, each of which is as nearly as possible self-contained. Each module will contain introductory, intermediate, and advanced materials.
Let these modules for D1 be M1 (D1), M2 (D1), M3 (D1) ... etc. and for D2 be M1 (D2), M2 (D2), M3 (D2)... etc. and so on for all other disciplines.

4. Working now in conjunction with experts in each S, determine the need for each M (D) in each S. The result may be a matrix such as this one:

Disciplines

		D1	D2	D3	D4	D5
	S1	M1, M8	M2	none	M4	none
Practical Specializations	S2	M5, M9	M1	M10	none	M2, M3, M9
	S3	none	M1	M1, M5, M12	none	none

5. Determine the academic responsibility for each knowledge module. Some responsibilities will be clear cut; i.e., if cost accounting is a module it is the responsibility of a school or department of accounting in a university. Other modules will not correspond to single responsibility centers.

The knowledge in all modules must be arranged into courses. Some or all of certain modules may simply not be available in the university. In a general model, one would have to evaluate whether a particular educational responsibility center is the probable most economical choice to convey the knowledge in a module; here, we assume some arbitrary and acceptable module allocations can be made if necessary.

6. Group modules and component courses by educational responsibility centers.

Each educational responsibility center would convert the modules assigned to it into a part of a curriculum. The accounting faculty should be prepared to give some guidance in respect to how much time is available to teach the curriculum and how large a portion of the curriculum can be allotted to any particular knowledge component of it.

7. Revise the curriculum to fit the university structure of responsibility.

The procedure through step (6) which makes use of the existing administrative structure to develop the curriculum should limit adjustments in (7) to the relatively major ones. If, for example, most module's contents are scattered among several responsibility centers, implementation of the curriculum may be impossible, and whether an administrative change or reorganization must be a part of the overall curriculum package is an appropriate decision.

8. Revise the curriculum to use as much existing material and methodology as is feasible.

What cannot be taught using existing materials must rely upon development of materials that are suitable.
The administration of a curriculum review process is a delicate responsibility. Strong support beyond the university for certain changes is helpful in getting such changes approved. Without this support, and without recognized faculty curriculum authorities, a new curriculum may become lost in a forest of issues and priors the

faculty feels are more important. In general, a curriculum process imposed and conducted by a few persons will not succeed. If participatory budgeting works for management, participatory curriculum planning works in universities. This means that individual faculty must create a curriculum they feel serves their own teaching and research interests. To them, the curriculum must be attractive to teach.

The Advanced Managerial Accounting Curriculum—Recent Developments and the Need to Reconsider Content, Sequence and the Blending of Theory and Practice in Courses Beyond the Introductory Level

A Critique
Alfred Rappaport

Ed Summer's paper is divided into the following sections:

Recent developments bearing on management accounting education
Conditions affecting managerial accounting options in education
Appraisal of present managerial accounting curricula
Possible future trends in managerial accounting curricula

In shorthand terms these sections may be labeled "history," "constraints," "evaluation," and "forecast," respectively. A disussant generally has three strategies open to him. First, he can develop a critical analysis of the main paper. Secondly, he can state that he is about to do a critical analysis of the main paper, while he embarks upon a discussion which has little connection with the paper. Finally, he can candidly admit that he wishes to develop his own view of the assigned topic rather than critiquing the main paper.

While I do question several of Ed Summer's assertions and forecasts, our overall viewpoints are sufficiently close to advise against my presenting a detailed critique of his paper. Thus, I have chosen the third approach, i.e. an independent approach to the assigned topic. This choice is further guided by Bill Ferrara's suggestion that "the orientation of every paper, critique, panel, small group session and summarization should be to identify and examine curriculum problem areas and to suggest approaches through which these problems might be resolved."

In brief, I would like to offer seven major suggestions for (advanced) managerial accounting curricula:

1. The perspective for accounting should advance from the financial-managerial dichotomy, to one which addresses the *informational inter-dependencies* within an organization and between the organization and its environment.[1]

2. The scope of managerial accounting should be broadened from one with an almost exclusive emphasis on profit-seeking firms to include not-for-profit organizations such as government, health care, and educational institutions.

3. Textbooks generally consider in some detail informational requirements for operational control and management control, however, additional consideration needs to be given to information for strategic planning.[2]

4. Since effective planning and control systems require the estimation of parameter values in standard, ready-made models, but also require that models be tailored to fit the specific system, students need not only be familiar with models but with the art of modeling as well.

5. Just as management accounting information serves as *a* basis for product-market decisions, the economics of investing in management information *per se* needs to be more carefully considered as another organizational resource allocation decision.

6. Inflation can no longer be viewed as a transitory phenomenon and should be explicitly considered in managerial accounting courses.

7. The notion of "relevant costs" should be explored not only in a competitive market context, but also when price or reimbursable costs are externally determined as is the case for regulated industries and companies involved in government contracts, respectively.

FOOTNOTES

1. The approach is detailed in Prem Prakash and Alfred Rappaport, "Informational Interdependencies: A Perspective for Accounting," *Accounting Review* (July 1975).

2. These terms are used as in Robert N. Anthony, *Planning and Control Systems: A Framework for Analysis* (Cambridge, Mass: Harvard University Press, 1965).

The Advanced Managerial Accounting Curriculum—Interaction with other Disciplines: Quantitative, Behavioral, the Business Administration Core

Edwin H. Caplan

For many years the primary emphasis in accounting education was on preparing students for careers in public accounting. This emphasis in objective led in turn to an emphasis in content and resulted in accounting curricula that were devoted almost exclusively to the study of financial accounting principles and practices. While students were required to take one or two courses in "cost accounting," these courses tended to concentrate on cost accumulation for inventory purposes and thus were more related to financial accounting than to managerial accounting. While I suspect that this extreme emphasis on financial accounting may still be found in some schools, it appears that we are now witnessing a significant change in attitude about the nature and importance of management accounting. This change is currently reflected in both the content of managerial accounting courses and in the variety of such courses available in many accounting programs. It is also reflected in the non-accounting parts of the curriculum.

There are several reasons for the increasing attention being given to management accounting education. In the first place, it is now widely recognized that a thorough understanding of management accounting concepts and techniques is an important part of the education of accountants regardless of whether they intend to enter the field of public accounting or to begin their careers in management accounting. Smaller CPA firms often provide controllership services to their clients. The large public accounting firms have specialized departments which offer a variety of management accounting services. Even members of the audit staffs of these firms need to be sufficiently knowledgeable about management accounting to identify problem areas when they see them and to be able to talk intelligently with their clients about management accounting matters.

Another reason for the increased importance of management accounting education is that management accounting tools and methods of analysis have become much more sophisticated. Modern management accounting requires not only a knowledge of accounting techniques but also the ability to apply concepts from several related disciplines. Furthermore, the approach and content of management accounting courses is becoming more and more differentiated from the approach and content of financial accounting courses. This means that, unless sufficient opportunity is provided for students to study management accounting, their education is bound to be deficient in this area no matter how many courses they may have taken in financial accounting.

A third reason for the growth of interest in management accounting education can be found in the changing organizational role of the management accountant. This role has been tremendously upgraded from one of performing repetitive clerical tasks to one of providing information required to improve the quality of management decision-making and organizational performance. Management accounting has taken on a new stature with career opportunities that are often as challenging and as rewarding as those provided by other areas of accounting. An important outgrowth of the changed role and increased responsibilities of management accountants has been recognition of the need to develop acceptable standards of competence. The "Certificate in Management Accounting" program, recently established by the National Association of Accountants, represents an attempt to define professional qualifications in management accounting and to identify the minimum levels of education, knowledge, and experience necessary to achieve professional recognition as a management accountant. Although predictions about the future are always dangerous, I believe that this program will contribute greatly to the recognition of management accounting as an area of professional study. Moreover, it is likely that the CMA Examination itself will ultimately have a substantial influence on management accounting education.

In summary, it seems clear that management accounting education is becoming increasingly important in its own right and that it can no longer be viewed merely as an adjunct to the study of financial accounting. Further, the content of the management accounting curriculum is evolving in response to a new set of needs and a broader interpretation of the organizational role of the management accountant.

Objectives of Management Accounting Education

Perhaps the best way to illustrate the extent to which management accounting has moved beyond simple cost-accumulation techniques is to examine the objectives of management accounting education as discussed by a recent American Accounting Association Committee:

Management accounting education should aid the student in integrating accounting and measurement concepts with managerial performance. The student should be confronted with the need to develop appropriate economic criteria for performance in light of management's end structures. The impact of decisions on economic objectives and of economic objectives on decisions should be stressed.
More specifically,

A. Management accounting should be related to the planning functions of managers. This involves:
1. Goal identification
2. Planning for optimum resource flows and their measurement.

B. Management accounting should be related to organizational problem areas. This includes:

1. Relating the structure of the firm to its goals.
2. Installing and maintaining an effective communication and reporting system.
3. Measuring existing resource uses, discovering exceptional performance, and identifying causal factors of such exceptions.

C. Management accounting should be related to the management control function. This includes:

1. Determining economic characteristics of appropriate performance areas which are significant in terms of overall goals.
2. Aiding to motivate desirable individual performances through a realistic communication of performance information in relation to goals.
3. Highlighting performance measures indicating goal incongruity within identifiable performance and responsibility areas.

D. Management accounting should be related to operating systems management, by function, product, project, or other segmentation of operations. This involves:

1. Measurement of relevant cost inputs and/or revenue or statistical measures of outputs.
2. Communication of appropriate data, of essentially economic character, to critical personnel on a timely basis.[1]

Even a cursory reading of the above objectives indicates that management accounting is considered by the Committee to have become an integral part of the management function. Moreover, these objectives support the proposition that education for management accounting must be an inter-disciplinary process involving the application of knowledge from such fields as economics, organization behavior, and quantitative methods.

Given the developments described in the preceding paragraphs, what should be the scope and content of management accounting education? Since my assignment was to focus on the relationship between the management accounting curriculum and the business administration core and behavioral and quantitative areas, the balance of this paper will be primarily concerned with this aspect of the subject.

We need to recognize one caution at the outset. Past experience has demonstrated that when management accountants adopt an overly narrow perspective of their role, this perspective places significant limitations on their contributions to the organizations which they serve. For example, accountants in some organizations have been reluctant to become involved with the development of computer-based information systems. As a consequence, these systems were often established outside of the management accounting function. Thus, two parallel information systems evolved—the conventional management accounting system and the computer information system—each operating independently of the other. The result of these parallel systems is a proliferation of information sources and reports and a situation in which neither system has the capability of meeting the needs of management.

An unfortunate by-product of such dual information systems has been the downgrading of management accounting as accountants attempt to compete with—or ignore altogether—the more efficient and comprehensive computer-based system. On the other hand, where management accountants have accepted the responsibility for developing and operating computer systems, they have greatly increased the usefulness of the management accounting function to the organization. Although the particular illustration selected here refers to computer science, this discussion applies with equal force to a number of other areas—from operations research to human resource accounting.

It is unreasonable to expect that every management accountant can possess highly specialized competence in every area. Nevertheless, management accountants are often in the best position to furnish such services and a well-trained management accountant should at least be knowledgeable about these closely-related subjects. This would suggest that management accounting education must be sufficiently *extensive* to provide the student with the ability to deal with a rather wide range of related concepts—and it must be sufficiently *intensive* that the student will be able to apply these concepts in practical situations.

Comparison of Two Approaches to the Management Accounting Curriculum

In examing the management accounting curriculum, we are fortunate to have available two references which approach the issue from somewhat different viewpoints. I have already mentioned the CMA Examination which was specifically designed to measure the threshold of knowledge deemed necessary for careers in management accounting. This examination consists of five parts: (1) Economics and Business Finance; (2) Organization and Behavior, Including Ethical Considerations; (3) Public Reporting Standards, Auditing and Taxes; (4) Periodic Reporting for Internal and External Purposes; and (5) Decision Analysis, Including Modeling and Information Systems. (The examination assumes that a management accountant requires a higher level of skills in connection with the topics covered in parts four and five then is necessary with those topics covered in the first three parts.) It is, of course, possible for reasonable men to disagree on the details of the topics covered by the CMA Examination. However, I believe that this examination as it is presently constituted does, in fact, identify the major content areas underlying modern management accounting.

A second reference is The Common Body of Knowledge Study (CBK) published in 1967 by the American Institute of Certified Public Accountants.[2] Two years later, an AICPA Committee attempted to express the conclusions of the CBK Study in terms of a specific accounting curriculum.[3] While technically it is incorrect to refer to this curriculum as the CBK Study, we shall do so here for purposes of brevity.

The CMA Examination is in a sense an output measure while the CBK Study sets forth a curriculum which can be evaluated in terms of the desired output. Therefore, it would be interesting to compare the knowledge content of the CMA Examination with that of the CBK curriculum. In particular, we can ask: Assuming that the CMA Examination does represent a reasonable identification of the topics appropriately included in management accounting education, does the CBK curriculum provide an acceptable approach to accomplishing this education?

The table on the following pages compares the content of the CMA Examination with the curriculum recommendations contained in CBK. Before examining the table, two comments are in order. First, it is not entirely clear whether the authors of CBK intended to design a curriculum for accounting education in general or for public accounting education in particular. However, as a minimum, the CBK curriculum was certainly aimed at preparing students for careers in public accounting. The fact that much of the proposed curriculum is also applicable for careers in management accounting seems to support our earlier comments concerning the need for increased attention to management accounting topics in the education of public accountants. Second, the basic proposal contained in CBK involves a five-year program. A four-year program is also presented but appears to have been viewed by the authors as decidedly a second choice. Nevertheless, the comparisons which follow are based on the four-year curriculum in order to remain consistent with the objectives of this conference. As might be expected, the five-year curriculum devotes more time to topics related to the content of the CMA Examination but even the four-year program comes remarkably close in this regard.

In the following paragraphs we will examine each of the content areas presented in the table in more detail.

Economic and Business Finance

Most accounting educators would agree with the CBK recommendation that three to four semesters of economic theory (both micro and macro) plus a course in money and banking should be part of any accounting curriculum. I am somewhat concerned that, in many schools, courses in economic theory—particularly at the intermediate level—offered by departments of economics tend to be designed more for prospective graduate students in economics than for business undergraduates. At the risk of being accused of contributing to academic proliferation, I am inclined to suggest that a course in intermediate economic theory taught by a business economist would probably be more useful for accounting students than similarly titled courses in economics.

The CBK Study recommends four semester hours in business finance; however, it appears that at least two courses—6 semester

Comparison of Examination for Certificate
in Management Accounting and Common
Body of Knowledge Curriculum

Examination for Certificate in Management Accounting	Common Body of Knowledge Recommendations (Note: "hours" refers to semester hours)
Part 1: Economics and Business Finance A. Enterprise Economics B. Institutional Environment of Business C. National and International Economics D. Working Capital Management E. Long Term Finance and Capital Structure	Economics Elementary Micro- and Macro-Economic Theory 6 hrs. Intermediate Economic Theory and The Monetary System 6 hrs. Social Environment of Business 3 hrs. Business Law 4 hrs. Finance 4 hrs.
Part 2: Organization and Behavior, Including Ethical Considerations A. Organization Theory and Decision Making B. Motivation and Perception C. Communication D. Behavioral Science Application in Accounting E. Ethical Considerations	Behavioral Science 6 hrs. Organization, Group and Individual Behavior 6 hrs.

Examination for Certificate in Management Accounting	Common Body of Knowledge Recommendations
Part 3: Public Reporting Standards, Auditing and Taxes A. Reporting Requirements B. Audit Protection C. Tax Accounting	Elementary Accounting 3-6 hrs. Financial Accounting 6 hrs. Cost Accounting 3 hrs. Tax Accounting 3 hrs. Auditing 3 hrs.
Part 4: Periodic Reporting for Internal and External Purposes A. Concepts of Information B. Basic Financial Statements C. Profit Planning and Budgetary Controls D. Standard Costs for Manufacturing E. Analysis of Accounts and Statements	See Part 3 above
Part 5: Decision Analysis, Including Modeling and Information Systems A. Fundamentals of the Decision Process B. Decision Analysis C. Nature and Techniques D. Information Systems and Data Processing	Modern Algebra, Calculus, Statistics and Probability 12 hrs. Quantitative Applications in Business 6 hrs. Production or Operational Systems 2 hrs. Computers and Information Systems in Business 6-7 hrs.

hours—are necessary to achieve the level of competence required on the CMA Examination.

CBK calls for three hours of the social environment of business and four hours of business law. While the CMA Examination does not specifically refer to law, this subject is obviously important in management accounting. Adequate preparation with respect to these subjects should include a consideration of the social, legal, and political environment of business and can probably be accomplished in six semester hours.

In general, the CBK curriculum seems to provide reasonably adequate coverage for this part of the examination.

Organization and Behavior, Including Ethical Considerations

The CBK Study recommendation of six semester hours of behavioral science followed by six hours of organization behavior seems adequate. The six hours in behavioral science is most likely to consist of one introductory course each in social psychology and sociology. My own preference would be to require one additional course in either of these two disciplines. If three courses are not feasible then I would rather see the student take all six hours in *either* psychology or sociology in order to gain a more intensive exposure to behavioral science concepts than is possible at the introductory level.

The recent "Report of the Committee on Behavioral Science Content of the Accounting Curriculum" of the American Accounting Association discusses this subject in detail.[4] The discussion need not be repeated here except to emphasize the Committee view that there are some important relationships between behavioral science and accounting and it is desirable that all accounting students develop an understanding of these relationships.

It is unlikely that contemporary undergraduate education for business is very successful in dealing with ethical considerations. Auditing courses may consider the ethical responsibilities of public accountants but this topic is developed in a rather specific context. One can only hope that recent events will cause educators to look more closely at their responsibilities for at least attempting to influence student attitudes concerning ethical behavior in the business world.

Public Reporting Standards, Auditing and Taxes

*Periodic Reporting for
Internal and External Purposes*

These two sections of the examination relate primarily to the accounting content of the curriculum and are not part of our consideration. As a general observation, it might be noted that the three semester hours of management accounting proposed in the CBK Study are clearly inadequate for accounting majors regardless of their career objectives. In my opinion, two courses in management accounting together with the computer and information systems courses discussed below represent an absolute minimum.

*Decision Analysis, Including
Modeling and Information Systems*

I doubt that it would be possible for an accounting student to over-prepare in this area. However, in view of the time constraints on a four-year curriculum, the CBK recommendations seem realistic. These recommendations include approximately seven semester hours devoted specifically to computers and information systems. Assuming the student will gain additional exposure to computers in other courses, this requirement should suffice. The CBK Study also recommends 12 hours of mathematics and statistics and 6 hours of quantitative applications in business. Again, this appears to represent a satisfactory minimum assuming that the quantitative models covered in these courses are applied in other courses.

The "Report of the Committee on Measurement Methods Content of the Accounting Curriculum" of the American Accounting Association[5] provides an excellent analysis of quantitative topics and their relation to accounting. The Committee identified seven topics as representing a minimum level of mathematical competence and seven additional topics which were considered to be desirable. The seven essential topics plus certain of the additional topics should furnish sufficient background for the CMA Examination and the required material can probably be covered in the time available in the CBK curriculum.

To summarize the above observations: With the exception of the important deficiency in management accounting courses, the recommendations of the CBK Study are generally consistent with the content of the CMA Examination. Therefore, it seems to follow that the CBK curriculum provides adequate coverage of accounting-related disciplines. (In fact, it is interesting that the CBK curriculum involves stronger preparation in the accounting-related areas than it does with respect to management accounting itself.) This coverage appears appropriate regardless of the career objectives of the accounting student. However, it is likely that students who are planning for careers in management accounting will wish to take additional course work in some areas.

Conclusion

Despite the optimism of the preceding remarks, this paper concludes on a somewhat pessimistic note. If it is correct to state that management accounting education must be concerned with concepts from the disciplines discussed here, then how should these concepts be incorporated into the curriculum? For far too long, accounting educators have solved this problem—and eased their consciences—by requiring students to enroll in courses taught by mathematicians, computer scientists, organization theorists, etc. Such courses are undoubtedly important in providing background knowledge, perspective, and basic skills but by themselves they cannot accomplish the desired results. Instructors in these other disciplines know little about accounting and should not be expected to establish the necessary connections between their subjects and accounting. Accounting instructors, on the other hand, usually know little about these other disciplines and seldom make any effort to assist students in applying what they have learned in other courses to accounting situations. Without guidance from the accounting faculty, the most common outcome is that students never do see the relevance of these disciplines to accounting. Thus, they are not motivated either to learn, or to retain and apply what they have learned.

It is hardly a coincidence that all three of the American Accounting Association Committee Reports (which dealt with curriculum issues) referred to in these pages make the identical point—*management accounting courses must include the application of relevant concepts from related disciplines as an integral part of the course content.* Until this is done, much of the time devoted by students to the study of these related disciplines will be largely wasted. In order to accomplish a better integration of such disciplines with accounting, three steps are necessary. First, text materials must be developed that truly accomplish such integration—not just in chapters patched on at the end of an otherwise conventional management accounting textbook or even in paragraphs patched on at the end of otherwise conventional chapters. Second, effective methods need to be developed which will enable accounting instructors to become competent and comfortable in using the text materials. Finally—and this may prove to be the most difficult step of all—accounting faculty must be encouraged to take advantage of these opportunities to upgrade their own skills.

In short, it is my view that the most important strategy for accounting curriculum change in this area involves finding better ways for incorporating behavioral, quantitative, and similar topics into the accounting portion of the management accounting curriculum.

FOOTNOTES

1. American Accounting Association, "Report of the Committee on Courses in Managerial Accounting," *Accounting Review*, Supplement to vol. XLVII (1972), pp. 6-7.

2. Robert H. Roy and James H. MacNeill, *Horizons for a Profession* (New York: American Institute of Certified Public Accountants, Inc., 1967).

3. American Institute of Certified Public Accountants, *Report of the Committee on Education and Experience Requirements for CPAs* (New York: March 1969). For an appraisal of this Report see "Report of the Committee to Examine the 1969 Report of the AICPA," American Accounting Association, *Accounting Review*, Supplement to vol. XLVII (1972), pp. 237-57.

4. American Accounting Association, "Report of the Committee on Behavioral Science Content of the Accounting Curriculum," *Accounting Review*, vol. XLVI (September 1971), pp. 247-85.

5. American Accounting Association, "Report of the Committee on Measurement Methods Content of the Accounting Curriculum," *Accounting Review*, vol. XLVI (September 1971), pp. 213-45.

The Advanced Managerial Accounting Curriculum—Interaction with other Disciplines: Quantitative, Behavioral, the Business Administration Core

A Critique
Don T. DeCoster

The development of a management accounting curriculum is one of the biggest challenges that accounting educators face. It is my impression that while accountants have given lip service over the years to developing and expanding the management accounting curriculum there has been little positive action. With the exception of the Master's level accounting courses directed at facilitating a business manager's decisions the majority of the accounting curricula remain directed at developing the professional, certified accountant. The expansion of the management accountant's role in our society has not been met with corresponding curriculum advances.

My experience leaves me with little doubt that management accounting is considered by the majority of both faculty and students as a poor country cousin to financial accounting. One cause of this attitude is that management accounting has evolved from the cost accounting courses which are primarily concerned with inventory valuation and income determination. In these courses the role of data in decision making, while covered, does not comprise the bulk of the content. Another cause is the employment opportunities for accounting graduates. Most faculty and students believe that the best students should enter the public profession and that marginal students should enter industry positions. It is almost a stigma for an undergraduate student to have to go to work in a management accounting position.

If my suppositions are correct, a starting point for any curriculum development might be a finer delineation between financial and managerial accounting. Perhaps we could say that financial accounting is concerned with income determination and measurement while management accounting is concerned with facilitating decisions for income optimization. Or, perhaps we could say that financial accounting is concerned with insuring optimum resource allocations between firms while management accounting is concerned with optimum resource allocations within a firm. Or, perhaps we could say that financial accounting is concerned with historical, stewardship and compliance accounting while management accounting is concerned with planning and controlling a firm's decisions and actions. Certainly we can say that the attitudes of the financial accountant about data accumulation, measurement, and consumption should be significantly different from the attitudes of the management accountant. To borrow a psychological phrase, "they require different response sets." Management accounting should no longer be considered a subset of cost accounting which is a subset of financial accounting.

This recognition of a true dichotomy between financial and management response sets does not automatically imply that the accounting curriculum should have two distinct, separate tracks resulting in two different accounting majors. The professional accountant, whether his interest area is in management, public, or governmental activities should be well-grounded in the entire body of accounting knowledge. The student should be exposed to the full spectrum of accounting fundamentals. A functional fixation on financial accounting as is so common today, will, I believe, be detrimental to the long run development of the profession.

There are three areas we should consider in examining the interaction of the management accounting curriculum with other disciplines. The first area deals with the content of the management accounting core course(s). The second area deals with the subject areas the student should take in support of the accounting area. The third area deals with timing and sequencing of the student's course work.

The Management Accounting Core

Professor Caplan pointed out the definite lack of emphasis in the Common Body of Knowledge Study on management accounting courses. The CBK recommends a 3 semester hour course in cost accounting. In my opinion this is grossly inadequate. Most cost accounting courses could best be described as "advanced bookkeeping for manufacturing firms with a passing glance at the use of data for decision making." We can sense the inadequacy when we picture the three hour course to introduce cost terminology, cost flow systems, job costing, process costing, multiple product costing, standard costing and variance analysis, problems of overhead costing, and an introduction to differential costing for decision making. Further, an examination of these topics shows that in this 3 hour management accounting course the majority of topics deal with income and inventory measurement.

Critical topics such as the theory of decisions, inventory control models, optimum production scheduling, advanced capital budgeting, problems of decentralized firms and transfer pricing, comprehensive budgeting including forecasting and simulation models, advanced pricing and production decisions integrating microeconomic theory, and the role of accounting in motivating actions are too often omitted or barely introduced into the accounting major's curriculum. These omissions create too great a concentration upon the income measurement problem and too little emphasis upon income optimization approaches. While some of these topics, such as regression analysis, linear programming, and human interactions, are included in the supporting business courses at most schools, it is not at all clear the students get the opportunity to integrate them with their accounting knowledge.

One area not mentioned by either Professor Caplan or the Common Body of Knowledge Study deserves special consideration. The management planning, decision making, and control aspects of not-for-profit organizations are almost untouched in the accounting core. This is *not* a call for the teaching of Fund Accounting per se. I am not thinking about the techniques of governmental accounting, either national or local. Rather, I am concerned about the special decision problems of programmed budgets, project decisions and accounting, cost/benefit analysis where there is no revenue function, and social costs.

When the management accounting core is fully developed to include these crucial and necessary topics, it will be impossible to teach the content in 3 semester hours. To teach this management accounting area will take a full 6 semester (9 quarter) hours, as a bare minimum.

Support Areas

Professor Caplan has done a good job of relating the Certified Management Accounting Examination with the Common Body of Knowledge Study. There is little that I can add here except to make a few specific comments and observations.

First, I believe that the intended coverage of the CMA exam serves as a useful model for content integration. The subject content seems complete and applicable as a benchmark for comparing accounting's management core and its supporting area.

Second, the Common Body of Knowledge Study integrates relatively well with the CMA exam except in the accounting area where the management accounting content of the CBK study is inadequate and in Part 2 of the Exam where the courses recommended by the CBK study may or may not relate directly to the exam studies.

Third, I agree completely with Professor Caplan that the Business Finance area should probably be 6 hours and that the behavioral science area should be concentrated in a single field of study so that at least one course is at the junior level.

Fourth, there is the need to consider two "policy" courses in the student's last year of study to integrate his previous accounting knowledge. One course might deal with policies applicable to financial accounting and the other with policies applicable to management accounting. These courses would *not* be advanced problems or advanced theory. Rather they would be patterned after case type courses where the student is forced to decide upon accounting policies and to select the relevant data.

Finally, for the management accountant two areas of the Common Body of Knowledge Study are weak. The Production and Operations Systems recommendation of 2 hours seems to me to be weak and no mention is made of the marketing, distribution and transportation function.

In summary, we do have some suitable guidelines in the CMA exam and the Common Body of Knowledge Study. They serve as an excellent starting point and probably will require little adjustment to develop a curriculum approach acceptable to most accounting educators. Further, I believe they are not significantly different from the recommendations of the AACSB. This would certainly make it easier to obtain full faculty approval.

Timing of Courses

The content of the courses is not the sole determinant of the quality of a student's education. The sequence in which the courses are taken is also important. Professor Caplan did not specifically mention the timing of courses so I would like to make a few suggestions and comments.

First, the student should have the following courses *before* he undertakes the "advanced" (junior level) financial and management accounting courses:

	Semester Hours
Algebra and Calculus	6 to 9
Statistics and Probability (including regression & correlation)	3 to 6

	Semester Hours
Computers and Information Systems (Basic or Fortran Language and machine familiarity)	3
A specific behavioral science (probably sociology or psychology)	6 to 9
Economics, both macro and micro	6
Social Environment and Law	6
Elementary Accounting (both intro to financial and to managerial)	6

Second, that the following accounting courses be taken concurrently (usually in the junior year):

	Semester Hours
Financial Accounting Core	6
Management Accounting Core	6

If we can establish these two aspects of the accounting core running parallel through one year we could overcome some of the functional fixation on financial accounting that occurs and lead the students to better adopt the concepts of different accounting data for different purposes.

Third, that to the extent possible the following support courses be taken concurrently with the accounting core:

	Semester Hours
Organizational and Group Behavior	6
Production Systems	3
Business Finance	3 to 6
Advanced Statistics and Quantitative Applications to Business	3 to 6

	Semester Hours
Advanced Micro Economics	3 to 6

Fourth, that the two accounting policy courses be taken as close to graduation as possible and that the student have completed *all* required accounting courses before being allowed to enroll in these policy courses.

Summary

It would seem to me that the tasks a committee should pursue are a further delineation of financial and management accounting, the development of a "management accounting core" that includes many of the topics often omitted, and the development of a timing sequence of both accounting and nonaccounting courses. The CMA Exam and the Common Body of Knowledge Study are good starting points but they are not completely adequate.

There is no doubt that a good curriculum and a poor teacher provide a poor education and that often a poor curriculum and a fantastic instructor can create a sound education. This is self-evident but we should keep this in mind. Any curriculum revision cannot exceed the bounds of the educator's ability to implement it or the ability of the average student to absorb it.

Models for Financial Accounting vs. Models for Management Accounting: Can (Should) They Be Different?

Nicholas Dopuch

The title of this paper was given to me as: Models for Financial Accounting vs. Models for Managerial Accounting—Can (Should) They be Different?*Given the stated purpose of this symposium, the issue seems to be a legitimate one to consider. However, upon reflection it became clear to me that the task of identifying and then contrasting the appropriate models for financial and managerial accounting may be too ambitious for one session. Indeed, as I scanned the topics for some of the other sessions, particularly the ones which preceded mine on the first day, I came to the conclusion that much of our efforts at this symposium will revolve around the problem of identifying the appropriate models for financial and managerial accounting.

As an illustration, consider the topics of the two earlier sessions of this day. One dealt with the course content for advanced financial accounting and the other dealt with the course content for advanced managerial accounting. I could not imagine how the speakers would develop their themes without first assuming some model for the two types of courses. Similarly, their discussants would either agree or disagree with the main themes based on their own conceptions of the appropriate models for the two areas. A good example here is the discussion by Rappaport who effectively offered his own model for managerial accounting.

This is not meant to be a critical remark since anyone who seriously evaluates the content of an accounting course must adopt some model which suggests which topics should be included and how these topics should be discussed. What becomes evident, however, is that a number of alternative models exists which can be adopted in either financial and managerial accounting, and so we face the problem of how to evaluate these models. In effect, a determination of whether the financial and the managerial models

---

*I wish to express my appreciation to N. Gonedes for the valuable comments he made on earlier drafts of the paper.

are alike or different presupposes that we possess criteria which allow us to select the *appropriate* model in each area. The fact that we do not possess such criteria is the main theme of this paper.

In developing this theme I found it practical to take advantage of existing literature on the subject which I believe to be relevant, especially that literature which is consistent with my own biases. It will not come as a surprise, then, that several of the references will be to items I had a hand in writing. Thus, I will draw on the thinking imbedded in my revised textbook,[1] which was co-authored with Demski and Birnberg, on the ideas expressed in the AAA Managerial Committee report of 1969-70, 1970-71[2] which was also written with considerable aid from Demski, and on some of the rationale concerning empirical research in accounting contained in a paper written with Nick Gonedes.[3] The latter was presented at the 1974 University of Chicago Conference on Financial Accounting Objectives. The first two items deal with managerial accounting whereas the last deals only with empirical work in financial accounting.

In an effort to indicate that my arguments are actually consistent with the current train of thought in accounting, I will begin my assessment of the issue at hand by contrasting the approaches to financial accounting theory reflected in ASOBAT[4] and more recently the Trueblood Objectives Report[5] against what was the dominant approach to accounting theory for at least the first half of this century. First, I will give my summary of this dominant approach, leading up to references which can be viewed as immediate antecedents to ASOBAT.

Prior to the appearance of ASOBAT, financial accounting theory generally consisted of a set of proposed income concepts—e.g., historical and replacement costs, exit prices, and discounted values and how these various concepts should be implemented. Indeed, Myron Gordon once argued that financial accounting theory could be used to refer to the theory(ies) underlying the measurement of income and wealth.[6] This orientation can be traced back to Canning who I believe was the first person to explicitly argue that financial accounting measurements could be evaluated within the context of an ideal concept of income. In his view, the "true" income of a firm could be measured by the changes in the discounted value of the net cash receipts generated by the assets held by that firm. Following Canning, we have been exposed to decades of literature dealing with various concepts of income and the relative desirability of each, given the standard proposed by Canning, as well as the optimal methods for implementing each in practice. Some representative references here are Zeff[7] and Revsine[8] (correspondence of replacement cost income to economic income), Solomons' discussion of economic versus accounting concepts of income,[9] and more recently, the Davidson-Bierman paper[10] on the selection of historical cost allocations based on economic income notions. All of these analyses were conducted at an a priori level.[11]

I have no intention of delving into the details about which income concept is the ideal one, and which accounting measurements become closest to achieving this ideal in practice. What is important is that alternative concepts (models) exist and these must be evaluated somehow within our accounting courses dealing with financial accounting. And one possibility, of course, is to evaluate them in terms of Canning's ideal concept.

During the 1960's, however, a shift in orientation regarding alternative accounting measurements became noticeable. Probably the first indication of this shift was the Edwards and Bell[12] discussion of replacement cost income versus historical cost income. Recall that Edwards and Bell did not argue that either replacement cost or historical cost income necessarily approximated economic income. Rather they made the assumption that both measurements of income could provide useful information to users who were interested in evaluating the efficiency of management. In other words, E&B adopted a user orientation as the basis for their proposals. A user orientation is also a reasonable description of some of the rationale behind the Chambers[13] and Sterling[14] proposals that accounting income measurements be based upon exit, or market values of assets. Again, neither argued that exit value income necessarily provided the best approximation of economic income, although it could under certain conditions. Instead they adopted a set of assumptions about investor and management decision needs, and on the basis of these, each came up with exit value income as the income concept most relevant to those classes of decisions.

Unfortunately, the user-orientation approach followed by Edwards and Bell, Chambers and Sterling, and by others since, presents us with a more difficult kind of problem. Apparently, it is possible to make a case for any concept of income if the researcher is given sufficient latitude in his assumptions about both the decision models of users and the competitive markets which exist for assets. Indeed, Littleton once made a strong case for historical cost income under the assumption that users are primarily interested in the efficiency of management's past decisions to acquire, hold, and sell assets in less than perfectly competitive markets. Note that in a perfectly competitive market in which all agents have homogeneous expectations, the various current value concepts of income can converge. Apparently, then, a proponent of replacement cost income has his own idea as to the kind of market conditions which exist for capital and trading assets, and these conditions differ from those assumed by proponents of exit price income, and both sets of conditions are not consistent with those of a perfectly competitive market with homogeneous expectations.

I do not wish to make too much of the distinction between the earlier researchers who followed Canning's approach and those who attempted to link particular income concepts to assumed decision makers and their decision needs. Both groups attempted to specify a normative income concept which could serve as the basis of accounting theory. The point is that, at the time the ASOBAT Committee faced its charge, it was clear that we lacked the appropriate criteria to indicate which of the various income concepts was the ideal one to adopt for accounting theory. Regardless of which of the two approaches was followed, we can appreciate the committee's attempt to get us out of our dilemma by moving still further toward a user orientation. This was accomplished by adopting a set of criteria for evaluating information proposals which did not rule out any particular concept of income as being useful to different classes of decision makers. Recall that the criteria the committee advanced were relevance, verifiability, quantifiability, and unbiasedness. On the basis of these they adopted the Edwards and Bell proposal to report both current cost and historical cost measurements. Unfortunately, they never explicitly discussed why they believed both sets of cost measurements were relevant, verifiable, etc., but perhaps they assumed this was obvious.

Now the Trueblood Committee went much further in its recommendations about what information should be disclosed to users of financial statements. That committee argued that all four of the various income concepts which have been proposed—economic income (i.e., discounted values), replacement costs, exit prices and historical costs— may be relevant to users' needs, not to mention certain non-financial data as well (e.g., social benefit measurements). Whether we accept the logic of the Trueblood Committee report is unimportant. The point is clear, however, that some respectable accountants have now adopted the view that progress in accounting is more likely to be achieved if we concentrate on theories of disclosure which explicitly link various sets of accounting information to diverse (heterogeneous) users, rather than via the route of trying to define an ideal concept of income which is appropriate under conditions of uncertainty, and in less than perfect markets.

Let us label this new development as an attempt to define theories of "relevant accounting." What sort of problems are presented by this type of approach to theory development? If we try to develop these theories at an a priori level, it soon becomes apparent that the relevant accounting approach presents the same types of problems encountered in trying to evaluate which of several competing income concepts is the ideal one for accounting. That is, once we are again given sufficient latitude in specifying assumptions about the kinds of decision problems faced by users of accounting information, the types of capital markets in which they deal, and the particular objective functions they adopt in making decisions, we can make a strong case for disclosing information on every conceivable event that did or might affect the operations of a firm, whether of a strict financial or non-financial nature. Obviously, there are costs associated both with producing information and the processing of that information by users, so some type of cost-benefit analysis must be imposed on the relevance criterion. Indeed, we might say that the ASOBAT Committee recognized this issue in part since the other three criteria they specified for evaluating potential information for disclosure—quantifiability, verifiability, unbiasedness—are more in the form of constraints on the relevance criterion, rather than being independent criteria in their own right. It is much less apparent that the Trueblood Committee adopted any such constraints on their recommendations regarding the types of information that should be disclosed in accounting reports.

But this is not at all surprising. Neither the Trueblood Committee nor any other committee can be expected to develop an optimal set of information to communicate in financial statements if the derivation of that optimal set depends on considerations of relative costs and benefits of producing alternative amounts and types of information. We simply do not know enough of about how (or whether) users' decisions are affected by different sets of information so we cannot specify exactly how competing alternatives will produce changes in the value of their objective functions. Moreover, accounting information can be viewed as a type of public good. Consequently, optimal decision about the production of accounting information must consider issues relating to social costs and benefits. Finally, very few accountants who propose alternative information for disclosure have any idea about the relative costs imposed upon firms should they be forced to change their information production decisions.

But these are the types of issues which must be considered if information is to be evaluated within the context of a cost and benefit analysis. It has only been in recent years that papers dealing with a theoretical analysis of information within a framework of a cost and benefit analysis have even appeared—e.g., the papers by Fama and Laffer,[15] Gonedes,[16] Demski,[17] and the one by Gonedes and myself.

The gist of the first two is summarized in our paper. Briefly, if information is viewed as a special type of public good, there are special market conditions under which information will have a competitive equilibrium price and the associated equilibrium decisions about producing information will be Pareto optimal. Changes in this equilibrium price of information in response to proposed disclosures may be used to assess the value of these proposed disclosures, and this value could then be compared to the marginal cost of providing them. Unfortunately, one of the market conditions required for this mechanism is the exclusion of non-purchasers of information from the use of that information. If nonpurchasers of information are allowed to use the information, the competitive price will always be identically equal to zero. Since no one is precluded from using the financial reports of a firm even if he has no financial interest in that firm, we may assume that the implied competitive price of publicly disclosed financial information is equal to zero. Note that this does not mean that publicly disclosed financial information has no value—it merely means no one has to pay a positive price for its receipt.

Demski's work also deals with the problem of evaluating information alternatives at a social level. He argues that under such a condition it is not theoretically possible to obtain *general* criteria for socially optimal information production decisions (an application of the Arrow "impossibility" theorem).

The crux of all this is simply that no concrete financial accounting model presently exists which can be used in a practical way to determine a firm's optimal information production decisions. This, in turn, suggests that there may be no single financial accounting model which is capable of indicating the optimal set of information which should be presented to accounting students Let me be more specific. We are presented with proposals to disclose a variety of alternative accounting measurements, but we have no definitive method for evaluating these proposals. Given that any reasonable proposal could be relevant to the decisions of some subset of decision makers this simply means that no theoretical basis exists for excluding any of them from consideration in accounting courses. Yet we must perform some type of screening or otherwise students will have to spend their entire college career in accounting.

What are some of the options? For our purposes, let me indicate but two feasible approaches. First we could structure our courses around the present thinking of what is generally acceptable practice, including references to the policy statements of such political bodies as the SEC, (APB), FASB, CASB and others. This is more or less the approach followed in textbooks. Apparently, this is not a completely acceptable basis for our financial accounting courses, or otherwise there would be little need for this symposium!

But is this approach necessarily that bad? It is true that if we confined the content of financial courses to what is currently acceptable, the students would not be exposed to new developments in accounting measurements and disclosures which eventually may be adopted in practice. However, such a restrictive approach need not be followed—indeed, a restrictive approach is probably not even feasible in this day and age. The SEC and the FASB (the latter no doubt motivated by the former) have adopted a much more liberal attitude toward accounting measurements and disclosure, and their actual opinions and their exposure drafts are even now sufficiently abundant to keep the students abreast of what is on the immediate accounting horizon. Thus, both the rationale for what is currently acceptable practice, and the proposals under review by policy-making bodies may be an appropriate basis for structuring financial accounting courses.

Keep in mind that what is being suggested is that policy making bodies be allowed to do our screening as to what accounting proposals should be discussed within the financial accounting courses. Some may argue that these bodies lack the capability of carrying out such a function since they exist primarily to achieve compromise solutions which are acceptable to a set of competing interests. In general, many would agree that policy making bodies should not be expected to arrive at optimal decisions about what information should be disclosed to decision makers (except by coincidence). Indeed, at a social level the appropriate concept of optimality is not even obvious. Nevertheless, these bodies are in a position to determine which of the many proposals that are exposed in the accounting literature have generated the most concern among financial analysts, investors, accountants and management. After all, a number of proposals for additional disclosures in financial statements constitute nothing more than emotional pleas, and it is impractical to embrace these until there is some reasonable probability that they will attain acceptance in practice.

Let me now turn to a second option. Rather than attempting to select which of many alternative proposals in accounting should be considered in our financial courses, we could adopt the strategy that the primary purpose of our courses, especially the advanced ones, is to teach students some operational methods for evaluating accounting proposals. Of course, this too is not a completely new approach in accounting since much of what we call accounting theory consists of an evaluation of alternative income concepts using either an ideal construct of income as a standard, or by determining which income construct is more consistent with an assumed set of conditions covering user decision models and the markets for assets. In recent years, however, additional methods of evaluating alternative accounting measurements have been employed, both at the a priori level, through the introduction of information economics, and especially at the empirical level. This can be illustrated by just mentioning some of the developments at the empirical level.

At a conference held at the University of Illinois in 1971, Hakansson presented a review of the empirical work done in accounting from 1960-70.[18] In his review Hakansson noted that a variety of accounting problems had been subjected to empirical analyses using a variety of empirical models. One of his conclusions was that conflicting results were obtained for the same type of accounting problem. This could be explained as a consequence of deficient theory underlying the empirical models, deficient statistical methodology, or both. Hakansson tended to place most of the blame at the theoretical level. Gonedes and I also did a review of empirical research in accounting in our paper presented at the Chicago conference. The purpose of our review was a little more pointed in that one of our objectives was to determine whether empirical evidence existed which might be used to guide policy making bodies, such as the FASB, in determining which of a set of competing accounting alternatives should be used in financial statements. As a consequence, our review of the empirical works had to consider under what conditions the empirical model was appropriate for a particular study, and, given that, could we then detect problems in the statistical methodology. The conclusions of our paper are unimportant for the purposes of this symposium. What we did discover, however, is that empirical researchers have used a variety of criteria to assess different accounting methods, and since no single empirical model exists which can answer all of the many questions which may arise, we can expect that alternative criteria will continue to be employed in empirical studies.

For example, a number of studies attempted to assess the *effects* on security prices of using different methods of accounting. Some were based on the so-called API analyses using capital asset pricing models and some were based upon variations of the Gordon dividend discounting model. Recently, a few researchers have even extended the API analysis to encompass issues of which alternative accounting method is most *desirable*. In addition to tests using changes in security prices, we also observed attempts to examine alternative methods via: (1) experimental or laboratory studies of *effects*, (2) examinations of the *significance* of different accounting methods, (3) assessments of the relative *objectivity* of different methods, and (4) determinations of the *consistency* of different methods within an assumed measurement framework (e.g., consistency within the historical cost framework).

Each of the various approaches to an evaluation of an accounting issue may provide information about that issue—of course, some did seem more robust than others in this respect. The point is, however, that a sufficient variety of approaches have been used in empirical work in financial accounting so that the methods of evaluation could constitute the basis for designing an advanced financial accounting course. Note that I stated "could." There must be other feasible options besides the two I have mentioned, with an obvious one being a combination of the two. But I cannot see an end to this process until some discipline provides us with a super theory which indicates which decision model is optimal for making investment decisions under uncertainty. I know of no such model, and so I would expect that investors will continue to use a variety of different models which rely on a variety of different kinds and sources of information. In effect then I have convinced myself that a determination of *the* optimal financial accounting model is at least beyond my present capabilities.

But this conclusion does not particularly disturb me. After all, we do have in existence a measurement system which has been with us for a number of years, and its survival over time must provide some evidence that its outputs are desired by a number of users. At the same time, that system is continually being bombarded by proposals ranging from how it may be extended to its complete rejection in favor of some alternative one. As long as accountants recognize these two facts, I would encourage them to experiment in their own way as to how they should teach the rationale of the present system (and I believe one exists) and how proposals to extend, modify, or replace the system can be evaluated.

The Managerial Model

As you will observe later, my observations about the appropriate managerial model will force me to a similar kind of conclusion. If we go back in time and examine the earlier textbooks on cost accounting, we could easily argue that early treatments of the subject were nothing more than extensions of financial (historical cost) accounting theory. How else could we ever justify the extensive detailed calculations which are required in actual process costing systems? Surely a standard cost system would be much more useful to management and would require fewer detailed calculations in process costing situations; yet, some early textbooks treated standard costs as a special topic.

In recent years, cost texts have moved in the direction of

providing information which is useful to management in its two primary decision areas: planning and control. I have no quarrel with this movement, but at the same time I recognize the problems it has created in trying to structure a managerial course.

The one advantage in linking cost accounting to financial accounting was that the linkage provided a model for the "managerial" course (a loose use of the term). Questions about cost classifications and cost accumulations could be resolved within the context of acceptable financial accounting theory. However, those of us who have been identified with managerial accounting soon recognized that cost classifications and cost accumulations which are relevant for financial accounting may not be completely appropriate for managements' decisions about outputs, capital acquisitions and inventory policies, or for establishing control over individual responsibility centers. Thus we were forced to look elsewhere for a basis or model which could guide the structure and content of managerial courses.

Initially the task of choosing an accounting model which is appropriate for managerial decisions seemed straightforward. For example, there is general agreement among recent textbooks that management is faced with at least three basic types of decision situations in the planning area—determining the output levels and mixes of products; the level of investment in capital assets, and when and how much inventory to acquire. Once decisions are made in these areas, management is then concerned with designing a control system which can communicate responsibilities for implementing their decisions and which provide measurements of the degree to which actual results conformed to expected results. Hence, few people would disagree with the statement that the accountant should provide the appropriate data which can be used to obtain cost estimates needed to make various planning decisions, and which can serve as standards of performance in the control system. Superimposed on this structure is a set of utility functions which guide the selection of the decision models which can be used in planning and control.

Now it is possible to refine this initial classification—for example to distinguish between strategic versus other types of planning decisions—but that will merely add to the problem I wish to develop. Let us accept the notion that the primary objective of the managerial accountant is to provide data which are *relevant* for planning and control decisions of management and that we have a common conception of the types of decision problems encountered by management at the planning and control stages.

Relevance is certainly an appropriate criterion to adopt in managerial accounting, as it seemed to be in financial accounting.

Indeed, relevance became the basic guideline employed by the 1967-68 managerial committee of the AAA [19] in carrying out their charge to develop a report on information needed to implement management's decision models. In that report, the committee proceeded to identify certain types of decision models used by management, including control models, and then suggested the kinds of accounting (and other) data that would be useful in implementing the identified models.

I certainly cannot disagree with such a strategy, since it is essentially the one we follow in our textbook. But in the process of doing so it became apparent to us that an identification of the decision models used by management and a specification of the data which are relevant for implementing those models are more difficult tasks than we have been led to believe. In particular it is not always evident which model(s) management should use in a specific decision situation, nor is there always just one set of data which is relevant for implementing a specific decision model. We have tried to highlight the nature of the problem in our revised text, but an appreciation for the complexity of the problem is more easily grasped if I can refer to our 1969-70, 1970-71 report on managerial accounting.

Those who are familiar with the content of that report will recall that our major objective was to demonstrate that information choice issues will arise even if we know the exact structure of a decision maker's decision model. For example, there is an initial information issue at the time a decision maker adopts a particular decision model. Should the accountant take the model as given or should he provide information to the decision maker which would motivate the adoption of a different model? Some of you may reject this possibility on the assumption that a decision maker should be the one who determines which decision model is appropriate under a given set of conditions. And yet, I could easily point to papers wherein the authors imply that they know which model is optimal in a given decision situation, and I would guess that these authors would supply information to a decision maker which would lead him to select that model. Of course textbooks are no less guilty here, since most textbook authors take stands on the types of decision models which should be used by management (e.g., see any textbook discussion on capital budgeting). But the main point is that different models exist for the same situation, so some criteria are needed in order to make a choice.

But even if the decision maker and the accountant agree on the type of model which is optimal for a specified decision situation, this still will not eliminate all information issues. Every decision model requires estimates of the parameter values to be used in the model.

Knowledge of the specific model may indicate which parameter values need to be estimated—e.g., revenue per unit, variable cost per unit, capacity requirements per unit, etc.—but there is no guide as to which one of several different estimates should be used. Different estimates of the same parameter value, say variable cost per unit, are possible either because different estimation models are used (linear vs. non-linear, multiple regression vs. visual fits) or different sets of observations are used (cross-sectional vs. time-series), to mention just two possible sources of differences. At the time a decision model is to be implemented, a choice between competing estimates must be made. This choice cannot be made, however, unless we possess some model which indicates how different estimates or forecasts should be evaluated ex ante to the actual decison. Unfortunately, this is a relatively new area of research in accounting.

The same question about estimation methods arises if we shift to the control phase of accounting. Apart from the choice of estimation models and appropriate sets of data to use, there is the further question of whether the reported estimates should be "biased." For example, should the reported estimate be reduced to provide additional motivation for efficiency? Should it be adjusted upwards and downwards to conform to personality characteristics of individuals? Should the reported estimate used in control systems be expressed as a single value (i.e., point) estimate, or should it be expressed as a probability distribution?

The above are some of the more obvious questions which may arise in choosing parameter estimates that may be used in planning and control models. Similar kinds of information choice questions arise when we must consider other aspects of control system design. For example, should the system be designed according to a strict definition of an autocratic management system, or should it allow for participative types of management systems? The former requires a very refined system of responsibility accounting, whereas the latter allows for certain amounts of interactive responsibilities. Similarly, the former has a definite influence on how deviations from standards are reported and analyzed, in the sense that standards are taken as *the* benchmarks of performance. In contrast the latter type of control system recognizes that standards are nothing more than estimates which are subject to measurement error. Incidentally, it is not clear that either one of these management control systems leads to the highest level of economic efficiency in all situations. In fact, one of our "behavioral" Ph.D. students [20] found both systems in operation within the same firm at the same operating level, even though the controller's department had designed a strict responsibility (autocratic) type of control system. One of the questions considered in that study is whether the accountant should adapt his system to individual management styles, and if he does not, whether the consequences of not doing so can be measured and evaluated. These are not trivial questions since it is not clear which control system is more generally optimal, although we all have our own priors.

I could go on and illustrate other types of information issues which arise at the other stages of the control process—e.g., alternative methods have been proposed for disaggregating variances, for assessing the significance of variances from standards, for assigning joint and other kinds of common costs to products, and so on. But I believe the above illustrations are sufficient to indicate that numerous information choice problems exist in managerial accounting even though we may agree on the types of decision problems faced by management, and even though we may know the characteristics of the decision model management wishes to employ. Thus, I cannot but agree with the observation made by the 1961 managerial committee regarding the concept of relevance, "... the term relevance is more a statement of the problem rather than a solution to it."

It appears then that the same type of problem which exists in financial accounting also exists in managerial accounting. A wide variety of proposals have been made concerning the kinds of information which should be provided to management. Many of these are competitive in that different kinds of information are proposed for the same decision setting. In designing our managerial accounting courses we must decide whether we can determine which of these proposals is optimal and, as such, should be included in the courses, or whether the courses should be designed with the objective of providing students with the capability of evaluating various proposals on their own. This second alternative differs from the first primarily in its orientation; i.e., the student would be exposed to the different proposals for information which exist at the planning and control stages and his responsibility would be to develop an ability to critically evaluate them.

Unfortunately, neither alternative is easy to implement given our current state of knowledge. The first assumes that there exist theories which will unequivocally indicate which decision model is appropriate in a particular decision situation, which cost estimation produces optimal estimates, which control system is optimal for a specific type of operation, and so on. I certainly do not know of the existence of these theories. The second alternative assumes that various criteria exist which can be used to evaluate different proposals, and on the basis of these make an optimal choice once the details of an actual decision are known. But do we possess such a set of criteria in managerial accounting? Here again I am skeptical.

One of the more general statements we could make is that information proposals should be evaluated within some type of cost and benefit framework. This notion is about as operational as the concept of relevance. In order to evaluate a specific information proposal in those terms we would have to be able to predict what signals would be produced if a proposal is adopted, how the produced signals will affect the probability assessments of the decision maker, how the revised probability assessments will lead to the selection of a decision, given the utility function of the decision maker, and what will be the marginal cost of adopting the proposal. Note that the decision effect of the information proposal can only be expressed in probabilistic terms. Just the mere task of formally stating this "theory" of evaluation constituted a major article by Feltham and Demski.[21]

Of course, a complete application of this formal approach to information evaluation is not practical, as is indicated by Feltham and Demski. About all we can do at present is develop simplifications of this approach which allow us to evaluate certain subsets of an information choice problem, but recognizing that any resulting evaluation of an information proposal is constrained by the restrictive assumptions which are employed. This sounds quite technical, but actually several cost textbooks already contain simplified assessments of alternative information proposals. For example, in the area of cost estimation, we might assume that a choice of parameter values for a cost estimation equation can be made by assessing whether the equation will lead to predictions which are consistent with a decision maker's loss function for penalties incurred through estimation errors. If we assume that the loss function is quadratic and that we are using past data to derive our estimation equation, this simply means that we choose our parameter values according to the least squares method of regression. Alternatively, we might choose parameter values which assume a loss function linear in absolute errors, in which case we wish to obtain a regression line which minimizes the sum of the absolute deviations from the line. Notice that a choice of parameter values along these lines can be made without reference to any specific decision model in which the cost estimates will be used.

In the area of planning models, a simplified form of evalution is provided by sensitivity analysis, where we vary the structure of the model or its parameter estimates in order to determine whether the optimal decision is affected by such changes. If the optimal decision is not sensitive to certain changes in the information used in the model we assume that no decision benefits would be forthcoming were the changes to be adopted. The method can be used for any decision model and may even be used at the control stage to assess the decision significance of variances from standards. One useful illustration of this method is in a study in which the researchers analyzed actual captial investment decisions of a group of firms. They found that essentially the same accept/reject decisions would have been made whether the decision-makers used payback or one of the discounting methods of investment analysis.[22] Many of the illustrative examples of capital budgeting problems found in textbooks exhibit a similar phenomenon.

This is a rather negative type of procedure for evaluating information proposals since the main difficulty in using it occurs when we observe that decisions are sensitive to different disclosures of information. For example, suppose we use the Vancil approach to the analysis of the lease vs. buy (and borrow) decision and the optimal choice is to buy (and borrow).[23] However, we then apply an approach recommended by Johnson and Lewellen[24] and note that the optimal choice is to lease. We could present both analyses to a decision maker and let him make his own decision, which effectively shifts the burden of choosing the appropriate model to him. However, many of us would be motivated instead to argue the merits of the two approaches and choose the one which seems most consistent with whatever theories exist in economics and finance. That is, we would revert to the a priori method of evaluation.

A priori arguments about the superiority of one method over another, sensitivity of decisions to different constructions of models or different parameter estimates, and making choices of estimation models on the basis of assumed loss functions are three methods of evaluation which can be found in several textbooks already on the market. But none of the three is very robust. We need more definitive methods of evaluation in managerial accounting, including various criteria which could be employed in empirical studies of different information proposals. Unfortunately, empirical work in managerial accounting is practically non-existent. A partial explanation of this deficiency may be that firms have not been very cooperative in supporting empirical work by managerial accountants. But that does not explain why we do not have much empirical evidence generated in laboratory experiments. Actually, only a small percentage of the behavioral studies in accounting have dealt with a managerial issue. I have no explanation for this fact. Whatever the reason, the evaluation of information proposals in managerial accounting definitely lags behind that observed in financial accounting since a great deal of empirical research exists there (good and bad).

The evaluation of proposals in managerial accounting also suffers another disadvantage relative to financial accounting.

Recall that in financial accounting several influential policy-making bodies exist which make pronouncements concerning the types and amounts of information which should be disclosed by firms. While we may not agree with all of these, their existence provides us with a particular kind of criteria with which we may compare alternative proposals. No such influential body exists regarding managerial accounting. In effect, a firm is free to adopt any type of information proposal it wishes, on the assumption that its benefits exceed its costs. While Bob Anthony may believe that the Cost Accounting Standards Board will eventually constrain the firm in designing its information system, I see little reason why the CASB's influence need be any greater in this regard than that of the FASB. Both boards may be viewed as external constraints which force the firm to provide information according to well-defined criteria. However, except for cost considerations, a firm is not prevented from designing its information system in a manner which it deems useful for its planning and control decisions, and then adapting the output of that system to meet these outside constraints. I am very skeptical that all of what the CASB determines to be good cost accounting will also turn out to be good for management's decisions.

In any event, I see the major problem in managerial accounting to be essentially the same as the one I outlined for financial accounting. Alternative information proposals exist in both areas of accounting, and we simply cannot determine which alternative is optimal either for investors or for management (part of the problem here is defining "optimality"). I would also conclude that the problem is much more acute in managerial accounting since our criteria for evaluating information proposals there are much less developed. Hence, I would be even stronger in recommending that managerial courses be structured in such a way that the student recognize that much of what he will be exposed to is highly speculative.

Conclusion

As I suggested earlier, I would not be able to conclude whether the financial model and the managerial model are the same or whether they are different. The reason is simply that I do not know what are the appropriate models for each area.

However, I can conclude that there are some common issues which arise in both areas of accounting. Our initial objective is to provide information which promises to be decision-relevant for external and internal parties. This requires that we have some notions as to the kinds of decision problems faced by both classes of users. Apart from some general statements about these decision problems, however, we really do not know which specific decision models should be employed by investors and management in various decision situations. Hence, we cannot be unequivocal about which information systems will produce optimal information signals for both classes of users.

Given that, I do not see how I could possibly argue one way or the other on the kinds of questions which were suggested in the program for this session. For example, in the announcement for this symposium, the following were listed as possible considerations for my topic: monetary and non-monetary information; accrual and cash flow information; non-incremental and incremental information; quantitative and non-quantitative information. I assume that I was expected to determine whether financial and managerial models were different in terms of these kinds of considerations. But I could not argue either way without knowing what sets of information are optimal for external and internal users of accounting information. Indeed, as I look back at these information distinctions, I am not even sure I now know what accounting information constitutes.

But suppose we consider these distinctions for a moment. Regarding managerial accounting, there is no question that both monetary and non-monetary, accrual and cash flow, and nonincremental and incremental information are produced by firms' internal accounting systems. I am a little less sure about whether both quantitative *and* non-quantitative information are produced by internal accounting systems, primarily because I do not know what the latter term implies.

Similarly, I can point to references in which proposals are made in financial accounting for the disclosure of both monetary and non-monetary information (e.g., social "cost-benefit" accounting includes both), accrual and cash flow information (income vs. various fund flow disclosures); and non-incremental and incremental information (income is an incremental notion). But here again I do not know whether non-quantitative information should be or is currently disclosed by accountants in financial statements since I have no definition for that category of information.

In any event, I do not believe that these distinctions lead us to the heart of the problems which exist in both areas of accounting— namely, that a large number of information proposals are available which purport to result in decision benefits for external and internal users, and our main task is to develop criteria which can be used to evaluate them within the context of some cost and benefit framework. Whether these proposals involve considerations of only monetary or non-monetary information, accrual or cash flow information, etc. is a secondary issue to me.

FOOTNOTES

1. N. Dopuch, J. Birnberg, and J. Demski, *Cost Accounting—Accounting Data for Management Decisions*, 2nd ed. *(Harcourt, 1974)*.

2. "Report of the 1969-70, 1970-71 Committee on Managerial Accounting," Supplement to vol. XLII, *Accounting Review* (1972).

3. N. Gonedes and N. Dopuch, "Capital Market Equilibrium, Information-Production and Selecting Accounting Techniques: Theoretical Framework and Review of Empirical Work," in Proceedings of the Robert M. Trueblood Memorial Conference on Financial Accounting Objectives; Supplement to *Journal of Accounting Research* (1974).

4. American Accounting Association, *A Statement of Basic Accounting Theory* (1966).

5. American Institute of Certified Public Accountants, *Report of the Study Group on Objectives of Financial Statements* "Objectives of Financial Statements" (1973).

6. M. Gordon, "Scope and Method of Theory and Research in the Measurement of Income and Wealth," *Accounting Review*, vol. XXXV, no. 4 (October 1960), pp. 603-18.

7. S. Zeff, "Replacement Cost: Member of the Family, Welcome Guest, or Intruder?" *Accounting Review*, vol. XXXVII, no. 4 (October 1962), pp. 612-14.

8. L. Revsine, "On the Correspondence Between Replacement Cost Income and Economic Income," *Accounting Review*, vol. XLIV, no. 3 (July 1970), pp. 513-23. He has since modified his view and has adopted a "user-oriented" approach as described in his book, *Replacement Cost Accounting* (Prentice-Hall, 1973), especially Chapter 4.

9. D. Solomons, "Economic and Accounting Concepts of Income," *Accounting Review*, vol. XXXVI, no. 4 (July 1961), pp. 374-83.

10. H. Bierman, Jr., and S. Davidson, "The Income Concept—Value Increment or Earnings Predictor," *Accounting Review*, vol. XLIV, no. 2 (April 1969), pp. 239-46.

11. C. Nelson, "A Priori Research in Accounting," in *Accounting Research 1960-70: A Critical Evaluation*, eds. N. Dopuch and L. Revsine (Center for International Education and Research in Accounting, University of Illinois, 1973).

12. E.O. Edwards and P.W. Bell, *The Theory and Measurement of Business Income* (University of California Press, 1964).

13. R.J. Chambers, *Accounting, Evaluation and Economic Behavior* (Prentice-Hall, 1966).

14. R.R. Sterling, *Theory of the Measurement of Enterprise Income* (University Press of Kansas, 1970).

15. E. Fama and A. Laffer, "Information and Capital Markets," *Journal of Business*, vol. 44, no. 3 (July 1971), pp. 289-305.

16. N. Gonedes, "Information-Production and Capital Market Equilibrium," *Journal of Finance* (forthcoming).

17. J. Demski, "General Impossibility of Normative Standards," *Accounting Review*, vol. XLIII, no. 4 (October 1973), pp. 718-23.

18. N. Hakansson, "Empirical Research in Accounting, 1960-70: An Appraisal," *Accounting Research 1960-70*.

19. "Report of Committee on Managerial Decision Models," *Accounting Review*, Supplement to vol. XLIV (1969).

20. A. Hopwood, "An Empirical Study of the Role of Accounting Data in Performance Evaluation," Supplement to the *Journal of Accounting Research* (1972).

21. G.A. Feltham and J. Demski, "The Use of Models in Information Evaluation," *Accounting Review*, vol. XLV, no. 4 (October 1970), pp. 623-40.

22. M. Sarnat and H. Levy, "The Relationship of Rule of Thumb to the Internal Rate of Return: A Restatement and Generalization," *Journal of Finance*, vol. XXIV, no. 3 (June 1969), pp. 479-89; especially, p. 489.

FOOTNOTES

23. The approach is described in N. Dopuch, J. Birnberg, and J. Demski, *Cost Accounting* . . . , Ch. 6. The reference to Vancil can also be found there.

24. R.W. Johnson and W.G. Lewellen, "Analysis of the Lease—or—Buy Decision," *Journal of Finance*, vol. XXVII (September 1972), pp. 815-23.

Models for Financial Accounting vs. Models for Management Accounting: Can (Should) They Be Different?

A Critique
Robert N. Anthony

Nick says that he is not "able to conclude whether the financial model and the managerial model are the same or whether they are different" because he does not know "what are the appropriate models for each area." Accounting teachers can't wait until these ideal models are discovered, however. They must design the best curriculum they can conceive of for next year's students, based on today's state of the art. Despite his disclaimer, Nick has in fact shed much light on the curriculum problem, and he has also suggested some important questions for further discussion.

First, he points out that in financial accounting, a body of generally accepted accounting principles does exist. In a theory course, it is appropriate to discuss methods of evaluating alternative principles, and in accounting research it is appropriate to examine these principles critically, but in the bread-and-butter part of the curriculum, it is essential that these principles be taught as they exist today, and as they are likely to exist in the near future. The student must understand what accounting *is* as well as what it might become.

Further, financial accounting is a single system that is tied together by the debit-and-credit mechanism, and the basic equation, Assets = Equities. Financial accounting reports are derived by summarizing and rearranging data drawn from this basic system. Even though one financial statement is based on a funds flow concept and another on the accrual concept, the underlying data for both statements come from the same set of accounts.

As Nick points out, no comparable unified body of principles and no single system exists in the field of managerial accounting. He discusses three quite separate topics: cost accounting, planning decisions, and the control system. Each of these requires different accounting information.

Cost accounting is tied to financial accounting, and the governing concept is that the full cost of a product or other cost objective is its direct costs plus a fair share of its indirect costs.

Planning decisions require information which is variously labelled differential costs, incremental costs, or relevant costs. This information is fundamentally different from full cost information. Nick says that with respect to a given problem, such as the buy-or-lease problem, various authors may differ as to what the proper decision model is, but there is nevertheless general agreement that the appropriate numbers to use in the model, whatever it is, are differential costs.

Control systems require a third type of information. Although there are differences of opinion as to whether autocratic management is preferable to participative management, there is general agreement that the information in a control system for either type of management should be structured in terms of personal responsibility.

Stated in terms of types of information, rather than in terms of types of problems, managerial accounting deals with three fundamentally different types of information: full cost information, differential information, and responsibility information. I suggest that our managerial courses currently do not recognize clearly enough that these distinctions exist.

Finally, Nick calls attention to a question that I think has great importance in curriculum design, namely, the proper scope of accounting. He points out that accounting systems now include nonmonetary information as well as monetary information, and he raises the question of whether our subject should encompass nonquantitative information as well as quantitative information. This question is worth a lot of discussion.

The former restriction to monetary information provided a clear dividing line between what should be and what should not be included in accounting courses, but it left accounting confined to too narrow an area. The current courses are broader, but the act of broadening them has blurred the line between accounting and nonaccounting. We need a new definition of accounting. I feel sure, for example, that we do not want to spend much time teaching how to write a business letter, nor are we competent to teach how to compose an advertisement, or to describe the data that are needed to control a complicated chemical process, even though these topics clearly are included within the boundaries of information. Accounting must be defined so that it excludes certain types of information, but also so that within its boundaries there is a coherent, important subject area. Such a definition has not emerged.

Next Steps

The foregoing suggests a basic question that needs to be answered prior to a detailed reconstruction of the curriculum; namely, what is the proper boundary of our subject area? I think accounting should include nonmonetary as well as monetary information (e.g., personnel data as well as payroll data), that it generally should be limited to systematic (as opposed to nonrecurring) information, that it generally should be limited to economic information, and that it should include all aspects of information processing. Conversely, I don't think our subject should include information on technical production matters (such as formulas for chemical compounds), or advertising techniques, even though advertising does convey information. The question of how to draw the proper line is a slippery one, and is worth extensive discussion.

The foregoing also suggests a way of constructing a set of management accounting courses with a minimum amount of overlap. Consistent with the three types of cost mentioned above, these courses could be:

1. Cost accounting, in the conventional sense of cost finding.
2. Management control.
3. Analysis for decision making.

There could be elementary and advanced courses in the second and third areas. There should also be courses on information processing.

It is not a great exaggeration to say that budgeting, cost accounting, cost administration, planning and control, management control, and administrative control courses as taught today differ only in their title; they all have substantially the same content. This does not make for a respectable curriculum.

Exhibit 1 sketches out a curriculum and indicates how the above courses would fit into it.

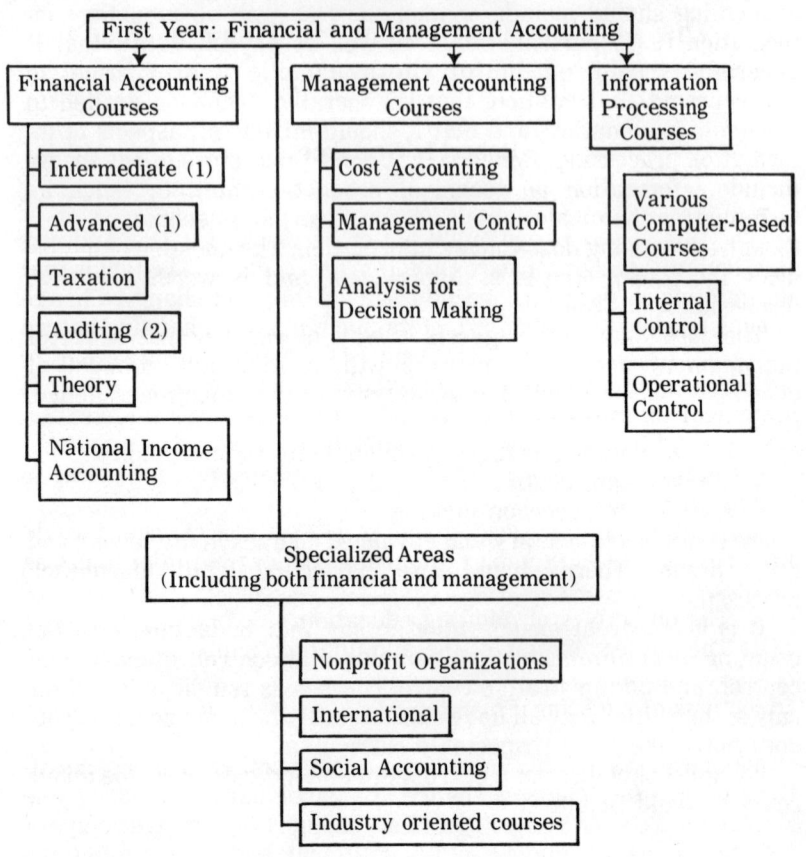

Exhibit 1
A Tentative Accounting Curriculum

First Year: Financial and Management Accounting

Financial Accounting Courses
- Intermediate (1)
- Advanced (1)
- Taxation
- Auditing (2)
- Theory
- National Income Accounting

Management Accounting Courses
- Cost Accounting
- Management Control
- Analysis for Decision Making

Information Processing Courses
- Various Computer-based Courses
- Internal Control
- Operational Control

Specialized Areas (Including both financial and management)
- Nonprofit Organizations
- International
- Social Accounting
- Industry oriented courses

(1) Intermediate and Advanced clearly need to be restructured, possibly in modules.

(2) Logically, a good case can be made to put auditing under information processing, but there are manning problems if this is done.

The Auditing Curriculum—Is There a Need for Change?

Robert L. Grinaker

The title of this paper might better be phrased, "The Auditing Curriculum—an Appropriate Direction for Change." The fact is that the auditing curriculum currently is in the throes of change. Change is evidenced by a number of factors, including the changing nature of textual materials, the increasing interest in auditing research, the increasing emphasis in auditing courses on such topics as statistical inference, perceptual phenomena, and communication theory. Auditing professors characterize the change by asserting that auditing courses are moving from emphasizing procedures to emphasizing concepts.

Because the auditing curriculum *is* in a state of change, I would like to explore the direction of this change under two major topics as follows:
1. The objectives of auditing education.
2. The subject matter of the auditing curriculum.

Objectives of Auditing Education

Whenever an activity involving a great number of independent-thinking people undergoes change, the participants can easily lose sight of the activity's objectives. If so, change may be made only for the sake of change, may be totally irrational, and may threaten the very existence of the activity involved. When thoughtful participants are involved, more likely than a simple loss of objectives is the loss of consensus on what those objectives should be. When this is so, groups of participants take off in a variety of directions toward an equal variety of objectives. Although the latter condition may be viewed as chaotic, the experimental aspects provide essential experience for selecting the best objectives when consensus is again sought.

In my judgment, the auditing curriculum is not yet ready for consensus on pinpoint targets. Too many educators are involved in creative and constructive experimentation. Consensus now on narrow objectives may tend to inhibit creativity. A sad consequence may be that the refreshing variety of textual materials now available in auditing will revert, in terms of variety, to the status of the intermediate accounting text. Nevertheless, I do assert that auditing education is ready for consensus on a single broad objective, viz., that the principal purpose of auditing education is to prepare students for professional auditing careers.

Even the most concept-oriented auditing educators recognize the ultimate goal of preparing a professional auditor. The principal arguments turn not on the ultimate goal, but rather on the appropriateness of subject matter to "university education" versus "firm training." Shenkir, for example, in advocating reform in auditing education, states as follows:

> ... reform should then result in a concept-oriented course. Contrary to traditional thought, such a course is compatible with the environment that an accounting graduate enters upon graduation. I refer to the environment of his future educational or professional training opportunity with CPA firms.[1]

The for-profession-preparation concept is finding growing support among accounting educators generally. Rumblings heard from a number of campuses indicate a growing sentiment for establishing schools of professional accounting. Moonitz makes the following recommendation:

> Professionalize the accounting curriculum, at least to the level of the quality found in the better law schools and engineering schools. What this means is that each and every course (after the introductory lower-division course) must be taught in a manner to enable the student to use the material he has learned and to operate with it at some detectable and measurable level of competence.[2]

Professionalization of the auditing portion of the accounting curriculum poses a number of issues:
1. Identification of the auditing profession.
2. Professional guidance of the auditing curriculum.
3. Professionalization of the educational processes.

Identification of the Auditing Profession

If we assume that auditing educators adopt as a common curriculum objective the preparation of students for professional auditing careers, we are faced with the problem of identifying the

auditing profession. Professional auditing, today, is practiced on three broad fronts: viz., (1) public auditing, (2) internal auditing, and (3) governmental auditing, particularly as exemplified by the General Accounting Office. The curriculum impact of these various phases of auditing practice present a number of questions for the auditing educator:
1. To what extent are the professional practices similar and different, particularly, with respect to -
   a. the specific nature of the work done?
   b. environmental factors impacting on practice?
   c. factors influencing demand for service?
   d. ethical and legal responsibilities for the quality of work?
2. To what extent are the underlying bodies of knowledge similar or different?
3. To what extent are these professions represented by an authoritative professional organization? To what extent do these organizations work together in identifying and solving common problems?
4. What is the relative importance of each profession, particularly, with respect to -
   a. the number of practitioners, current and prospective?
   b. the perceived societal benefits of the services performed?

Answers to the foregoing questions are essential to rational curriculum development. To assume that auditing is auditing, and, hence, that any auditing course will provide adequately for any phase of practice may be a gross oversimplification. The question of whether public auditing, internal auditing, and governmental auditing are special branches of a general discipline is important. For example, are these phases of practice comparable to medical specialities? If this be so, a common discipline core must exist upon which special education can be built. Of course, the further question is posed of how much special education, if any, is required for each phase of practice? On the other hand, these special phases of practice may represent substantially different disciplines which only by happenstance carry auditing as a common title. If this be so, the educational requirements for each profession would be substantially different. It would be tragic, indeed, if these be different professional disciplines under the common rubric, auditing, and if we in education were to distend and distort any single curriculum to cover all disciplines.

I am convinced, however, that more and more common ground will be found among the auditing professions. Evidence of such common ground appears to surface (1) in a comparative analysis of discipline definitions and (2) in the fact that operational audits are now being conducted in significant numbers by public accounting firms. A comparative analysis of discipline definitions is made in a subsequent section of this paper. The involvement of public accounting firms in operational auditing is evidenced by the following publications:

1. Comptroller General of the United States, *United States General Accounting Office—Standards for Audit of Governmental Organizations, Programs, Activities and Functions*, U.S. Government Printing Office, 1972.
2. Committee on Relations with the General Accounting Office, *Auditing Standards Established by the GAO—Their Meaning and Significance for CPAs*, American Institute of Certified Public Accountants, 1973.
3. Committee on Governmental Accounting and Auditing, *Audits of State and Local Governments*, American Institute of Certified Public Accountants, 1974.

Currently, most operational audits by CPA firms involve the examination of local grantee agencies for the benefit of responsible grantor federal agencies—e.g., audits of local antipoverty agencies which received grants from the Office of Economic Opportunity (OEO). The operational aspect of such audits is summarized in the foreward of *GAO Standards:*

> . . . demand for information has widened the scope of governmental auditing so that such auditing no longer is a function concerned primarily with financial operations. Instead, governmental auditing now is also concerned with whether governmental organizations are achieving the purposes for which programs are authorized and funds are made available, are doing so economically and efficiently, and are complying with applicable laws and regulations.[3]

It is expected that the *GAO Standards* will be adopted by an increasing number of state and local governmental units. Consequently, these standards will become increasingly applicable to all audits of governmental units.

In summary, it may be the case that all auditors are concerned with both financial and operational auditing. If so, all aspects of auditing practice can be founded on a base of common discipline knowledge. Nevertheless, research should be directed to identification of similarities and differences in all aspects of auditing practice. A truly rational curriculum depends on this information.

Professional Guidance of the Auditing Curriculum

If we hold the assumption that the principal objective of auditing education is to prepare students for professional auditing careers, we can also assume that auditing education should be responsive to expressed needs of the auditing profession and that these needs be reflected in a large portion of the curriculum. I do not hold this same position with respect to *accounting* education. To understand accounting does not require experience in the practice of *accounting*. Many of the best accounting minds are educator-scholars with little or no practical experience. Furthermore, accounting is not easily learned on the job. Typically, much of accounting experience is quite limited with respect to accounting problems encountered. Also, accounting measurements are essential to all aspects of human life and are made by many people quite apart from those who practice as professional accountants. Conceivably, the accounting discipline could—like mathematics—be taught and researched for the benefit of society with the only professional accountants being scholar-educators.

Comparable statements cannot be made about *auditing*. While some might argue for development of a broad auditing discipline which deals with problems of appraising the reliability of general information flows, such is not the current perception of the auditing discipline. Rather, the auditing discipline is conceived as a professional activity for the appraisal of operations and information flows for the benefit of interested parties who are unable to perform the required appraisals for themselves. Hence, auditing is a professional activity. To the extent that a body of theory exists, it exists solely to serve the professional activity. For these reasons educators should aggressively seek counsel and guidance in curriculum matters from professional practitioners.

While I am convinced of the validity of the foregoing thesis, I also am convinced that counsel from professional auditors is seldom sought or given in curriculum development. When curriculum judgments *are* expressed by practitioners, they come with less than a unified voice. Some tell us, "Give 'em the things they can read in the literature, we'll teach 'em the rest. It's mostly common sense anyway." Others tell us, "Please prepare us a professional auditor; salaries today are simply too high for us to afford extensive firm training, whether it's on the job or in formal courses." Of course, it is impossible to respond to such inconsistent messages. Unfortunately, very little helpful guidance is found in the prefessional literature. For example, the description of auditing courses in the Beamer report easily matches a university catalogue for vagueness.[4] Also, in my judgment, little or no curriculum guidance can be found in the auditing portion of the CPA examination. Although the examination trend is clearly toward concepts and away from procedures, questions require either regurgitation of the literature (e.g., SAS #1) or only rather superficial analysis. Although auditing education has had little benefit of an exchange between educators and professional practitioners, it is not the fact (1) that educators will not listen, or (2) that professional practitioners are devoid of judgments concerning the quality and content of auditing education. Clear and direct statements from practitioners do, indeed, get attention from auditing educators. Consider, for example, the following statement from the Beamer report:

> We believe that there is no way to successfully simulate an audit engagement in the classroom and that long detailed practice sets traditionally take more scarce time from an already crowded curriculum than is warranted by the results generally achieved.[5]

This is a very clear statement and I believe that educators, rightly so, have received the message and appropriately modified their course content.

I also am convinced that professional auditors have judgments concerning the quality and content of auditing education and that these judgments are essential to rational development of the auditing curriculum. At the very least, educators should know the extent to which the profession is satisfied with the auditing knowledge of accounting graduates. This question could be the subject of a worthwhile research project.

Meanwhile, we have *some* indication that the profession is not altogether pleased with the current auditing graduate. Huge sums are being spent by the profession for continuing education. These expenditures include substantial amounts to prepare accounting graduates to perform in entry level positions. What is the profession really saying by conducting such educational activities? Is it saying that such training is inappropriate for the university and, hence, we will take it on? Or, is it saying that the university is not doing the job it should; hence, we must fill in whatever gaps we find? Informal contacts lead me to the conclusion that professional leaders have sharply divided opinions on this issue. Nevertheless, more conclusive answers should be sought.

Given that professional inputs are essential to rational development of the university auditing curriculum and that auditing educators will heed clear and consistent judgments by professionals on curriculum matters, I strongly urge that the auditing profession(s) prepare formal curriculum statements dealing both with objectives and course content. In this regard, a joint effort by public, internal, and governmental auditors would be very helpful to educators faced with the problem of identifying similarities and differences in the educational needs of each profession.

Professionalization of the Education Processes

If educators heed the admonishment to professionalize the auditing curriculum, we might also consider the implied imperative to professionalize at least a portion of the teaching-learning activity. Moonitz recommends that experience be moved into the educational program as one means of upgrading accounting education. Moonitz also recommends an internship with subsequent return to the classroom as the appropriate means for accomplishing this upgrading objective.[6] The professional internship is not, of course, a new concept to accounting education. However, a clinical experience required generally for all auditing students would, indeed, be something new.

Despite a promising outlook for internships, I would like to recommend a "teaching practice of accounting" as an even more promising vehicle for clinical experience in accounting education. To be effective, of course, such a practice would have to be staffed by first-rate professional auditors with a concurrent interest in professional education. When compared to the internship, significant advantages of the "teaching practice" are the following:

1. A common experiential relationship provided for students and faculty.
2. Readily available research opportunities, particularly for faculty and doctoral students.
3. The ability of a school to expand its faculty base through professional fees to include experts in a wide variety of fields, such as EDP and SEC.
4. The wealth of readily available consulting talent from non-accounting faculty. Furthermore, a ready consulting outlet for non-accounting faculty might well serve to enhance the image of the accounting discipline in the eyes of its sister business disciplines.

I would further recommend that the teaching practice include taxes and MAS services as well as auditing.

Establishment of teaching practices would pose a number of problems. For example, the concept would have to have full support from the profession to mitigate any perception of a competitive threat. Certain ethical problems would have to be thought through. For example, would general institutional advertising by the university be viewed as of benefit to the teaching practice? Organization would pose problems. My first thought is that the teaching practice be organized as a non-profit foundation, with all cash throw-offs to be used for accounting education and research. Persons responsible for conducting the practice might be termed accounting residents.

A significant constraint on the teaching practice might be the inability to handle large engagements and thus lose the enriching experience provided by such engagements. This problem might be overcome by forming a consortium of teaching practices throughout the nation or even the world.

One final word of comment on the teaching practice issue. The AICPA is now on record as supporting strong professional programs and the professional school concept. A statement issued last summer on this issue by the AICPA's Board of Directors reads in part as follows:

> The Institute strongly endorses any action which provides such strong professional programs. As one way, and perhaps the preferable way, of achieving an increased emphasis on the professional dimension of the discipline, the Institute endorses and encourages the establishment of professional schools of accounting at qualified and receptive colleges and universities.[7]

A significant problem involved in establishing a truly professional program is obtaining adequate financing for faculty, students, and facilities. To carry on the same programs under a different rubric would be self-deluding. Bluntly stated, programs for specialized professions simply cost more money than is provided by current allocations within the university. If we look to the regular university budget, increased funding is simply "not there." Hence, we must look to private sources, principally public accounting firms. Unfortunately, if allocated to *all* worthy schools, such private financing will be too thinly spread. Hence, donors will be required to discriminate and the choices involved will not be happy ones. The currently rich, strong programs likely will win the significant support and become even stronger. Those schools struggling toward excellence will be "also-rans" and will continue to struggle in frustration. Tragically, I think, chances will be indeed small for the also-ran schools to break into the ranks of the elite.

Although *direct* financial support for all worthy professional schools (or professional programs) would be clearly impossible, encouragement of teaching practices would provide *indirect* financial support and might well be the answer to an otherwise difficult dilemma.

The Subject Matter of the Auditing Curriculum

For purposes of further discussion, I would like now to assume that auditing is a *professional* activity and, hence, that auditing education—if it is to have any justification—*must* be professionalized. From this assumption, I will assert that effective auditing education requires that the profession be clearly defined, with reasonable consensus among practitioners and educators. If the auditing profession is not so defined, it will surely be defined by individual instructors, or perhaps worse, by the textbook writers. Inasmuch as auditing instruction is undergoing a period of transition, a variety of definitions may be developed which could prove more chaotic than constructive. As one consequence, the profession may be forced to assume the worst with respect to *all* auditing graduates and provide *all* of them with expensive training in matters more appropriately handled in university education. At the worst, the better prepared students may become bored and frustrated and leave the profession; at the best, significant training costs may represent wasted money.

To place the matter of definition in perspective, consider the problem of a faculty member charged with development of a professionalized auditing curriculum. In his deliberations, what better guidance could he seek than an authoritative definition of auditing? To explore this question, let us begin with a comparative analysis of some typical definitions of the auditing activity.

The Auditing Activity—Comparative Analysis of Definitions

Typical of definitions of the auditing activity are the following:

1. By the Committee on Basic Auditing Concepts, American Accounting Association:

> Auditing is a systematic process of objectively obtaining and evaluating evidence regarding assertions about economic actions and events to ascertain the degree of correspondence between these assertions and established criteria and communicating the results to interested users.[8]

2. By the Committee on Auditing Procedures, AICPA:

> The objective of the ordinary examination of financial statements by the independent auditor is the expression of an opinion on the fairness with which they present financial position, results of operations, and changes in financial

position in conformity with generally accepted accounting principles.[9]

3. By the Institute of Internal Auditors:

Nature of Internal Auditing:-

Internal auditing is an independent appraisal activity within an organization for the review of operations as a service to management. It is a managerial control, which functions by measuring and evaluating the effectiveness of other controls.

Objective and Scope of Internal Auditing:-

The objective of internal auditing is to assist all members of management in the effective discharge of their responsibilities, by furnishing them with analyses, appraisals, recommendations, and pertinent comments concerning the activities reviewed.

Among the activities listed as appropriate for the internal auditor is the following:-

Appraising the quality of performance in carrying out assigned responsibilities.[10]

4. By the Controller General of the United States:

... demand for information has widened the scope of governmental auditing so that such auditing no longer is a function concerned primarily with financial operations. Instead, governmental auditing now is concerned with whether governmental organizations are achieving the purposes for which programs are authorized and funds are complying with applicable laws and regulations.

These standards provide for a scope of audit that includes not only financial and compliance auditing but also auditing for economy, efficiency and achievements of desired results.[11]

5. By Willingham and Carmichael:

A primary function of the public accounting profession is to render independent and expert opinions on the fairness of presentation of . . . stewardship reports. In our complex, modern society this function—called the *attest* function—fulfills the role of adding to the credibility of representations on resource stewardship and, hence, increases the reliance which can be placed on the reports. To *attest*, then, means to assume responsibility for the credibility of representations. To warrant this assumption of responsibility, the attestor must make an examination of the objective evidence underlying the data reported. This examination—called an *audit*—is the central subject of this book.[12]

Willingham and Carmichael, for purposes of distinction, go on to define an operational audit:

An operational audit is a comprehensive and constructive examination to appraise management organizations, techniques and performance. Such an audit is a measure of the extent of achievement of organization objectives. The primary product of the operations audit is a report recommending improvements to increase the efficiency and effectiveness of operations.[13]

Willingham and Carmichael also comment that, "Operational audits are performed by all types of auditors. However, internal auditors and governmental audit agencies have been more active in this area than independent public accountants."[14] In regard to this latter comment, please recall (See the preceding section on *Identification of the Auditing Profession*) that public accounting firms are experiencing a growing involvement in operational audits, in particular the examination of local government grantee agencies for the benefit of responsible grantor federal agencies. The standards imposed for this work are *GAO Standards* and clearly include the concepts of "economy, efficiency, and achievement of desired results."

Although the foregoing definitions involve a wide variety of subject matter, certain characteristics appear to be common to all of them.

1. Each definition implies assertions by responsible persons or entities concerning actions, objects, or events (generally, economic in character). The assertions are in the form either of operational activities or of formal reports on such activities.

2. Each definition implies that the activities or reports conform to some criteria—for example, *financial statements* in conformity with fairness and generally accepted accounting principles and

activities in conformity with economy, efficiency, and achievement of desired results.

3. Each definition implies that the assertion is communicated to an interested party appropriately related to the entity in question—for example, (a) an assertion that financial statements are in conformity with generally accepted accounting principles by management to shareholders and creditors, (b) an assertion of economy, efficiency, and achievement of desired results by operational management to higher-level management, (c) an assertion of economy, efficiency and achievement of desired results by management of a local government grantee agency to the responsible grantor federal agency.

4. Each definition either specifies or clearly implies that an auditor examine the assertion for conformity with the specified criteria and, based upon the examination of objective evidence, form a judgment to be communicated to the interested party.

These common characteristics indicate that a consensus definition of auditing is feasible. I strongly urge that such a definition be prepared by a consortium of auditing practitioners and educators. A consensus definition would have a significant and constructive effect on auditing education.

The Definition as Guidance for Curriculum Content

Although a consensus definition of auditing would be greatly more helpful, the foregoing definitions and comparative analysis should provide significant guidance for curriculum content. The following content topics seem to be suggested:

1. The various environments which create demands for auditing.
2. The nature of assertions and related criteria to be evaluated.
3. The auditor as a person—his personal and professional characteristics.
4. The investigative aspects of auditing—accumulation and evaluation of evidence.
5. The reporting aspects of auditing—communicating results to interested users.

Detailed consideration indicates that the foregoing topics can be developed based on one of two major assumptions. First, it may be assumed that most of the topics comprise new information. Under this assumption, very little in the way of prerequisite knowledge would be expected. Second, it may be assumed that most of the topics involve a synthesis of prior knowledge. Under this assumption, much in the way of prerequisite knowledge would be expected of the auditing student.

I am inclined toward the latter view and assert that auditing, as a body of knowledge, is largely a synthesis of more basic knowledge. Based on this assertion, I would like to explore more fully the following three topics:

1. The criteria against which assertions concerning economic actions, objects, and events are to be evaluated.
2. The investigative aspects of auditing.
3. The reporting aspects of auditing.

The criteria. Every definition of auditing includes the concept of conformity of certain assertions with specified criteria. Those conformity criteria which appear to be clearly evident from the foregoing analysis of definitions are the following:

1. Conformity criteria for financial statements: fairness and consistent application of generally accepted accounting principles.
2. Conformity criteria for operations: economy, efficiency, and effectiveness (effectiveness to mean achievement of desired results).

Unquestionably, the current auditing curriculum specifies the consistent application of generally accepted accounting principles as prerequisite knowledge. Despite the fact that these principles are often vague and difficult to identify, we take them in auditing as clear and precise criteria. With respect to these principles, we also assume considerable sophistication on the part of the auditing student. Such knowledge, of course, is essential to the discussion of auditing, per se. This is simply because inquiry in any field requires that the investigator be thoroughly familiar with the subject matter under investigation; an audit investigation is no exception.

Unlike accounting principles, prerequisite knowledge of the fairness criterion is not so readily provided. As enunciated in the Continental Vending case, "fairness" is now identified as a criterion distinct from generally accepted accounting principles. However, fairness, like beauty, is in the eyes of the beholder. Until the fairness criterion is operationally defined, auditors will have to deal with it case by case. Eventually, the fairness criterion should be incorporated in generally accepted accounting principles. In the meantime, we must deal with it in the auditing curriculum, probably by reference to dictum in the Continental Vending case.

The criteria of economy, efficiency, and effectiveness pose difficulties similar to fairness. These criteria also are too general for operational application. *Auditing Standards Established by the GAO—Their Meaning and Significance for CPAs* appears to have been written to deal specifically with the vague nature of these criteria. Consider the following statement from that publication:

Because audits for efficiency and economy do not deal in

absolutes, and because there can be differing views of an operation and its results, sufficiency of evidence cannot be clearly defined. In a financial audit, the fact that an item of inventory can be observed may be the only evidence the auditor requires of physical existence. In audits for efficiency and economy, *criteria* for evaluating evidence, for deciding what is to be measured, and for making the measurements will, for the most part, not have been specified. It is in the *standardization* and acceptance of new concepts of measurement that the GAO standards may be most challenging to auditors. (Emphasis added.)[15]

Note that the problem is identified as a lack of specified criteria and that the challenge is to develop appropriate standards. Until more specific operational criteria are developed and standardized by the profession, the criteria of economy, efficiency, and effectiveness will be a substantial challenge for auditing education. In any event, inasmuch as all auditors (public, internal, and governmental) are now significantly involved in operational auditing, operational auditing and its criteria can no longer be ignored in the auditing curriculum.

In my judgment, the auditing curriculum cannot deal effectively with operational auditing without considerable reliance on prerequisite knowledge. Actually, required prerequisite knowledge may pose more problems for the traditional auditing instructor than for the students. In this regard, I will assert that the core requirements from a modern business curriculum provide the ideal prerequisite knowledge for operational auditing. Consider the following array of nonaccounting courses from the four-year accounting program proposed in the Beamer report:

Subject	Semester Hours [16]
Communication	6-9
Behavioral sciences	6
Economics	6
Introduction to the computer	2-3
Mathematics (Modern algebra, calculus, statistics and probability)	12
General education	25-18
Economics (intermediate theory and the monetary system)	6

Subject	Semester Hours
(Continued)	
The social environment of business	3
Business law	4
Production or operational systems	2
Marketing	2
Finance	4
Organization, group and individual behavior	6
Quantitative applications in business (optimization models, statistics, sampling, Markov chains, statistics, decision theory, queueing, PERT, simulation)	6
Written communication	2
Business policy	3

Surely, it is reasonable to assume the above courses will give adequate consideration from a number of viewpoints to issues of economy, efficiency, and effectiveness. An operational auditing course might well be viewed as a synthesis of all prior coursework. Thus, those who would develop a course in operational auditing might do well to consider techniques employed in business policy or other capstone courses in business administration.

The investigative aspects of auditing. In my judgment, the investigative aspects of auditing offer great opportunities for the advancement of auditing education and for establishment of auditing as a scholarly discipline. The American Accounting Association Committee on Basic Auditing Concepts takes the position "that auditing is based, in part at least, on the discipline and philosophy of the scientific method."[17] If the foregoing position is appropriate, then the methods of scientific research and such research tools as general logic and statistical inference should be established as prerequisite knowledge for the auditing curriculum. Presenting the investigative aspects of auditing based on scientific research methodology as a prototype would have a significant impact on auditing courses and would provide an abundance of challenging research opportunities for the educator-scholar with obvious direct benefits for the professional auditor.

Internal control evaluation is a topic uniquely applicable to auditing. Conceptually, the role of internal control in the investigative aspects of auditing is easily understood. Nevertheless, internal control principles are very complex, are difficult to teach, and are even more difficult to relate logically to other auditing procedures. I am convinced that problems encountered by the educator in evaluating internal control and in relating internal control to other auditing procedures are almost as troublesome to the professional auditor. I also am convinced that the difficulty lies in an inadequate statement of principles. To be truly useful, a statement of internal control principles should serve as a readily applicable framework for analyzing and evaluating any particular control system. In my judgment, the internal control section of SAS 1#(Section 320), although quite definitive, fails this test of usefulness.

Analysis and evaluation of internal control is especially difficult when the environment is modified by an EDP system. The following is stated in the 1972-73 report of the American Accounting Association Committee on Auditing: "Full appreciation of internal control evaluation of EDP systems requires a depth of knowledge ordinarily beyond the training and education of the average college student."[19] If the auditing curriculum is truly to be professionalized, this condition cannot continue to prevail. It would be most helpful if internal control principles for EDP systems were expressed in a framework similar to that for general control principles. As a minimum, control principles for EDP systems should be stated in the same framework as SAS #1 (Section 320).

In summary, a clear statement of internal control principles suitable as a tool for analyzing particular systems (including EDP systems) would have a significant and constructive impact on auditing education. Also, in my judgment, such a statement would be of immediate and direct benefit to the professional auditor. Study of internal control principles would be greatly facilitated by prerequisite knowledge of accounting systems, including EDP systems.

The reporting aspects of auditing. A substantial portion of professional auditing literature deals with reporting the results of the audit investigation, particularly with respect to the examination of financial statements. The literature is sufficiently complex so that its application to case situations requires rigorous analysis. Furthermore, the reporting literature facilitates understanding of the objectives of the examination of financial statements. Comparable benefits should be obtained from the study of similar reports of internal and governmental auditors, particularly, those reports emanating from operational audits.

A significant future direction for the auditing curriculum would be time devoted to critical analysis of reporting practices by all professional auditors—public, internal, and governmental. Such analysis would serve not only to improve the communication skills of auditing students but would also provide a sharpened awareness of the objectives of the various audit functions. Analysis should surface such problems as the current dilemma for financial auditing created by the inconsistent relationship between unaudited financial statements, disclaimers of opinions, and piecemeal opinions. Prerequisite knowledge of communication theory would be most helpful to the analytical processes involved.

Summary and Conclusions

Although the auditing curriculum is in a state of change and is not yet ready for pinpoint objectives on all issues, the curriculum is sorely in need of professionalization—i.e., to be more responsive to the educational needs of various aspects of professional practice. To be more responsive, auditing educators need certain information as follows:

1. Information concerning identification of similarities and differences in the various aspects of auditing practice—public, internal, and governmental.

2. A consensus definition of the auditing discipline, preferably prepared by a consortium in which all aspects of auditing practice are represented.

3. An appraisal by professional practitioners of the current quality of auditing education.

4. Curriculum guidance from practitioners on a continuing basis.

Also, in my judgment, professionalization of the auditing curriculum requires a clinical experience for all accounting students. Although a number of problems are posed, I submit that this clinical experience can best be obtained through the establishment of teaching practices of accounting.

The auditing curriculum also is faced with a number of critical subject matter issues as follows:

1. Certain conformity criteria are in need of development— particularly, criteria of (a) fairness with respect to financial statements and (b) economy, efficiency and effectiveness with respect to operations.

2. Because operational auditing is becoming a significant part of all aspects of professional practice, it must receive greater emphasis in the auditing curriculum.

3. Scientific research methodology should be adopted as a prototype for the investigative aspects of auditing.

4. If internal control is to be taught effectively, a more analytically useful set of principles need be developed.

FOOTNOTES

1. William G. Shenkir, "The Auditing Course in the Accounting Curriculum: A Professor's View," paper presented at the Twenty-Third Annual Meeting of the Southeast Regional Group, American Accounting Association, pp. 7-8.

2. Maurice Moonitz, "The Beamer Report—A Golden Opportunity for Accounting Education," *Journal of Accountancy* (August 1973), p. 67. Reprinted from the California CPA Quarterly, March 1973.

3. Controller General of the United States, *United States General Accounting Office—Standards for Audit of Governmental Organizations, Programs, Activities & Functions* (U.S. Government Printing Office, 1972), p. i.

4. *Report of the Committee on Education and Experience Requirements for CPAs* (New York: American Institute of Certified Public Accountants), pp. 56-7.

5. Ibid., p. 57.

6. Moonitz, p. 68.

7. *The CPA Letter, March 11, 1974* (New York: American Institute of Certified Public Accountants).

8. Committee on Basic Auditing Concepts, *A Statement of Basic Auditing Concepts (ASOBAC, Studies in Accounting Research 6,* (Sarasota, Florida: American Accounting Association, 1973), p. 2

9. Auditing Standards Executive Committee (formerly Committee on Auditing Procedure), *Statement on Auditing Standards 1* (New York: American Institute of Certified Public Accountants, 1973), p. 1

10. Institute of Internal Auditors, *Statement of Responsibilities of*

the *Internal Auditor,* (Orlando, Florida: The Institute of Internal Auditors, 1971).

11. Controller General of the United States, pp. i and 2.

12. J.J. Willingham and D.R. Carmichael, *Auditing Concepts and Methods* (New York: McGraw-Hill Book Company, 1971), p. 4.

13. Ibid., p. 27.

14. Ibid.

15. Committee on Relations with the General Accounting Office of AICPA, *Auditing Standards Established by the GAO—Their Meaning and Significance for CPAs* (New York: American Institute of Certified Public Accountants, 1973), p. 8.

16. Committee on Education and Experience Requirements for CPAs, p. 58.

17. Committee on Basic Auditing Concepts, p. 2.

18. Auditing Standards Executive Committee, p. 13.

19. "Report of the Committee on Auditing," *Accounting Review,* Supplement to vol. XLIX (1974), p. 157.

The Auditing Curriculum—Is There a Need for Change?

A Critique
Alvin A. Arens

Professor Grinaker has written a clear and well-stated proposal for changing the auditing curriculum. For the most part, our views correspond on the major problems facing curriculum development in auditing. Our disagreements are more a matter of degree than on the basic substance of his ideas.

In discussing the author's paper, the first few pages will be directed to limited comments about objectives and professional guidance in curriculum development in auditing. Subsequently, the major area where our views differ will be discussed, which is the significance of the need for change and its implications.

Objectives in Auditing Education
I am in substantial agreement with Professor Grinaker in his statements of the objectives of the auditing course. The principle objective should be the preparation of individuals for a professional career in auditing. Recently in the Education Research and Academic Notes section of *The Accounting Review*, R.K. Mautz expressed similar views about the objectives of accounting education. His comments seem to me to be equally applicable to auditing.

> Applied accounting needs an educational system that gives attention to preparation for a professional career. In that preparation, conceptual understanding is important, but also important are technical skill and a professional attitude . . .
> From a practitioner's point of view, the ideal recruit to the profession would have (1) a conceptual understanding of accounting; (2) technical skill in the procedures of accounting analysis, in handling quantitative data, and in the utilization of record keeping techniques and tools; (3) business judgment; (4) an operational understanding of

professional responsibilities, including his obligation to raise professional standards; and (5) the basic virtues of integrity, ambition, loyalty, and honor. He needs all of these in some kind of balance. Great conceptual understanding without technical skill will not get him very far. Likewise, technical skill or an operational understanding of professional responsibility by itself is not enough.[1]

Since at many universities, the teaching of professional ethics and legal liability has been done in the auditing course, the above characteristics of the professional accountant seem particularly relevant to curriculum development in auditing.

There are two groups besides the professional auditor whose needs should at least be considered in the auditing curriculum. First are the accounting majors who have not yet decided upon a career as a professional auditor or some other career in accounting. A part of the process of education is providing students with information to help them make career choices. Auditing is significantly different from financial and managerial accounting in this respect because at many universities there is only one auditing course in the curriculum. The second group that should be accommodated is the students who definitely do not plan to enter into a career in auditing, but plan to be accountants. There are a large number of accounting majors who are employed in corporate or governmental accounting who will be closely involved with auditors throughout their careers. A commonly encountered problem for accountants without any exposure to auditing is the difficulty of comprehending the auditor's objectives and his requirements to complete the audit. If only one auditing course is to be included in the curriculum, the needs of the individual with no auditing career plans must at least be considered.

Differences Between Concepts in Public Accounting, Internal Auditing, and Governmental Auditing

A major contribution in the Grinaker paper is the identification of the need to place a greater emphasis on governmental and internal auditing in the auditing curriculum. A major shortcoming of many auditing courses is the complete exclusion of the discussion of any aspect of governmental and corporate auditing.

As a part of discovering more about the overall objective of a professional career in auditing, I concur with Professor Grinaker that the possible differences in the basic subject matter of corporate, governmental, and independent auditors is a matter of considerable concern in auditing education. In most auditing courses, the emphasis has been on auditing by CPA firms. This occurs for different reasons, which include the personal backgrounds of most auditing teachers, the emphasis in the standard auditing textbooks, the strong influence on the profession by the AICPA, and the relatively recent emergence of extensive governmental and corporate internal auditing. It is certainly possible that the emphasis on auditing by public accounting firms in auditing courses is a self-fulfilling prophesy that discourages the most competent students from entering corporate or governmental auditing.

Professor Grinaker's urging of additional research into the differences and similarities between different sectors of the profession is an excellent one. The results of extended research in this area could have a significant effect on the curriculum development.

Until adequate research is completed to determine the concepts common to all segments of the auditing profession, it is my feeling that examples used to illustrate concepts should be drawn from governmental and internal auditing by the auditing teacher. It would not be wise to attempt to expand the coverage in most auditing courses to include the study of these two sectors of auditing separately. There is always a danger of spending so much time in a course on superficial surveys of the differences and similarities of auditing in the various sectors of society that it becomes impossible to spend sufficient time on the most relevant basic auditing concepts.

Professional Guidance in the Auditing Curriculum

The two major points that Professor Grinaker makes about professional guidance are, first, that auditing education should be responsive to the expressed needs of the auditing profession, and second, that inputs from professional auditors are essential to the auditing curriculum. I agree wholeheartedly with both of these points and I would like to expand on them somewhat.

There is a difference between responding to the needs and inputs of professional auditors and permitting professional auditors to determine the responsibility of universities in auditing education. It is important for educators to remember that there may be a difference in the responsibility of educators to their students, the profession, and the employment needs of individual professional auditing firms, corporations, or governmental units.

It is reasonable to expect auditing practitioners to want students who understand the existing rules and standards before they enter the profession. This permits the employer to effectively utilize the employee more quickly in his professional work.

In an article bemoaning the lack of research being taught in accounting classes as compared to the study of practice, Robert R. Sterling makes the following point:

> This complimentary relationship (between practice and education) is due mainly to educator's predilection to prepare students for practice; we educators teach our students acceptable practice so that they can get jobs. Practice complements education in that it provides educators with information on what are the acceptable practices and practitioners practice what educators teach them . . . strictly interpreted (this practice) would prohibit change. Since changes do, in fact, occur, we know that there are exogenous inputs to the circle. The source of these inputs is practice, not education or research. That is, practitioners add to (and subtract from) their store of accepted practice and then educators observe, codify, and teach these additional accepted practices.[2]

Assuming that educators who are concerned primarily with the long run needs of the students determine the appropriate curriculum, I agree that we must seek the counsel of professional auditors in making our curriculum more meaningful. Those involved in the practice of auditing can certainly provide relevant inputs into auditing courses designed for a professional career in auditing.

The University Auditing Curriculum as a Part of Continuing Auditing Education

In recent years, practitioners have begun extensive professional development programs in auditing that probably should affect the auditing curriculum at universities. These programs are becoming highly sophisticated and have become highly significant in most professionals' total auditing education.

These training programs in all sectors of the auditing profession point out a major change that should be taking place in university level auditing education. Educators must begin to recognize that the university courses in auditing are now only one part of the formal learning programs of the auditing professional. Traditionally, the university courses were the termination of formal training and subsequent auditing education was on a self-taught informal basis.

Today, the university education is only the beginning of a continuing education process.

For university auditing courses to be an effective part of a professional's long-term continuing education needs, it is essential that the information taught be part of an overall integrated education program. This implies that the auditing taught in universities must be reasonably uniform from university to university if the public, internal, and governmental auditing are each to continue to hire students from different universities and assume a certain level of auditing knowledge in their training programs. In addition to being reasonably uniform, the auditing curriculum of each university must also be relevant and meaningful to the students if the education is to be a significant part of their overall integrated auditing education.

Evaluation of Existing Auditing Education

Throughout the paper, Professor Grinaker apparently takes the view that the auditing curriculum throughout the United States is undergoing major changes that are likely to result in a high quality relevant auditing curriculum. As a result of this optimistic view of experimentation and innovation in auditing courses, he is hesitant to recommend achieving consensus on the specfic coverage in a basic auditing course at this time.

Although I concur that some innovative changes are taking place in university auditing education, the need for achieving a consensus is of much greater importance to me than to Professor Grinaker. First of all, as was previously expressed, I believe that a reasonably uniform auditing education is an important goal to achieve. Secondly, I believe that auditing courses taken as a whole throughout the country need to be made more relevant to the present needs of the profession.

In teaching professional development courses for the past eight years, I have frequently inquired as to which courses in the accounting curriculum were most relevant and useful to the participants and which were least relevant and useful. Although there is great disagreement about which courses have been most relevant, I have observed fairly consistently that the least useful was the basic auditing course. Discussions with college recruiters and professional development personnel about the effectiveness of auditing courses have indicated that for the most part, students typically regard their college audit course as boring and irrelevant.

Although the typical attitude about college auditing courses seems to be highly unfavorable, occasionally a participant in a staff training program or a recruiter or a professional development educator will praise a particular auditing course as being highly relevant and meaningful. Informal investigation of these instances leads me to believe that an auditing course that is well-received by one student or one recruiter is likely to be highly acclaimed by most students and recruiters. Another way of expressing this is that apparently some interesting and highly relevant auditing courses are being taught, but many, if not most, are not well-received or respected by most students, recruiters, and professional auditors.

The reasons for the perceived lack of usefulness of many auditing courses are probably numerous but the following are certainly major factors:

1. The practice of auditing has changed significantly during the past two decades. Many auditing courses have not changed concurrently.

2. Professional development courses by CPA firms have been significantly increased during the past decade. Many auditing courses have not been modified to recognize this change.

3. The auditing course is a secondary responsibility of most faculty who teach auditing. This in itself causes great difficulty because considerable time is necessary to keep current in the professional literature and to develop more relevant auditing courses.

4. Many auditing courses are taught by full-time practitioners who do not have an adequate academic background in auditing or teaching. Auditing courses taught by full-time practitioners are frequently taught on the basis of what was relevant to the practitioner when he started practice.

5. In many cases, the auditing teacher received his experience several years ago and has not had an opportunity to update his experience. As a result, his experiences may no longer be relevant and the course may be outdated.

6. Relatively few of the teachers currently involved with auditing had a conceptual auditing course of any kind in their graduate academic program.

Although there has been a slow but gradual increase in the favorable comments about auditing courses by former students, recruiters, and professional development personnel, the progress has been alarmingly slow. Given the conditions of a rapidly expanding explosion of knowledge in auditing and an increasing pressure on faculty to keep abreast of many different current developments in his subject field, it seems unlikely that the auditing course in most colleges and universities will be highly regarded in the near future.

Education by CPA Firms

In order to gain a different perspective about the general quality of education at the college level, an examination of auditing education by CPA firms may be useful. Virtually all of the larger and medium sized firms offer recent accounting graduates their first professional development programs relatively early in their public accounting career. For practical purposes, most of these programs can be regarded as entry level professional development.

An examination of several of these programs developed by the AICPA and several other large firms leads me to the conclusion that there are substantial similarities in the content of most basic staff training programs. The primary emphasis in these programs is in the auditing area rather than in financial accounting, managerial accounting, or taxation. In the auditing portion of the program, the emphasis appears to be on the study of basic auditing techniques and procedures with particular emphasis on the purpose and relevance of different audit tests.

In examining the materials of these basic staff training programs, it appears to me that the basic assumption being used by the CPA firms is that the individuals taking the programs either had no auditing course or alternatively a highly conceptual auditing course that provided useful background as a basic understanding of the materials in the program.

Discussions on an informal basis with many who have taken a basic university auditing course indicates to me that for the most part, their auditing course was not highly conceptual and was not taught at a more abstract level than their staff training programs. To the contrary, many auditing courses are apparently taught in a procedural manner in a sterile atmosphere. Although it remains unclear to me what should be taught in a university auditing course, I am convinced it should be different from that which is currently being taught at many universities. Unfortunately, at this point, we may have achieved more uniformity than relevance.

Proposal to Improve Audit Education

A reasonable approach to revising the auditing curriculum would be in the context of the recommendations set forth by Professor Grinaker. The primary objective should be to develop a curriculum in auditing that would prepare the student for a professional career in auditing. Therefore, the course must be reasonably uniform from university to university, relevant to the professional auditor's needs, and be a useful part of a continuing education package.

Given this objective, it is my belief that a concentrated effort by leaders in auditing from both the academic community and auditing practice must jointly attempt to develop a solution to the problem. Although there are presumably alternative solutions that might improve auditing education, the following research and education proposal is one that I believe could prove highly beneficial.

One part of the auditing research project should be of the nature recommended by Professor Grinaker. This would be the identification of the similarities and differences in the underlying bodies of knowledge of public accounting, internal auditing, and governmental auditing. The impact of this research would be the starting point in establishing the responsibility of universities in the education of professional auditors. Presumably, the university education courses should emphasize those concepts that are most common to all three sections.

Another phase of the project, which can be done concurrently with the previous research, is to determine the nature of the professional development programs in auditing now being taught by the three professional sectors that are served by university auditing education. To the extent that there are significant similarities in certain portions of professional development programs, this may indicate that universities could more appropriately perform the education. Naturally, there may be some aspects of audit education that are common to all professional education programs that are still inappropriate for university education.

The third part of the program is meant to delineate those concepts in auditing that should be performed as a part of a basic auditing course and those that are best left for professional education because of time constraints or the inability to teach the ideas affectively in a university environment. This phase should probably not take place until the two previous phases are completed.

If this phase is to be successful, it is essential to have inputs from various sources. There should be competent educators whose primary concern is with auditing concepts and the changes taking place in the profession. But there should also be educators who teach auditing as a secondary interest, but who will be useful in evaluating whether the concepts suggested for a basic auditing course are teachable by most educators who will teach auditing. Naturally, practitioners who are actively involved in continuing education in the three sectors of the economy should have a significant impact. Recent college graduates who have taken part in professional development programs also can contribute useful ideas.

If at the completion of phase three, the primary auditing education responsibilities of universities should be clearly established and agreed upon by the groups represented. I believe this would be a significant accomplishment, but this would not be sufficient to provide any reasonable assurance that the auditing concepts would be taught or communicated to auditing professors. The assumption that published recommendations about an auditing curriculum would be widely studied and implemented by educators is probably invalid. A more effective method of implementation is necessary.

The fourth and perhaps most important phase is the presentation of these concepts and alternative ways of teaching them to auditing educators throughout the country. Some logical place for this to occur would be at the annual, national, and regional meetings of the American Accounting Association. Another would be at accounting conferences held in some states or regional areas. These programs could be of the nature of a one or two day professional education program for auditing educators. It is my belief that a major shortcoming in accounting education in recent years is the failure to provide educators with continuing education programs that will assist them in being more effective in the classroom. This recommendation is meant to provide that assistance.

In addition to providing instructional assistance, the programs would be meant to facilitate a dialogue among educators in auditing from different institutions. One of the difficulties in implementing change in auditing education is the lack of communication among auditing teachers due to the limited number of auditing teachers on a given faculty. The presentation of a well thought out recommended auditing curriculum that relates to continuing education by practitioners should provide an excellent vehicle for discussion of the goals of auditing education and the need to change the curriculum.

Even if phase four could be accomplished, a mechanism is needed to assure that the recommended curriculum is dynamic in nature. This can be done by having a continuing committee made up of representatives from the groups previously mentioned which would meet periodically to discuss changes in technology or other considerations necessitating a change in the curriculum. Presumably, this could be an ongoing American Association Committee.

Assuming that the first four phases could be accomplished, a major difficulty would be in determining adequate teaching material for such a curriculum. This would probably be a problem for a while, but I am confident that some enterprising author would provide a textbook for such a course.

Existing Materials For The Proposed Research

Although the approaches are considerably different from the proposal presented here, there have been several recent efforts in producing a useful basis for education in auditing.

The first of these is "A Statement of Basic Auditing Concepts," by the 1970-71 Committee on Basic Auditing Concepts of the American Accounting Association. Included in the preface is the following comment:

> The study contains concepts that should be explored in both undergraduate and graduate courses in auditing to provide the student with a better appreciation and understanding of the audit process.3

Although this study has not, to my knowledge, been widely read and implemented in the classroom by educators, there are many ideas that should be meaningful to any group developing a curriculum consistent with a long-term plan for continuing education in auditing.

A second source of existing materials is the 1971-72 Committee Report of the Auditing Education Committee of the American Accounting Association which had the following charge:

> To survey existing auditing concepts, literature, and practice (including the report of the 1970-71 AAA Committee on Auditing Concepts) with a view to determining the proper scope, content, and implementations of auditing theory and methodology in the accounting curriculum at both the graduate and undergraduate level.4

The committee, which was chaired by Professor Grinaker, developed a recommended set of prerequisites, considered the differences between auditing education versus on-the-job training and set forth a detailed basic auditing course outline. It did not study the basic auditing concepts that are common to CPA's, governmental and internal auditors. In addition, a study of existing professional development programs by CPA firms, governmental and internal auditors was not done before the recommendations were made. Although some of the material from the 1971-72 Committee Report would be useful for the proposed study, it is my belief that most auditing educators would be unwilling or unable to teach the recommended topics and concepts in the report.

Professor Grinaker's section in his paper, on the subject matter of the auditing curriculum, is also a relevant source of ideas for additional research on the subject. His ideas on the definition of auditing, their use in developing topics for a relevant auditing course, and the consideration of prerequisite knowledge are all potentially useful for the suggested proposal.

Each of these three sources present ideas which are consistent with what appears to be a conceptual and relevant university auditing course. But, there has not yet been any significant research that I know of that attempts to tie these concepts into the integrated continuing education needs of the professional auditor. This is now needed if we are to professionalize the auditing curriculum.

FOOTNOTES

1. R.K. Mautz, "Where Do We Go From Here?" *Accounting Review* (April 1974), pp. 357-58.

2. Robert R. Sterling, "Accounting Research, Education, and Practice," *Journal of Accountancy* (September 1973), p. 46.

3. Report of the Committee on Basic Auditing Concepts, *Accounting Review*, Supplement to vol. XLVII (1972), p. 16.

4. Report of the Committee on Auditing Education, *Accounting Review*, Supplement to vol. XLVIII (1973), p. 1.

The Taxation Curriculum—Is There a Need for Change?

Ray M. Sommerfeld

This paper will be devoted to a very imprecise but hopefully interesting discussion of the sorry state of affairs in which tax education finds itself today. The thesis of the paper is simply that educational institutions have not responded appropriately to the needs of society relative to tax education. Proof of the thesis will not be offered by way of a rigorous analytical model but rather by some random observations made in the great social science laboratory, *viz.*, the world in which we all find ourselves (for reasons which we cannot comprehend!).

Tax advisors were born the child of need and nurtured to maturity on the pap of experience. Had they not fallen heir to sizable fortune so early in life, their educational preparation might have been viewed with less selfish interest. Alternatively, their educational preparation might then have been deemed wholly unnecessary! The facts remain, however, that : (1) approximately 32 per cent of the gross national product of the United States is now diverted from the private to the public sector by means of taxation; (2) approximately 110 million *federal* tax returns are filed annually (the number of state and local returns, a multiple of that figure, is unknown); (3) some 200,000 persons offer their services to the public as "tax experts"; (4) 25 to 30 per cent of the gross revenue of C.P.A. firms in the United States is attributable to "tax work"; and (5) tax lawyers and tax accountants are increasingly being called upon to advise governments in matters of policy.

Considering the economic and social s gnificance of taxation, it behooves academicians and educational institutions to re-examine both educated citizens in general and
tax advisors in particular. Before turning our attention to the question of what might be done in the future, we might first examine the traditional answers of the past.

Traditional Tax Education

If a researcher were systematically to ask businessmen, including a reasonable sample of lawyers and accountants, how best to prepare for a career as a tax advisor, my unvalidated suspicions are that the vast majority of answers would fall into one of three well defined "tracks." The most frequently cited track probably would consist of an accounting degree, followed by a law degree, and topped by experience. The other two tracks would, alternately, exclude accounting or law but both would include experience. These alternatives can be schematically represented as in Figure 1.

Figure 1

Formal Education:	Track 1	Track 2	Track 3
Undergraduate	Accounting	Any major	Accounting
Professional	Law School	Law School	None
Practical Experience	Required	Required	Required

If one were to investigate the academic preparation of each of these three tracks for tax content, the results would surprise everyone but the accountant-lawyer who had been there. He would know from first hand experience that his total academic exposure to taxation most likely consisted of one pedantic introduction to taxation taught by the oldest, youngest, or most-part-time faculty member of an accounting department. The text he used was not unlike a big Sears' catalog, sans those colorful pictures which prove that integration has arrived. His law school exposure was equally rich in rewards. Usually one course, at the very most two, which covered essentially the same ground he last met three years earlier in an accounting department, but this time with a text that jumbled the entries in the catalog so that you never knew from day to day if the topic was boots or brassieres. This joyous mixture of statutory, administrative, and judicial law—called the case approach—did at least prepare one for the disturbing fact that real-world problems never came in the nice, neat packages that presented themselves for solution at the end of each chapter in that well respected undergraduate textbook.

Inadequacies of the Traditional Patterns

Given the formal educational background that is typical to each of the three tracks of Figure 1, we need not ponder long the reason why practical experience is the single common ingredient to the three modes of educating the traditional tax advisor. Practical experience is, after all, the source of 95 per cent of his knowledge. If this conclusion is at all factual, one might argue forcibly that institutions of *higher* education should not demean themselves to undertake the practical task of training tax advisors because the world of experience has already proven itself quite capable of performing that function. I contend that this conclusion is fallacious on at least three grounds.

First, if the critical criterion for educational institutions turned upon the inability of experience to provide a satisfactory substitute, all universities could close their doors tomorrow morning. Indeed, one might argue that the invention of the printing press made professors and classrooms an expensive redundancy. If the world were willing to provide interested persons with the requisite time, materials, and guinea pigs, then surgeons, scientists and philosophers could be molded from a world unhampered by educational institutions. Several forces keep this from happening. Most importantly, educational institutions substantially increase the *efficiency* of knowledge-gathering process. In addition, educational institutions serve as a certifying agency which facilitates the flow of commerce that would move very slowly if the credentials of each would-be expert had to be determined independently.

Second, the world of experience actually has found that the formal classroom is still most helpful. But, in the instance of taxation, the classroom has been created largely outside the structure of the university in a free-university, crazy-quilt pattern of tax institutes, professional development programs, IRS programs, and in-firm training courses. In short, the failure of the traditional educational institutions to fill the gap has created a whole new organizational structure of non-school schools.

Third, because the very restricted formal education of the tax advisor has been so heavily influenced by pragmatic constraints, it has slighted an entire dimension of basic knowledge or understanding which has important social, economic, and political consequences. Tax education, because of the economic reward system, has concentrated its attention on a single dimension of the taxing process: that is, on taxpayer compliance. The recent increase in social awareness, if not social conscience, has demonstrated the need for something more. Tax advisors now are being called upon to recommend changes in tax policy. The American Institute of Certified Public Accountants and the American Bar Association both have created units which try to deal with the policy issues. For many reasons, neither group has been particularly successful. A primary reason is the fact that the educational background of these persons simply has not been either adequate or appropriate for the new role. If any of this nonsense makes some sense, what then does this say for tax education in the future?

General Implications for Tax Educators

Business and law schools, including accounting departments, should recognize openly that taxation is neither an advanced course in accounting or law. What little most schools typically offer can only be an introduction to taxation.[1] Taxation perhaps is best described as a truly interdisciplinary study which encompasses at least some parts of law, accountancy, economics, and government. The overlap might be diagrammed as in Figure 2, below:

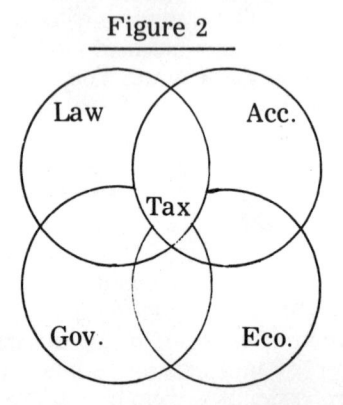

Figure 2

The more that I study the subject of taxation the more convinced I become that Figure 2 should be expanded to encompass what we now call linguistics but I am sufficiently ignorant of the content of that discipline that I continue to exclude it for fear of exposure. Besides, Figure 2 is already properly complex!

Explanation of the presence of the accounting circle seems to depend upon two facts. First, accountants collectively are the only group in today's society who have grappled with the multitudinous problems of income measurement at the micro (i.e., the individual or corporate) level. Secondly, the data from which many tax bases are derived is essentially accounting data. The accountant's knowledge of and facility with these data are what provided him with an initial entry into tax practice. It is interesting to observe that accountants seldom if ever get much involved with real property taxation. Courthouse records remain within the domain of the lawyer and the real estate appraiser and the accountant knows enough to steer clear. However, when it comes to income measurement, to payroll records, and to sales data, the accountant is not reticent for he knows better than anyone else the shoals that dot those troubled waters.

Explanation of the presence of the law circle in Figure 2 is equally obvious. Our taxes are, after all, based on statutory provisions which, in cases of dispute, must finally be interpreted in the judicial arena. The lawyer is the best equipped person in our society to deal with problems of statutory interpretation and judicial procedures. He too, therefore, was quite properly admitted to tax practice "in the beginning."

Only recently has it become apparent that compliance with statutory rules is not enough. Tax advisors trained in the "how to" answers are not doing a good job with the "why" and "how much" kinds of question. The latter problems traditionally have been reserved for the economist and the political scientist who have done reasonably well in those spheres but only so long as they remained abstract from the practical problems of taxpayer compliance. As the role of taxation expands, the need for the person who can bridge both the conceptual and the practical problem becomes increasingly clear. Unfortunately the institutional constraints of departmentalized academic disciplines and the heady professional jealousies of the interested parties make it difficult to chart a reasonably efficient course for the education of the would-be tax advisor.

Given a completely free hand, I believe that a very desirable educational pattern could be designed for tomorrow's tax advisor. This pattern would include the following:

From accounting—traditional courses in financial income measurement and some knowledge of managerial accounting concepts, information systems, and auditing.

From law—a thorough introduction to legal methods, statutory interpretation, conflict of laws, security regulation, business associations and property law.

From economics—intermediate macro- and microeconomic theory, public finance (both descriptive and theoretical) and an introduction to econometrics.

From government—courses in the administrative and legislative processes and some introduction to political parties.

From taxpayer compliance (which could be offered in most any department)—introductory tax concepts, specific I.R.S. and judicial procedures, and the substantive rules applicable to selected areas of taxation (see further discussion of this aspect of tax education in the subsequent section, *Education of The Tax Specialist).*

To round out this education I would turn to such traditional favorites as English composition (especially technical writing), mathematics and statistics, history, philosophy (including symbolic logic), psychology, and speech as well as the newer area of linguistics. By the careful deletion of the other courses which are presently required in each of the academic programs identified in the four circles of Figure 2 it would be possible to keep the total time required to complete such a program to about five years. The result, in my estimation, would be a far superior educational package for the tax advisor of tomorrow. The likelihood of this result occurring is so remote, however, that we would do well to consider less drastic modifications of our present institutional structure.

Specific Implications for the First Course in Taxation

Most first courses tend to be a combination of an introuction to elementary techniques and a survey of the field. In my estimation the first course in taxation should be no exception to that general rule. For taxation this means that the course should introduce the student to the role of taxation in society; it should acquaint him with the way in which taxes are apt to influence his life in particular as well as human behavior more generally; it should introduce him to the forces which have caused the subject to change in the past so that he might better anticipate the likely role of those same forces in the future; it should acquaint him with the existence of the Code and the subtleties of interpreting that document in carefully selected particular fact situations; and it should acquaint him with the legislative and administrative process by which taxation proceeds from one day to the next.

Acceptance of the creed stated in the preceding paragraph does not mean that the first course must be void of specific content in favor of glib generalities. To the contrary, acceptance of that creed will necessitate frequent reference to explicit provisions which aptly demonstrate exactly why and how taxes will affect anyone, how and why specific provisions have changed, and why interpretation of common words can be exceedingly difficult. On the other hand, acceptance of this creed will necessitate *rejection* of the belief that the first course should maximize the number of specific tax rules which a student can recall on a moment's notice. It also rejects the notion that even simple tax return preparation is a primary objective of the first course.[2]

In my estimation far too many introductory tax courses are still taught in a manner which emphasizes the less important material to the exclusion of more basic knowledge on which a professional education should rest. A majority of my colleagues seem bent on educational patterns which are appropriate only for those few students who plan to leave school and go immediately to work for a small or medium-sized accounting firm which prepares large numbers of individual tax returns. If you would, our traditional pattern is the equivalent of a medical school spending its time teaching routine laboratory techniques to medical students. While that kind of training may be wholly appropriate for certain students, it should not be the standard package for professional accountants.

Collectively we should begin to recognize the fact that the vast majority of our students need a wholly different kind of elementary tax education. I have already outlined for you the kind of first course which I prefer for all undergraduates. As a strong, second alternative, I would argue for a course which was less broad in general educational objectives but which still avoided the traditional commitment to the memorization of specific tax rules. That alternative would have as its objective the maximization of a student's awareness of tax opportunities and pitfalls. I personally consider this alternative a second choice because it sacrifices a basic appreciation of the role of taxation in our society for a more pragmatic view of how to live with tax rules—in other words, how to minimize your personal and or corporate tax liability. In spite of that major shortcoming, however, the alternative approach does have the merit of being relevant to the needs of a large majority of our students. Business managers in general, and even the audit and management services personnel in larger C.P.A. firms, will rarely be called upon to *solve* a tax problem. All but the most trivial tax problems will be referred to a tax expert for solution. This means, of course, that all other persons need to be educated in tax matters only to the extent which permits them to recognize every situation in which an expert should be consulted. Learning to recognize tax problems and opportunities requires a wholly different orientation from learning to solve them. Both orientations are viable but the educator must be more careful in the future than he has been in the past in determining which bill of fare he provides for which students. Educational teaching materials directed toward each of these orientations are already commercially available. Although these materials may not be as polished or as well developed as any of us would prefer, the choices are already extant if educators would only exercise their options.

Moving to the educational needs of students who intend to pursue a course of study which will best equip them to serve as professional tax advisors, however, we find that a major need for further improvement in teaching materials still exists. Before commenting upon those specific shortages, let me outline some general considerations pertinent to the educational preparation of a tax specialist.

Education of The Tax Specialist

Even in the second tax course, a student should not in my opinion be rushed into a detailed study of specific tax rules. At that juncture he should learn the skill which is commonly described as "tax research." This prescription calls for a detailed study of the intricate interaction between (1) facts, (2) law (statutory and judicial), and (3) administrative procedures, in the process of taxation. Stated in another way, this prescription calls for the tax student to appreciate in some depth the lawyer's approach to every significant tax problem.

A course in this kind of tax research would direct the student to:
1. Appreciate the critical role of facts to the resolution of every tax issue, including an appreciation for the ways in which facts can be determined and substantiated as evidence when needed;
2. Articulate precisely the issue or issues implicit in any fact situation studied and, in some cases, appreciate why an issue must be stated in the alternative;
3. Locate all of the potential authority which bears upon the issues under consideration;
4. Evaluate the authorities located and determine the relative strengths and weaknesses of the several authorities and, if necessary, resolve conflicting authorities; and
5. Communicate his professional conclusion in good form to any interested party.

A course like the one described above could readily be expanded to include an introduction to tax practice with substantial emphasis on the ethical questions implicit in any such practice. The practice portion of the course could also cover the more routine aspects of tax return preparation, the maintenance of client files, and an introduction to tax planning techniques.

Only after both completing a general introduction to taxation and acquiring the fundamental skills of tax research should a student seriously begin his study of specific substantive tax rules. Such a study should be part of either a graduate or a professional education. In addition, such a study should ordinarily be restricted to those few persons who intend to specialize in taxation and that study should be put as close to the exit-point of his formal education as possible. Exactly which tax rules the tax students studies is not, in my opinion, terribly critical. What is critical is recognition of the fact that no single school should even attempt to cover all of the possible areas of tax study. Areas which might be studied profitably include, but certainly are not limited to: corporate corporate shareholder relations (i.e., Subchapter C of the Code); consolidated corporate problems; partnership taxation (Subchapter K of the Code); estate and gift taxation; of multinational tax complications. Many alternatives could substitute for any of these topics; for example, some may prefer to study capital gains and losses; compensation devices such as pension, profit-sharing, and stock-bonus arrangements; oil and gas taxation; bank and insurance taxation; state and local taxes; or any of several other tax topics.

The student preparing to spend his life as a tax advisor needs to study only three or four tax areas in depth while he is enrolled in an educational institution. If he does, he soon will learn that the same techniques can be applied generally to other areas of taxation if he but has the time and the interest to pursue those topics. Neither the university nor the student should try to cover all of the areas; to do so would violate the fundamental efficiency criterion suggested earlier for any educational institution.[3]

The advanced course offerings available in the relatively few institutions which elect to offer graduate study in taxation should be selected on the basis of (1) the probability of use by students (i.e., the subject areas which are most likely to be encountered by a majority of the students generally should have priority over those courses which have more limited applicability); (2) the interest and expertise of the available faculty (and the quality of faculty is a major problem in tax education); (3) the ability of a subject to interest and motivate good students (in this regard I have observed that multinational taxation is one subject which tends to attract good students; thus, even though it still is of limited importance, I think it can be justified as part of a limited curriculum); and (4) the availability of first-class text materials. Fortunately there are excellent text materials available in some of the tax areas; other areas are desperately in need.[4]

Immediate Problems of Major Significance to Tax Education

Second to a change in the attitude and orientation of many tax instructors, the greatest need of tax education today is the development of quality teaching materials in the area of tax research. The only material commercially available has recently gone "out-of-print." This means, of course, that until adequate materials are again developed and made available, each instructor either must prepare his own material or refuse to offer such a course. Neither alternative is desirable and most will elect the second option.

In my opinion, all accounting majors who intend to engage in the practice of public accountancy theoretically should be required to complete something approximating the first two tax courses described earlier in this paper. Only disagreement with my conclusion, habit, or ignorance impede implementation of the first course. Implementation of the second course described here, however, is virtually impossible because (1) no text is available and (2) the library and faculty facilities necessary for such a course are woefully inadequate to the task at hand. The former problem could be corrected with even very limited financial assistance and a little time. The latter problem—i.e., inadequate faculty talent and grossly inadequate library facilities—is not so readily resolved. In the interest of time and space constraints and because I hold no ready answer to the latter problems, I will spare you the details of the few things which could be done to alleviate the problems in the short run in order to allow a few comments on a second major problem.

Perhaps the next greatest need of tax education today is a vast improvement in a few Ph.D. programs which would attract persons interested in either the teaching of taxation or tax research as a life career. When I use the term "tax research" in this context, I do not refer to the study suggested as the content for the second tax course. Rather, at this level, I refer to the educational preparation needed to answer the policy questions behind every tax law.

At the outset we need to identify the various kinds of research that are needed and begin to prescribe the educational package necessary for conducting those kinds of research. My *very* preliminary thinking in this regard suggests that there are at least five essentially different kinds of tax research which need to be done. They may be described as (1) descriptive statistics studies; (2) econometric modeling; (3) legal scholarship; (4) behavioral studies; and (5) social surveys. Some of the areas are in greater need than others and each requires a rather different academic preparation.

A group of tax-oriented professors certainly could refine and improve on this brief listing of the different "kinds" of tax research. Such a group could also identify some of the better examples of the research that has already been done in each area; suggest problems most in need of study now; and suggest the academic preparation appropriate for further work. Pending such a study, we each must work alone in seeking answers to isolated problems which individually interest us and which we are individually capable of solving. A more concerted effort directed toward the policy-research area would have substantial secondary benefits by attracting to tax education a larger number of the most capable Ph.D. candidates who could then begin to implement and refine the tax education package suggested here.

FOOTNOTES

1. Interestingly, a few legal organizations have apparently recognized this fact in a peculiar way; some States have removed all tax questions from their bar examinations!

2. The utilization of various IRS forms and the preparation of returns may remain as an incidental part of such a course, particularly when use of the forms facilitates the illustration of a more fundamental notion. Students seem to be impressed with the fact that their general knowledge permits them to complete a "real, live tax return" and this may provide an added incentive for their work; they fail to realize that anyone with a college education and an ability to read English should be able to complete most of the tax returns assigned to them in the average tax accounting class.

3. Incidentally, this author believes that the same conclusion is equally applicable to financial accounting education. As the number of APB FASB "opinions" expands, academic accounting preparation must become increasingly selective and conceptual. To try and cover each opinion in depth as part of basic education (i.e., "intermediate accounting") would not be a good use of scarce resources.

4. The fundamental problem is the fact that publishing houses are, after all, profit-making organizations. They are not about to risk their capital in ventures which hold little promise for large profits even if the ventures are necessary to a quality education for a few. Those firms, quite understandably, are only interested in publishing in areas where the number of consumers is large enough to at least hold a promise for meaningful profit. In this kind of market the financial support of a non-profit organization like the American Accounting Association could be critical.

The Taxation Curriculum—Is There a Need for Change?
A Critique
Donald H. Skadden

The field of income tax has become increasingly complex in the past 20 years. The body of knowledge has grown tremendously and has become ever more interrelated with the business, economic, political and social aspects of our national and international communities. Not only have taxes become more significant for the business manager and the professional accountant, but the field of tax practice has attained essentially a professional status in its own right. Today the tax field has its own professional organizations, its own body of professional literature, and its own statements of professional ethics. It seems entirely likely that the accounting profession will soon recognize taxation as a "specialization" and institute some examination or other procedure whereby one may be recognized as a "tax specialist."

The Introductory Course

Thus, it is particularly appropriate that accounting educators should now reexamine the tax courses in order that we can provide appropriate tax education for all our students, whether they be future auditors, future managers, or future professional tax advisors. The day is long overdue that we recognize that one three-hour course on detailed tax rules cannot provide the proper foundation for all three groups. Indeed, as Prof. Sommerfeld has pointed out, such a course probably is not appropriate for any one of the groups.

Sommerfeld's comments suggest at least two alternatives. We might develop a single course suitable for all three groups—a course emphasizing the economic and social implications of taxation; or we might develop two basic courses: a tax planning, tax awareness course for the future manager, plus an introductory course for the tax advisor. It should be emphasized that either of these approaches is predicated on the assumption that further tax education will be available for the tax advisor. One can easily detect the similarity to the situation surrounding the introductory accounting courses. Should we have one course for all, or should we have separate introductory courses for the accounting and non-accounting majors? If we have a single course, for which group should it be designed? Most educators seem to agree that it is usually not feasible, nor appropriate, to have separate introductory courses. The second question has not been so easily resolved. There has been substantial change in introductory accounting in recent years, and one of the strong reasons has been the desire to make the course more suitable for the non-accounting major. However, this assumes that the accounting major will take additional accounting courses.

Also, as accounting is necessary for the non-accounting major, it seems just as essential that all business students have some knowledge of the many ways that taxation impacts on almost every business decision. Certainly the accounting major who does not want to be a tax specialist, still needs to have considerable tax knowledge to perform effectively in positions such as auditor, business consultant, or controller. The business community does not seem to recognize that there can be a "non-tax accountant." They expect all accountants to be rather knowledgeable in the tax area.

Preparation for the Tax Advisor

Prof. Sommerfeld suggests that most businessmen, lawyers and accountants would probably identify one of three "tracks" as the most appropriate preparation for a career in the tax field. For the past nine years I have conducted a very unscientific, unstructured opinion survey on a very similar topic. I have queried several dozen tax partners from CPA firms plus tax managers from several corporations as to which of four tracks would best prepare a person for a tax career. Using the seven year time frame comparable to the normal law school program, I attempted to describe four rather typical preparation "packages." All started with a four-year undergraduate program in accounting. The remaining three years consisted of one of the following:
 1. A three-year law degree
 2. Three years of audit experience
 3. Three years with the I.R.S.
 4. One or two years in a business school graduate tax program plus one or two years of audit experience.
Invariably, number four was selected as the best of these four possibilities.

Suggested Research Projects and Other AAA Involvement

The hope has been expressed that one of the beneficial results of our two days together will be the identification of specific projects for further study and implementation. Many such projects are readily apparent in the tax field—I will suggest only a few.

1. In order to develop the best undergraduate tax courses and to coordinate them with the accounting curriculum, the general business curriculum, and with the graduate curriculum in taxation we need considerably more information about what tax knowledge is necessary for all those different students. A research team with a supporting task force should be commissioned to identify, develop, and describe the "Common Body of Knowledge in Taxation."

2. Research is needed on the relative effectiveness of various forms and levels of tax education—undergraduate, graduate, law school, professional development programs, on-the-job training.

3. Closely related to the first two projects could be a study of what tax specialists actually do (or should do) at various stages of their careers. A detailed analysis of the types of tax questions encountered in (say) the first, third, fifth and tenth years of tax practice could suggest many things about the nature and timing of education for the tax specialist.

4. Price-level accounting is the topic of considerable research by the FASB and others in the accounting and business communities. There are important income tax ramifications of price-level accounting that should be studied in depth. Although the AICPA Tax Division has recently appointed a task force to study this subject, a concurrent study by an AAA group would be most desirable.

5. Prof. Sommerfeld mentioned the rather inadequate role accountants have played in tax policy development. A standing committee of the AAA could bring to focus the educational backgrounds, the research capabilities and, most important, the essential independent viewpoint to provide meaningful imput into all levels of tax policy discussions.

Not-for-Profit Organizations in the Accounting Curriculum—Where and How?

Robert J. Freeman

The rise of not-for-profit (NFP) organizations, particularly governments, to their present role and significance in our economy will surely be noted by astute historians as a major phenomenon of this century. How many accountants would have ventured to forecast, say 30-40 years ago, that the NFP sector would account for approximately 40% of the economic activity of our "free enterprise" economy by 1974? How many would have predicted, even 10-15 years ago, that the NFP sector would emerge as one of our fastest growing "growth industries"—perhaps the fastest growing—not only in terms of full-time employment opportunities for accountants but of audit and management advisory service engagements of independent public accountants?

Not-for-profit organization financial management and accounting are as important today as that for profit-seeking organizations—and are apt to take on added significance in the years ahead. Thus it is appropriate that we consider the question, "Not-for-Profit Organizations in the Accounting Curriculum—Where and How?"

Accounting—Purpose and Objectives of
Accounting Education—The Accounting Curriculum

Logic dictates that we place the question at hand in perspective by first considering briefly (1) the definition and scope of accounting, (2) the purpose and objectives of accounting education—the ends to be achieved, and (3) the nature of the accounting curriculum—the means by which these ends are to be achieved. This is an essential first step, for the question at hand is but a subset of these broader, related considerations and should not be approached in isolation.

"Accounting"

After defining accounting broadly as ". . . the process of identifying, measuring, and communicating economic information to permit informed judgments and decisions by users of the information,"[1] the American Accounting Association (AAA) committee that prepared *A Statement of Basic Accounting Theory (ASOBAT)* accented the fact that:

> Information systems are designed to serve managers and others in carrying out the organizational objectives of entities in which profitability is not the sole or even an important objective as well . . . as in business entities.[2]

Similarly, after defining accounting almost as broadly, the Accounting Principles Board (APB) of the American Institute of Certified Public Accountants (AICPA) observed that, "Accounting includes several branches, for example, financial accounting, managerial accounting, and governmental accounting."[3]

Though semantics may be open to debate, the salient point is that "accounting" encompasses both not-for-profit and for-profit organizations. We may choose to emphasize one over the other in accounting education, just as a parent may favor one child over another or our profession may emphasize income determination to the detriment of asset valuation in accounting for private business enterprise. But if we choose to do so this should be the result of a conscious choice, and we should be prepared to defend that choice and bear its consequences.

Purpose and Objectives of Accounting Education

The Report of the 1964-67 AAA Committee to Compile A Revised Statement of Educational Policy stated the purpose of accounting education as:

> . . . to prepare students for careers in accounting and in related fields, and to prepare them to deal effectively with the problems they will face as practicing members of their profession and as responsible citizens of the social and economic community in which they live.[4]

After observing that, "The subject matter of accounting encompasses a body of knowledge that lies behind the information system underlying *all* economic activity,"[5] this committee set forth its views on the objectives of accounting education:

> Accounting education should provide men and women with a competency to embark upon careers in accounting or

in related fields. Such an education should be structured to accomplish the following objectives: (a) General Education, (b) Education in Business, and (c) Education in Accountancy.[6]

Addressing the third objective, education in accountancy, the committee noted that we must attempt to "... furnish students with sufficient training in accounting to recognize the problems they will face as accountants and to provide basic knowledge useful in solving these problems."[7]

These statements of the purpose and objectives of accounting education are obviously very broad and general, not specific and operational. Yet I submit that even these broad goals can not be attained in an educational environment that fails to provide *all* students of accounting an understanding of that for NFP organizations.

A more specific, operational statement of the objectives of accounting education is conspicuously absent from our literature. The ost relevant studies would appear to be *Horizons for a Profession: The Common Body of Knowledge for Certified Public Accountants*[8] (CBOK) and the Report of the AICPA Committee on Education and Experience Requirements for CPAs[9] (the Beamer Report). Both ave been criticized, however, as being preoccupied with the collegiate education of entry-level public accountants. For example, although the terms "profession" and "CPA" were intended to be interpreted broadly by the authors of both the CBOK study and the Beamer Report, the summary of the nationwide seminars concerned with the latter indicates that:

> The major criticism ... was that it was apparently directed explicitly at public accountants to the exclusion of other rapidly growing fields of interest—government accounting, industrial accounting, non-profit organizational accounting.[10]

Even a cursory review of the literature (or dialogue with our colleagues) indicates the difficulties inherent in preparing a concise, operational listing of the objectives of accounting education. The 15-year aftermath of the Ford and Carnegie reports has been a traumatic era in accounting education. As Anderson and Griffin noted early in this period:

> ... reform of the collegiate curriculum in business administration has developed into a modern Crusade. The acknowledged enemy is stultifying specialization; the

sanctioned goal, a liberal education. Unfortunately, as in most such movements, the participants have often disagreed over just what or who the enemy is, as well as the shortest and safest route to the objective, which is only vaguely defined.[11]

Several diverse schools of thought with respect to the objectives of accounting education are evident. One widely held view might be termed the "generalist-normative-academic" school. Most recent "trends in accounting education" articles are in this vein:

> The emphasis is moving in the direction of general concepts, hypotheses, and theories. Specific procedures are relatively unimportant.[12]

> *Highly specialized courses* such as consolidations, *municipal accounting,* budgeting, etc., were classified as optional and some highly specialized advanced courses were moved to the graduate level.[13]

Educators holding this view urge that we not overemphasize procedures and first-job skills to the detriment of conceptual understanding. They are particularly concerned that the "skills" approach may prepare the student well for his first job while leaving him unprepared to reason out unfamiliar problems, to adapt to the rapidly changing environment, and to rise to mid- or upper-level career positions. Some educators of this conviction have dispensed with virtually all procedural training or descriptive knowledge and teach only normative models; and in some cases the accounting subject matter has been reduced to 10-15 of the student's educational experience.

On the other hand, some of our colleagues feel that the pendulum has swung too far, that procedural skills and descriptive knowledge are now being unduly deemphasized. Holders of this view, which might be termed the "traditional-pragmatic-professional" school, value the rigor and career orientation of the more traditional approach to accounting education and emphasize the necessity of first-job training as well as conceptual and cultural training. As Professor Paton observed recently:

> . . . the study of accounting can facilitate the grasping of a rung on the professional ladder by the college graduate. I am convinced that this, in general, should be the objective of college training.[14]

Those of this conviction are concerned that accounting education has become too academic, and some urge us to seek additional educational autonomy, perhaps through establishing professional schools of accountancy. Many would agree with Aslanian and Duff that:

> The arrival of the academically oriented business school has relegated accounting in general, and financial accounting in particular, to a position of relative weakness.
>
> When one considers that accounting is the only functional area taught in the business school which prepares a student for entry into a legally recognized profession, the dimension of the plight of professional training comes into focus. For in this setting one finds a reward function which liberally rewards a member for academic publication and a political environment which forces the uniquely professional department in the school to adopt a nonprofessional orientation.
>
> ... a professional orientation must be restored to accounting education.[15]

Still other accounting educators, sometimes termed the "pluralistic"[16] school, suggest that our field has become so broad that no one can be expected to be competent in all of its aspects. They propose that undergraduate accounting majors be schooled in a fundamental common body of knowledge and well-grounded in professional ethics and standards; beyond that, each should select one or more fields of specialization (at the undergraduate level) in which to develop a depth of knowledge.

There are other schools of thought, to be sure, as well as variations of those cited here. We also find diverse views as to the role of collegiate accounting education vis-a-vis graduate-level, on-the-job, or formal continuing education. Clearly there is no unanimity among accounting educators as to the objectives of accounting education—objectives which the curriculum is designed to achieve.

"The" Accounting Curriculum

The point of what may appear to be a tangential excursion into the realm of the objectives of accounting education is that one contemplating the role of not-for-profit organizations in the accounting curriculum must necessarily consider the nature, objectives, and content of that curriculum. But the curriculum is, by definition, the means by which we seek to achieve the objectives of accounting education—objectives which have been only vaguely defined—and there is no universal *"the"* curriculum. Rather, to the extent permissible under accreditation rules and other institutional constraints, the prevailing views as to the objectives of accounting education shape the unique curriculum and educational thrust of each institution. Still further, there is not even agreement as to the length of time over which the curriculum is to extend. While the most common time frame is approximately four years—and is apt to continue to be so for some time—some believe a fifth year is needed[17] while others are convinced that three years is sufficient.[18]

In addressing the question at hand, therefore, we must conduct our deliberations in terms of an assumed *"typical* curriculum" rather than *"the* curriculum." This tack is not without precedent, of course: the economist's "economic man," the lawyer's "prudent man" and the accounting practitioner's "average user" are merely joined by the "typical curriculum."

Despite widespread differences of opinion as to the objectives of accounting education, the two most recognized curriculum models are remarkably similar. If one ignores differences in the number of courses or credits and expands their listings of elective courses, the curricula of both the 1964-67 AAA Committee[19] and the Beamer Report[20] may be summarized as follows:

Required Courses	Elective Courses
Elementary Financial	Governmental and Institutional (NFP)
Intermediate Financial	Budgeting and Controllership
Advanced Financial	Advanced Financial (Theory)
Cost	Advanced Cost
Tax	Advanced Tax
Auditing	CPA Review
Computer Applications Systems	Other Advanced Courses

In both cases the accounting courses are assumed to comprise 20-25% of the undergraduate curriculum; a four-year undergraduate curriculum is assumed here.

The Present Role of Not-for-Profit Organizations in the Accounting Curriculum

To what extent is the accounting student exposed to NFP organization accounting in the typical undergraduate curriculum? Relatively speaking, the exposure must be considered minuscule.

Not-for-profit organizations are considered (usually) in only one required course, Advanced Financial Accounting, and in two elective courses, the CPA Review and the Governmental and Institutional (Fund Accounting) courses.

Advanced Accounting

Advanced Financial Accounting textbooks commonly include one or more chapters capsuling the highlights of governmental accounting. These chapters may be omitted from the advanced course, however, especially where there is a separate elective course on not-for-profit accounting available. Further, it appears that the Advanced Financial Accounting course is increasingly being viewed as "specialized," and either made elective or moved to the graduate curriculum. Thus, even should we agree that the brief coverage of NFP organization accounting in contemporary Advanced Accounting texts imparts the requisite minimum knowledge that undergraduate accounting majors should receive— and I do not concede that point—we have no assurance that all of them will be exposed to even that capsule coverage.

CPA Review

Another course in which NFP organization accounting usually receives some attention is the CPA Review course. Though a survey in the mid-sixties[21] indicated that approximately half of the responding AACSB-member schools offered this type course, it is almost always an elective course and we have no data on the percentage of students selecting it. Still further, this course has a limited objective, preparation for the CPA examination, and is not the appropriate vehicle for imparting fundamental knowledge.

Governmental and Institutional,
Not-for-Profit or Fund Accounting

The only place in the typical curriculum where our students *might* receive in-depth exposure to NFP organization accounting theory and practice is the Governmental and Institutional, Not-for-Profit, or Fund Accounting elective course. A 1966 survey by Neeley and Robason[22] indicated that this is the elective course most common to accounting curricula, being offered by approximately two-thirds of the responding AACSB-member schools. Again, however, we have no data on the frequency with which the course is offered, the percentage of students electing it, or the trend in these regards over the past 8 years. One suspects that the percentage is small, and may well be declining.

Neeley and Robason identified two major constraints to offering the Governmental and Institutional Accounting course, even as an elective: (1) lack of faculty and student interest, and (2) the necessity of satisfying AACSB requirements within the usual 120 plus hours undergraduate curriculum. Neither reason—apathy or institutional constraints—is relevant from an academic standpoint, i.e., neither addresses the questions of whether the course is needed and, if it is, what role it should serve. Nonetheless, there is little doubt that the influence of such factors on curriculum decisions is significant.

Inasmuch as curricula may be expected to evolve to meet perceived needs, the reasons underlying this lack of faculty and student interest seem particularly germane to the question at hand. Among the more plausible reasons underlying this disinterest are these:

> Business administration and public administration are commonly housed in separate collegiate organizational divisions. It may not be agreed or understood by all concerned that "business administration" encompasses the business of both for-profit and not-for-profit organizations; indeed, not-for-profit organizations are often termed "non-business" organizations, and jurisdictional disputes with regard to Not-For-Profit Organization Accounting courses are not uncommon.

> Neither business administration faculty members nor students may be fully aware of the present and prospective importance of the NFP sector, either from the standpoint of one's role as a "stockholder" in them or of the employment opportunities in business administration within that sector. Rather, both may consider NFP organizations "second rate" in terms of employment opportunities, compensation levels, and the like.

> Faculty members may not consider themselves competent in NFP accounting, especially those aspects beyond that knowledge required to successfully complete the CPA exam. Too, there is some indication that the NFP course has not received the attention of leading faculty members at many institutions—but is often assigned to either the part-time or youngest faculty member as a "citizenship" duty—and that it has often been taught with a procedural emphasis designed

primarily to assure successful completion of the CPA examination.

The present need in a "thin" market situation for authors to write broad-gauge textbooks designed to serve simultaneously the accounting, public administration, and practitioner markets may have resulted in texts that do not appear to serve the accounting major adequately—especially if the professor follows the textbook "from cover to cover," neither omitting certain sections nor supplementing other sections of the textbook.

The growing body of competing electives, particularly in the more "glamorous" computer, behavioral, or other areas may well have detracted from the appeal of the Governmental and Institutional course.

This listing is not exhaustive, but it is indicative of the academic environment of the Governmental and Institutional, Not-for-Profit, or Fund Accounting elective course.

Adequacy of the Present Role of NFP Organizations in the Accounting Curriculum

The 1972-73 AAA Committee on Not-for-Profit Organizations observed that:

> At the great majority of colleges and universities, courses required of accounting students in their major field deal only with various aspects of accounting for profit-seeking entities... In many cases not even one elective course is offered in the NFP accounting area....23

Is the present role of NFP organizations in the accounting curriculum adequate in view of the present and prospective role of the NFP sector, and that of accountants, in our economy and society? I think not! Returning to our earlier analogy, it seems obvious that we do far more than merely favoring one child (profit-seeking accounting) over the other (not-for-profit accounting). Indeed, we choose to treat NFP accounting either as an orphan or as a badly neglected stepchild—but virtually never as a full member of the accounting curriculum family.

It is paradoxical, to say the least, that while the role and significance of the NFP sector have increased dramatically in recent years, an increasingly larger percentage of our graduates may never be exposed to even the rudiments of NFP accounting, much less to an extensive treatment of its theory, procedures, debatable issues, and horizons. *Is this the result of a conscious choice? Are we prepared to defend that choice and bear its consequences?* I submit that the answer is "no" on both counts, and that we in academia are far behind in this respect in attuning our curriculum to the present and future needs of our graduates. And I say this with concern, not contempt, for the problems of covering our rapidly expanding body of knowledge in what seems to be a constantly shrinking number of allotted courses and or credit hours seem at times to be insurmountable. As one leading accountant observed several years ago, " ... the greatest educational problem of the (accounting) profession is that there are almost too many things that accountants should be taught ... "[24]

On a more positive note, interest in and developments affecting NFP organization accounting are escalating in both the academic and practitioner facets of our profession. For example:

Both the Financial Accounting Standards Board (FASB) and its Advisory Council have representation from the NFP sector.[25]

The Trueblood Committee included a separate chapter on "Objectives of Financial Statements for Governmental and Not-for-Profit Organizations" in its report on the *Objectives of Financial Statements.*[26]

The AICPA has greatly increased its activity in the NFP sector. For example, it recently revised its voluntary health and welfare organization audit guide and, in addition, issued audit guides for hospitals, colleges and universities, and state and local governments.

The Comptroller General of the United States recently promulgated a distinct statement of governmental audit standards.[27] These have received broad endorsement from the AICPA Committee on Relations with the GAO,[28] and are apt to have a far-reaching impact on governmental auditing. Further, the Federal Government Accountants Association (FGAA) has set forth educational guidelines for its members, which include a course in governmental accounting,[29] and has partially underwritten the cost of preparing a new text on governmental accounting; and at least one writer has suggested that a certified governmental accountant (CGA) program should be instituted.[30]

The AAA has markedly increased its committee efforts in the NFP organization realm as compared with the pre-1966 period. Reports of these committees have had significant impact on practice and on the pronouncements of other organizations, and are increasingly being utilized as supplemental materials in governmental and institutional accounting courses.

The Municipal Finance Officers Association of the United States and Canada is in the process of establishing a new National Council on Governmental Accounting.[31] To function much as did the APB prior to formation of the FASB, the new NCGA could play a major role in the determination and promulgation of state and local government accounting standards and principles.

An ad hoc Committee on State Governmental Accounting Principles and Practices of The Council of State Governments, established just last month, is exploring alternative means by which state government accounting standards and principles might be researched, refined, codified, promulgated, and disseminated.

Whereas the Neeley and Robason study in 1966 was the first study of the Governmental and Institutional Accounting course in the accounting curriculum—at least in recent years—and has remained alone in that regard for the past eight years, at least two other studies of NFP accounting courses in collegiate accounting curricula are now in progress.[32]

Not-for-profit organization accounting has recently become a much discussed topic, both in the professional literature and on programs of various accounting educator and tes and Canada.
As in any area of concern, widespread recognition of a problem area and interest in changing the status quo are prerequisites to effecting change.

What Should Be the Role of Not-for-Profit Organizations in the Accounting Curriculum?

What *should be* the role of NFP organizations in the accounting curriculum? I contend that a conceptual understanding and working knowledge of the area is fundamental to both the "general education" and "education in accountancy" objectives of accounting education. *NFP organization accounting can no longer properly be considered a "specialized" or "graduate-level only" subject area.* Indeed, a curriculum in which all students do not receive instruction in at least the fundamental concepts and procedures of NFP accounting must be considered deficient.

This conclusion is consistent with those of both the CBOK study and the Beamer Report. The CBOK study concludes, with regard to its "thorough knowledge-good knowledge-fair knowledge" criteria that " . . . it is not suggested that the beginning CPA be an expert in municipal accounting . . . but merely that he have a *good* knowledge of fund theory and its applications."[33] Elsewhere in that study it is observed that " . . . trusts, governmental units, and estates all bear distinguishing features, knowledge of which is *vital* to one who is to be considered capable of dealing with their financial problems."[34]

Role in the Typical Curriculum

How does this translate in terms of the role of NFP organizations in the typical accounting curriculum? I suggest that we should modify that curriculum—now virtually 100% oriented to for-profit organizations—to the extent of requiring *at least* one course in not-for-profit organization accounting of *all* accounting majors. Devoting 10% of our curriculum to the public sector would not seem unreasonable in view of its contemporary and prospective role in our economy and in the lives of our graduates.

Such a course should not be limited to the municipal accounting course often found today. Rather, though it may emphasize the municipal model initially and use it as a point of departure and comparative frame of reference, the course should also cover the essential aspects of federal government accounting, as well as accounting for educational, health care, and other not-for-profit organizations. Further, the course should be balanced between its treatment of theory and practice, it should delve into controversial issues as appropriate, and it should cover those budgeting, reporting, and auditing aspects that are unique to the public sector.

Realizing that institutional constraints may preclude requiring a separate NFP course immediately in some situations, I suggest that the *absolute minimum* coverage in any program during the transition period should include the equivalent of the capsule coverage of most advanced financial accounting textbooks. I do *not* concede that this is adequate—indeed it could not impart "good" knowledge as I interpret that term—but requiring less would surely place us in a position of being derelict in our duty as educators.

Role in the Integrative Curriculum

Now let us wipe our "typical curriculum" slate clean for a moment and consider an alternative integrative approach as the possible long-run direction of accounting curriculum development. I believe it is significant in this regard that one of the eight modules in *A New Introduction To Accounting* focuses upon accounting for individuals and not-for-profit organizations.[35] In the same vein, it is interesting to note that Horngren's classic article, "The Accounting Discipline in 1999," includes the prediction, with respect to managerial (internal) accounting courses, that " . . . as governmental bodies, medical institutions and other non-business organizations grew in size and influence, they received increasing emphasis."[36] More recently, Moonitz has urged acceptance of the integrative approach.[37]

Though such a change in the direction and nature of the typical curriculum would be a long-run undertaking—especially in view of existing textbooks and courses, the extent to which accounting courses typically follow the textbook,[38] and the trend toward professorial specialization—it has much merit conceptually. Should the relevant aspects of NFP organization accounting be woven within the fabric of our typical curriculum—in elementary, intermediate, advanced, tax, cost, managerial, auditing, and computer applications courses—then I would be satisfied to return the not-for-profit course to an elective stance. Further, should this come about, the textbooks for that elective course might evolve to a higher, more sophisticated plane, as it would no longer be necessary for their authors to make the (now valid) assumption that the student has no prior knowledge of the subject field.

Specialization in Not-for-Profit Organization Accounting

Yet a third role of not-for-profit organizations in the accounting curriculum is that of equipping the specialist. There is a need for several colleges and universities to develop in-depth specialization options or programs in NFP organization accounting. Obviously faculty interest and competency, as well as institutional objectives and location, should be determinative in such a decision. Such an option might include separate courses in accounting for state and local governments, the federal government and its agencies, health care organizations, and educational institutions, as well as public sector budgeting, auditing, and computerized information systems. The primary opportunity in this regard would seem to be at the graduate level, as this type option or program should have appeal to many persons with undergraduate degrees who are employed in the public sector and wish to further their formal education on either a full- or part-time basis, as well as to graduate students in education, health care, public adminstration, or other university programs. To the extent that some students attracted to this type program may have non-accounting undergraduate backgrounds, a suitable "gateway" course(s) should also be developed. Further, a few schools might develop undergraduate specialization options along these lines, particularly those of the pluralistic school of thought located near major NFP organization employers.

Need for Further Research and Development Effort

Several areas deserving intensive research or development effort by accounting educators came to my attention in the course of preparing this paper. Four of these seem particularly relevant to this symposium and to the question at hand.

First, I became acutely aware that we have not articulated the objectives of accounting education in a concise, operational fashion. Rather, our efforts to date have resulted in very broad statements of our purpose and objectives. From these we have moved directly to specification of curriculum design and course content details. Further, views of respected educators with regard to our objectives vary so widely as to cause one to wonder how the model curricula set forth in recent years could be so similar. I suggest, therefore, that we should undertake a major study of the objectives of accounting education, perhaps similar to *ASOBAT* or the Trueblood Committee study of the objectives of financial statements. Admittedly this would be a very difficult task, one that might never be accomplished satisfactorily, but the present void between broad statements of purpose and objectives and of curriculum and course content details warrants exploration by a group of outstanding accounting educators.

While I would not be so presumptuous as to formulate the charge for that study group, I suggest that it should include both normative and descriptive research. Time-honored assumptions such as that 20-25% of the undergraduate accounting curriculum should be devoted to accounting subject matter should be questioned. Likewise, it should not be presumed at the outset of such a study that there can be only one curriculum model for accounting education.

Two, three or more alternative models might well be developed as a result of such an undertaking. Many other issues also warrant consideration by this study group. Perhaps we have gone too far in the direction of liberal education; perhaps AACSB requirements are unduly hampering accounting education; perhaps schools of accountancy having at least curriculum autonomy are necessary for the advancement, or even the survival, of the accounting discipline. Perhaps the reverse is true. Also as part of such a study, the lines of demarcation between the role of collegiate education and that of post-undergraduate, on-the-job, or formal continuing education should be drawn with a reasonable degree of clarity. (Again, this listing is intended to be indicative, not exhaustive, of the topics of such a major research effort.)

Three areas for research and development relating to the question of not-for-profit organizations in the accounting curriculum deserve attention. First, there is very little empirical data available as to the role of NFP organization accounting in existing curricula. Determining this, and the percentage of students that are (or are not) being educated in NFP organization accounting—and the extent of that education, if any—warrant careful research.

Second, if we are to move toward the integrative curriculum approach, much developmental work is needed to prepare appropriate NFP accounting materials to supplement existing financial, cost, managerial, computer applications, auditing, and tax courses. Such materials should ultimately find their way into standard textbooks on these subjects. Development of model syllibi, exercises, cases, and problems to be integrated into courses taught in this fashion deserves at least exploratory efforts. Should we not move toward the integrative curriculum approach, or should the notion ultimately find acceptance only in the introductory course, such materials would nonetheless prove quite useful both at the elementary level and in the Not-For-Profit Organization or Fund Accounting course(s). Indeed, there is a dearth of illustrative case and problem material relative to federal, educational, health care, and other NFP organization accounting.

Finally, there is need for research and development with respect to the feasibility and content of NFP accounting specialization options or programs, both at the undergraduate and graduate levels. Assuming there is a need for several colleges or universities to provide such programs, concentrated curriculum design and course development efforts will be required to bring the concept to viable reality. Here also, a major key to the success of such an endeavor is the development of additional case and problem materials, particularly those related to federal, educational, health care, and other NFP organization accounting.

Summary

Though NFP organizations play an immense and increasingly important role in our economy and lives, NFP accounting has only a bit part, at most, in the accounting curriculum script.

The absence of definitive and operational agreement on the objectives of accounting education makes it difficult, perhaps impossible, to specify the appropriate role of NFP accounting in the collegiate curriculum. Yet NFP accounting is clearly an integral part of the subject matter of accounting education, and I contend that even the broad purpose and objectives of accounting education are not met where all students of accounting are not schooled in at least its fundamental concepts and procedures. Thus, until the essential aspects of not-for-profit organization accounting are integrated into the financial, managerial, cost, tax, auditing, and computer applications courses, the Not-For-Profit or Fund Accounting course should be a *required* part of the basic undergraduate core curriculum. Where this is not immediately feasible, at least a capsule coverage of the topic (such as that included in most contemporary advanced financial accounting texts) should be incorporated within the common core of the accounting curriculum.

Beyond this, there is a need for several colleges or universities to develop in-depth specialization options or programs in NFP organization accounting. While the principal opportunity and need in this regard would seem to be at the graduate level, an undergraduate specialization option might well prove feasible in schools located near major NFP organization employers.

Finally, it has been suggested that further research is needed both to set forth more precisely the objectives of accounting education and to better determine the present role of NFP organization accounting in the curriculum. An intensive developmental effort is needed also to prepare syllibi, cases, exercises and problems in order both to further explore the feasibility of integrating NFP accounting subject matter into other courses in the accounting curriculum and to develop specialization options or programs in NFP organization accounting.

FOOTNOTES

1. Committee to Prepare a Statement of Basic Accounting Theory, American Accounting Association, *A Statement of Basic Accounting Theory* (Chicago: The Association, 1966), p. 1.

2. Ibid., p. 2.

3. Accounting Principles Board, American Institute of Certified Public Accountants, *Statement of the Accounting Principles Board No. 4,* "Basic Concepts and Accounting Principles Underlying Financial Statements of Business Enterprises." (New York: The Institute, October 1970), p. 17.

4. 1964-67 Committee to Compile a Revised Statement of Educational Policy, American Accounting Association, "A Restatement of Matters Relating to Educational Policy," *Accounting Review,* Supplement to vol. XLIII (1968), p. 56.

5. Ibid. (emphasis added.)

6. Ibid., p. 57.

7. Ibid.

8. Robert H. Roy and James H. MacNeill, *Horizons for a Profession: The Common Body of Knowledge for Certified Public Accountants* (New York: The American Institute of Certified Public Accountants, 1967).

9. Committee on Education and Experience Requirements for CPAs, American Institute of Certified Public Accountants, *Report of the Committee on Education and Experience Requirements for CPAs* (New York: The Institute, 1969).

10. W. Thomas Porter, Jr., *Higher Education and the Accounting Profession: A Summary Report on the Haskins & Sells 75th Anniversary Symposiums* (n.p.: n.p., 1971), p. 10. This criticism was reflected in 13 of the 53 symposium reports according to the author. A similar view is found in Geraldine F. Dominiak, "Wanted: Advice from Accountants Not in Public Practice," *Federal Accountant* (June 1970), pp. 49-56.

11. Hershel M. Anderson and Fred B. Griffin, "The Accounting Curriculum and Postgraduate Achievement," *Accounting Review* (October 1963), p. 813.

12. Ronald J. Patten, "The Trend In Accounting Education," *Managerial Planning* (November-December 1972), p. 34.

13. Helene M.A. Ramanauskas, "Trends In Accounting Education," *Woman CPA* (September 1970), p. 10. (Emphasis added.)

14. William A. Paton, "Accounting's Educational Eclipse," (Editor's Notebook) *Journal of Accountancy* (December 1971), p. 36.

15. Paul J. Aslanian and John T. Duff, "Why Accounting Teachers Are So Academic," *Journal of Accountancy* (October 1, 1973), pp. 50-1, 53.

16. For an excellent discussion of this viewpoint see John W. Buckley, "The Myth of the Compleat Accountant," *Federal Accountant* (September 1972), pp. 40-52.

17. Committee on Education and Experience Requirements for CPAs, p. 42. The committee did not specify whether the fifth year should be at the undergraduate or graduate level.

18. "Less Time, More Options: Education Beyond the High School," A report issued by the Carnegie Commission on Education (January 1971).

19. 1964-67 Committee to Compile a Revised Statement of Educational Policy, p. 77.

20. Committee on Education and Experience Requirements for CPAs, p. 58.

21. Paden Neeley and G.A. Robason, "Governmental Accounting: A Critical Evaluation," (Teachers' Clinic) *Accounting Review* (April 1967), p. 367.

22. Ibid.

23. Committee on Not-for-Profit Organizations, 1972-73, American Accounting Association, "Report of the Committee on Not-for-Profit Organizations, 1972-73," *Accounting Review,* Supplement to vol. XLIX (1974), p. 246.

24. Robert M. Trueblood, "A Far-Away Thing," *Tempo* (December 1968), p. 31.

25. "Financial Accounting Standards Board Proposed Rules of Procedure," (Official Releases) *Journal of Accountancy* (November 1972), p. 75; "FASB Adds Two Members; Advisory Council Named," (News Report) *Journal of Accountancy* (April 1, 1973), p. 12.

26. Accounting Objectives Study Group, American Institute of Certified Public Accountants, *Objectives of Financial Statements: A Report of the Study Group on the Objectives of Financial Statements* (New York: The Institute, 1973), pp. 49-51.

27. The Comptroller General of the United States, *Standards for Audit of Governmental Organizations, Programs, Activities & Functions* (Washington: United States General Accounting Office, 1972).

28. Committee on Relations With the GAO, *Auditing Standards Established by the GAO—Their Meaning and Significance for CPAs* (New York: American Institute of Certified Public Accountants, 1973).

29. "Federal Government Accountants Association Educational Guidelines," *Federal Accountant* (June 1971), pp. 73-8.

30. Orville R. Keister, "The Case for A Certifying Examination in Governmental Accounting," *Federal Accountant* (December 1971), pp. 107-11.

31. *A Report of the MFOA Task Force on the Sponsorship of the National Committee on Governmental Accounting and Related Programs* (Exposure Draft) (Chicago: Municipal Finance Officers Association of the United States and Canada, March 1973).

32. Paden Neeley and G.A. Robason, pp. 366-69.

33. Robert H. Roy and James H. MacNeill, p. 203.

34. Ibid., p. 209.

35. *A New Introduction To Accounting* (Report of the Study Group on Introductory Accounting sponsored by the Price Waterhouse Foundation, July, 1971, prepared and edited by Gerhardt G. Mueller), pp. 48-51.

36. Charles T. Horngren, "The Accounting Discipline in 1999," *Accounting Review* (January 1971), p. 7.

37. Maurice Moonitz, "The Beamer Committee Report—A Golden Opportunity for Accounting Education," (Statements in Quotes), *Journal of Accountancy* (August 1973), p. 67.

38. Alexander W. Astin, "Classroom Environment in Different Fields of Study," *Journal of Educational Psychology* 56 (1965), pp. 275-82.

Not-for-Profit Organizations in the Accounting Curriculum—Where and How?

A Critique
Lennis M. Knighton

Introduction

This is an impressive symposium, and Professor Freeman has presented an impressive paper. In the few minutes allotted to me, I want to underscore a couple of points raised in his paper, present a few additional considerations for your review, and outline what I feel this association might do at this juncture to support curriculum development in public-sector accounting.

Before taking up curriculum and educational matters, however, let me emphasize again the magnitude of our challenge and the importance of timely and appropriate responses from this association by citing a few impressive statistics. In 1940, the Federal budget totaled only about $10 billion. In the budget presented by the administration to Congress this past January to cover the forthcoming fiscal year, the total was over $300 billion. For every 1 percent increase in the Gross National Product, there is an automatic increase of 1.5 percent in Federal revenues due to the graduated income tax rates; and state and local expenditures over the past decade have increased at a faster rate than those of the Federal government. Together, the expenditures of all governments in the United States—Federal, state and local—now account for almost 40 percent of the total GNP. When you add to these figures the expenditures of other not-for-profit organizations, it is clear to me (and I hope to you also) that we are not talking about a tiny little segment of the world nor an area where a few accountants just might become involved some day. We are talking about an area that comprises almost half of all the economic activity of our society. It is equally clear that as academicians, we must give more than a passing nod in the accounting curriculum to the unique and complex problems facing accountants in the public sector and other not-for-profit areas.

Thus, my first proposition to you today is that we begin to teach our students that accounting is a discipline of public administration in the same way that it is of business administration. The day when it was appropriate to teach that accounting is the "language of business" is long past, if indeed that day ever existed. We must recognize and teach that the private sector has no monopoly on exciting and rewarding opportunities for accounting students. Indeed, some of the areas most in need of the dedicated professional in our field lie in the public sector. In a moment, I want to discuss a few of them briefly with you.

Who and How Do We Teach?

In attempting to determine what should be done with the curriculum in accounting, we must first ask: Who are we to teach? It seems to me that there are three major groups with which we must be concerned on campus. The first is the accounting major who will pursue a career in a public-sector or not-for-profit organization. The second is the accounting major who, while not working full time in the public sector, nevertheless will have significant involvement with public sector organizations. Included here are CPAs who will audit governmental and not-for-profit organizations, the professional accounting consultant (including CPAs) who will assist in the design of information and reporting systems, etc., and the professional accountant who becomes involved with advisory groups, special commissions, boards of trustees, and other such activities where they are looked to for competent advice on financial matters.

The third group of students for whom we must develop our curriculum is the non-accounting major who looks to us for service courses. Chief among these, of course, are students majoring in public administration, hospital administration, etc. For our discussions today, I will use Public Administration for my example.

Professor Freeman suggested three possible approaches to teaching public-sector accounting—namely, the use of a special course (as is done now in most instances where this is taught), the integration of public-sector material into other accounting courses, and the offering of a separate concentration within the accounting degree program so that some students can specialize here.

If we consider the three groups for which we must be responsible, and then look at the alternatives he suggests, it becomes apparent that no one approach can serve all three groups equally well. Clearly, the non-accounting major who wants some background in public-sector accounting to strengthen his program in public administration or some other field cannot best be served by having this material scattered throughout several accounting courses. Thus we have a real need to develop specialty courses for these students that articulate with and complement the other courses in their programs. In this regard, our job is very similar to that of offering special courses to MBA students who have a non-business background, except that the focus and emphasis in the course will differ somewhat.

From the standpoint of the accounting major, it is clear that one elective course, in which only a fraction of the students enroll, and which is devoted to only a few narrow areas of public-sector accounting, cannot do much more than say to the student, in effect: "We have another area over here, but we are not going to do much with it. If you are interested, we'll teach you a few things; but it really doesn't pertain to you very much." Such a course, as traditionally taught, has not been interesting to students or faculty, and it is not the answer to our problem today. Sure, we could revise the content of such a course to make it more comprehensive and more interesting, and we should. But even then, in my opinion, this approach is based on faulty assumptions.

First, there is a tendency to divide accounting into financial, managerial, governmental, etc. This type of classification of accounting subjects seems to suggest that governmental accounting is something other than financial and/or managerial, when in fact it is as much financial and managerial as is corporate accounting. There are some important differences between governmental and corporate accounting, to be sure, but they both are concerned with accountability, control, and performance evaluation.

Second, it is too often assumed that the only real difference between public-sector accounting and corporate accounting is the extensive use of fund entities and the need for accountants to use fund accounting in the public sector. Among academic accountants, this myth is undoubtedly caused and perpetuated by the fact that almost every course that is presently taught in this area deals almost exclusively with local government fund accounting.

For these and other reasons which cannot be explored in the limits of this discussion, I strongly favor an approach that calls for integrating public-sector accounting into the other materials of accounting courses for accounting majors. An advanced elective, in which other uniquely public-sector material could be taught, would still be appropriate; but it is not enough by itself to do the job that needs to be done.

Examples of the Integrative Approach

To further illustrate some examples of how I propose that these concepts and principles be integrated into the other courses in the accounting curriculum, let me very briefly run through a few examples.

One of the most interesting and important areas is that of performance evaluation. We spend much time teaching our students about the concepts and process of matching effort and accomplishment, where effort is measured in terms of expired cost and accomplishment is measured in terms of revenue produced. We compute earnings per share, return on investment, profit on sales, and other such indicators of performance as a basis of evaluating the enterprise and the results of its operations. Why not, at this point, take time to ask the student: How can we relate effort and accomplishment for a public-sector organization where revenue is not the expected result. In fact, why not introduce here the concept of a revenue that is not "earned" but results from the basic exercise of the powers of government or that is "contributed" voluntarily by someone who is neither a financial investor nor a direct beneficiary of the organization's programs.

We talk much about accrual accounting; and in the private sector, we take for granted that every enterprise will use an accrual accounting system. It often comes as a bit of a shock to learn that few governments today use a true accrual accounting system and that those who do have accrual accounting generally have only accrued expenditure systems, not accrued cost systems. Is it because governments are backward? Is it because they do not need anything more? Or is it because of the special problems associated with accrual accounting that we have this situation. Let me just ask a few questions—questions which make for good discussion in accounting classes. How do you accrue income taxes? How do you accrue liabilities (for the grantor) and receivables (for the grantee) under a matching grant program? What is the difference between accrued costs and accrued expenditures, and for what types of decisions is each relevant? When is depreciation a relevant item of expense if income is not being measured? How do you accrue the liability for major assets procured under a long-term contract— when the work is done, when a billing is received, or when the asset is completed and has been officially accepted? All of of these questions are critical to understanding basic accounting concepts and principles in the public sector. None of them require an understanding of fund accounting.

How do we measure and account for the outputs and accomplishments of public programs? We talk a lot about performance evaluation in industry, and we look at production and output measures as being an important part of the accounting system. With service industries becoming an increasingly larger segment of our economic system, we have begun to ask about output measures for non-manufacturing activities. Is this not the place also to ask about public-sector programs? At least in the private sector we have a pricing system, and we can convert our outputs to dollar revenues. What about public programs that are not "priced" in the market? Some of the most exciting and challenging work in accounting is being done here, but we are only beginning to understand the problems.

We spend time in cost accounting classes talking about cost centers and responsibility accounting. We discuss the implications for cost determination as well as cost control. Have you ever thought of discussing with your class how one would go about setting up appropriate cost centers, determining an appropriate basis for justifying overhead reimbursements, and accounting for the direct costs of a grant program with two or more sources of funding? The cost allocation problems of industry are difficult; but they are even more challenging in a governmental or institutional fabric because of funding structures, organizational and budgetary patterns, and the lack of cost systems.

Turning to fund accounting itself, I have always found it useful to pose a problem for students so that they have the opportunity to see why different fund entities are used to preserve the integrity of special revenues and borrowed monies. Instead of saying, "Governments use the following funds . . . ," etc., ask them what they would do to insure the integrity of three or four sources of funds, such as bond proceeds, a Federal grant, a restricted gift, and a special assessment. Let them explore the alternatives, and then teach them the basis of fund accounting. Bond sinking funds, which we in government call Debt Service Funds, make a good example of this principle.

Finally, let me give you one more brief example. We have a great opportunity in our auditing classes to study the scope of auditing beyond traditional financial audits. We can look at the AICPA Audit Standards and audit guides as well as the audit standards applicable to government programs and organizations, as set forth recently by the Comptroller General of the United States. There is no question but what CPAs are going to be doing a lot of performance auditing in the years ahead, and we can do much to prepare them for it—not through separate auditing classes, though these would be helpful if we could fit them into the curriculum, but primarily through the integration of new material into our present auditing courses.

I have given but a few simple examples, highly oversimplified perhaps, and certainly not in the depth I would like to explore them, in the hopes that you will be stimulated to think about this approach more carefully. We need to do much research into these possibilities, to develop guidelines and materials that can readily be used, and to assist our teachers in becoming interested and knowledgeable enough to accomplish this objective. Nowhere, in my judgment, can the funds now available to this association be better used than in this area.

Accounting for Public Administration

I want to make a special appeal today to accounting educators to give more thought to what our responsibility is to public administration programs. I wish I had time to give you a full one-hour lecture on this subject, but a few comments will have to suffice for now.

In recent years we have seen a significant shift in many public administration schools away from schools of public policy and public affairs to schools of public management. In other words, the trend is more and more to educate students in the subjects appropriate to management responsibilities; and accounting is certainly one of these critical subjects. This trend reached its most significant milestone only two weeks ago when the National Association of Schools of Public Administration, meeting in Syracuse, adopted a resolution calling for accréditation standards that clearly require a much stronger core of management courses than ever before. Thus, we stand in a position to be of vital help if we can respond quickly and effectively.

I would like to see this association launch immediately an effort to develop an outline, together with appropriate teaching materials or references to materials already available, that can be used for at least one core course in accounting (or preferably two courses) to be offered in a professional MPA program. Such a course cannot be the same as the MBA course, for MPA students are not much concerned with inventory costing methods, alternative depreciation methods, corporate equity accounts, and many other matters on which we spend much time in the typical MBA course. I have been trying to develop such a course and teach it for the past three years in our own program, and I obviously have some ideas as to its content. What we need, however, is not only my ideas but those of many others as well. We also need some research to support our conclusions, not just the weighted opinion of a few educators.

A Plan of Action

There are so many other facets of this subject which could be explored that it is difficult to cut our discussion off at this point. However, it is necessary that we consider a plan of action to follow up on what we have already discussed.

I suggest that this association fund a project that would have the following objectives:

Identify the critical issues in public sector and not-for-profit accounting that can be taught as an integral part of the accounting curriculum and suggest appropriate ways in which this integration might occur.

Develop or identify appropriate sources of teaching material to accomplish the integration in teaching, and/or recommend additional more comprehensive studies necessary to accomplish this objective.

Determine, in the light of current needs and developments in the public sector and among other not-for-profit organizations, the appropriate subject matter for an advanced elective within the accounting curriculum, both with and without the integrative teaching contemplated above.

Identify the unique needs and propose a model course outline for the core requirement in an MPA program which emphasizes management skills. (This might also include other programs, such as hospital administration, etc.)

Prepare a model curriculum, or propose a separate study to accomplish the same, for a specialization or concentration in public-sector accounting. Such a specialization might occur in the undergraduate program, but is more likely to occur in professional graduate programs or professional schools of accountancy.

Explore and make recommendations for cooperative research projects with other professional organizations, and with government agencies (such as U. S. General Accounting Office, Office of Management and Budget, etc.).

This proposal may encompass too much for an initial effort, but if we look at all of these aspects together, making appropriate recommendations for additional studies where necessary, we are likely to achieve our ultimate objectives much better. We cannot start with a little piece of the problem. We must look at the whole, define our problems and identify our opportunities, then set our priorities and move ahead.

In conclusion, it is my firm conviction that nowhere in the

development of accounting curriculum is there a greater opportunity for us to demonstrate that this discipline has something uniquely relevant and important to offer in making this world a better world than in the manner in which we respond to our challenges and opportunities in public-sector accounting.

Social Measurement in the Accounting Curriculum—Where and How?*

Ralph W. Estes

How should accounting educators respond to the developing phenomenon of social accounting? Should courses be modified, new courses instituted, programs altered? This paper will attempt to address these and other questions concerning the place of social accounting in accounting education.

What is social accounting? Not surprisingly for a developing area, there is a little agreement as to the boundaries. In this paper a rather broad definition will best serve, and social accounting will be taken to include:

1. accounting for and evaluating the impact of corporate social responsibility programs;
2. human resource accounting;
3. measurement of selected social costs;
4. measuring the full impact of an entity on society;
5. social reporting (reporting results of items 1-4);
6. accounting for public (governmental) programs.

About the only possible definition excluded is that of national income accounting, and it may not be possible to exclude even that meaning when considering the long run.

Short run and long run implications will be explored. The short run can be considered to run from the immediate present to somewhere around five or ten years. The long run of course picks up there, but we can adopt a focus of about twenty years.

This paper will not discuss in any depth the demand for social accounting, current practices, or detailed proposals for social measurement and reporting. These matters are already adequately covered in the literature; good bibliographies are contained in the following American Accounting Association committee reports:

Committee on Non-Financial Measures of Effectiveness, *The Accounting Review,* Supplement to Vol. XLVI (1971), pp. 164-211.

* Suggestions of Marc Epstein and David Linowes in the preparation of this paper are gratefully acknowledged.

Committee on Measures of Effectiveness for Social Programs, *The Accounting Review,* Supplement to Vol. XLVII (1972), pp. 336-96.

Committee on Environmental Effects of Organization Behavior, *The Accounting Review,* Supplement to Vol. XLVIII (1973), pp. 72-119.

Committee on Human Resource Accounting, *The Accounting Review,* Supplement to Vol. XLVIII (1973), pp. 168-185.

Nor will detailed prescriptions be attempted here. Projection of the broader role of social accounting in accounting education is treacherous enough; attempts at detailed course prescriptions might be fun but they would not be useful. As in financial statements, I'm "rounding to the nearest thousand."

The Short Run: Keeping Our Options Open

Obviously we cannot predict the ultimate of social accounting. Some of us believe it marks the beginning of a major expansion of the boundaries of accounting; others hold it to be a passing fad, a curiosity. Until our crystal ball clears a bit, our educational stance should be a flexible one. It would be wrong to completely restructure programs at this time; it would be equally wrong to make no changes and risk graduating accountants with inadequate preparation for the demands they may face.

I believe our primary response should be to weave new material into present courses. In addition, separate courses or seminars might be instituted at more schools (several already exist). Encouragement should be given to the writing of theses and papers on social accounting within present programs. Continuing education seminars should be developed. And we should periodically consider modifications in the "Common Body of Knowledge" and in requirements for the CPA certificate, although such changes do not as yet appear warranted.

Modifying Present Courses

Social accounting material might be introduced into present undergraduate courses as shown in Exhibit 1. At the introductory level descriptive material should be presented dealing with evaluation of the impact of corporate social responsibility programs and activities, human resource accounting, the concept of evaluating and reporting an entity's full impact on society, and the use of accounting in controlling and evaluating public programs. These modifications would be consistent with the recommendations of the Price Waterhouse Foundation study *A New Introduction to Accounting* as well as the concluding objective proposed by the AICPA Study Group on the Objectives of Financial Statements (the "Trueblood Committee"):

> An objective of financial statements is to report on those activities of the enterprise affecting society which can be determined and described or measured and which are important to the role of the enterprise in its social environment.

Management accounting courses should include consideration of the techniques for assessing the effects of corporate social responsibility programs (such as favorable loan or credit terms for inner city businesses, pollution control programs, recycling efforts, and plant beautification schemes); valuing human resources; and quantifying and even assigning money values to social costs. Here the approach should be analytical, and should give attention to survey and interview techniques, shadow pricing, economic research studies, cost-benefit analysis, psychological testing, present value analysis, and non-financial measures of effectiveness.

The intermediate financial course should include appropriate attention to increased disclosure in financial statements such as (1) the requirements recently promulgated by the SEC concerning the financial effects of compliance with environmental protection laws; and (2) the recommendations of the American Accounting Association's Committee on Environmental Effects of Organization Behavior to disclose environmental problems, abatement goals of the organization, progress in achieving these goals, and material environmental effects on financial position, earnings and business activities. These courses might also consider approaches to and ramifications of reporting human resource values, social costs, and other values not confirmed in market transactions.

Either in the section of advanced financial courses dealing with governmental and fund accounting or in separate government accounting courses, attention should be given to the emerging importance of program budgeting and PPBS to evaluate and control social programs.

Accounting theory courses should explore various approaches to valuing social effects, with emphasis on theoretical soundness more than measurement techniques. This also seems to be the most appropriate place to consider alternative approaches to measuring the total impact of an entity on society, and integration of values for

EXHIBIT 1
Social Accounting in Undergraduate Courses

	Introductory	Management	Intermediate	Advanced	Theory	Tax	Auditing	Information Systems
Accounting for corporate social responsibility programs	X	X				X	X	X
Human resource accounting	X	X	X					
Social cost measurement	X	X			X			X
Total impact of entity on society			X		X			X
Social reporting	X		X	X			X	
Accounting for public programs	X			X				

externalities along with presently measured financial / economic effects into a comprehensive reporting model.

Income tax effects of social responsibility programs should be covered in the tax courses. Special incentives and write-offs for investment in pollution control equipment and tax minimization through charitable contributions are among the effects which might be considered.

As noted above, the SEC now requires disclosure of the financial effects of compliance with environmental protection laws and an AAA committee has recommended even more disclosure relative to environmental problems. Today's auditor must be able to satisfy himself as to the fairness of such disclosures; tomorrow's auditor may attest to substantially expanded disclosure possibly including values associated with human resources and with social costs. The auditing courses should deal with acquisition and verification of appropriate evidence supporting these disclosures and with wording of qualifications when adequate evidence cannot be obtained. These courses should also add some study of state and federal environmental protection requirements so the auditor can determine whether his client is in compliance or whether the client faces possible litigation (the SEC requires disclosure of even those legal proceedings merely "known to be contemplated by governmental authorities"). Although the SEC has not spoken explicitly in the area of civil rights litigation, the auditor should also investigate whether his client's financial statements disclose possible litigation and contingent liabilities due to noncompliance with Equal Employment Opportunity Commission requirements and guidelines; attesting to this area of social reporting should also be considered in auditing courses.

The study of financial accounting, tax, and auditing is heavily influenced by regulations and pronouncements of governmental and professional bodies (GAAP, Internal Revenue Code, auditing standards, SEC regulations); courses in these areas will generally be dominated by attention to these requirements. Information systems, like management accounting, is not so constrained. There are no external rules; if it works it's valid. For this reason the study of information systems must encompass the *wants* of management as well as external reporting requirements. And more and more executives are asking for social accounting information. A recent survey by George Steiner for the Committee for Economic Development revealed that 76% of the companies surveyed had recently attempted to inventory or assess their socially relevant activities; while 46% of the responding executives thought that social audits of business firms would be *required* in the future. Many, probably most, of the attempts at social audits or assessments to date have been frustrated and delayed by the lack of desired information within the information system. In studying the design of information systems, we must begin to recognize this new and growing information demand, and structure the systems accordingly.

Materials for these proposed course modifications must come primarily from journal articles for now, but new accounting texts should include text and problems covering relevant facets of social accounting. There is also a growing body of case material dealing with social accounting issues available from the Intercollegiate Case Clearing House.

Accounting instructors need to become familiar with social accounting issues and problems if they are to make the course changes recommended. Diligent individual study of the literature is an effective but not efficient approach; a more practical answer would be an AAA workshop on social accounting for accounting educators, similar to the quantitative methods and behavioral science workshops.

Integration of social accounting material throughout the undergraduate curriculum appears to be the best way to deal with this developing dimension of accounting in the short run. Another possibility, which can be used along with the integration approach, is to create new courses.

New Courses

Separate courses in social accounting are more appropriate at the graduate level during the present stage of development. A separate course does not appear to be justified at the undergraduate level unless it is in the style of a special studies course, a course in current issues in accounting, an honors seminar, or the like.

Every instructor will structure his course differently, so I will not try to recommend an "ideal" course outline; instead I will briefly describe three courses presently offered at three different schools.

New York University. Lee Seidler's course "Socioeconomic Accounting" has the following catalog description:

Considers the development and application of measurement concepts and skills beyond the boundaries of present enterprise accounting. Principally concerned with attempts to increase the validity and objectivity of measurements of social importance. Topics include the determination and measurement of the social costs and benefits of enterprises, both public and private; development of techniques for the selection and control of government social programs; development and application of devices such as pollution taxes; measurement of the values of human inputs and outputs and interaction of social goals with conventional financial reporting. The role of the professional accountant in the social dimension is also considered.[1]

The students include both MBA and Ph.D. candidates, with about 25 per cent coming from public administration, education, and library sciences. Students undertake research projects alone or in teams on such topics as "The Social Audit of X Corporation," "A Social Income Statement for NYU," "The Delivery System for Public Education," and "The Metropolitan Transit Authority." A wide variety of materials is used ranging from Plato through Locke, Rousseau, Churchman, The Federalist Papers, U.S. statutes, court decisions, Flamholtz, Baumol, and cases. About one-third of the course deals with philosophical background; the emphasis on techniques of social measurement has increased each time the course has been offered.

University of Illinois. David Linowes of Laventhol Krekstein Horwath & Horwath introduced a course in "Socio-Economic Accountability" at the University of Illinois this spring. Topics covered include:

The General Concepts of Socio-Economic Accountability
The Accountant's Enlarged Professional and Social Responsibilities
Accountability of Public Institutions
Social Responsibilities of Corporations
Measuring Social Programs in Business—State of the Art
Socio-Economic Management Audits
Socio-Economic Operating Statements (A form of "Social Audit")
Accountability for Human Needs
Social Targets and Funding
Techniques for Stimulating Performance
The Power of Visibility (to induce desired results)
The Power of Innovation
The Beginning and Ending of Accountability

Linowes requires a "thesis" of about thirty pages on some aspect or application of socio-economic accountability. Materials range widely over the current accounting literature with emphasis on Linowes' *Strategies for Survival* (Amacom), Estes' *Accounting and Society* (Melville Publishing Co.), and Eli Goldston's Carnegie-Mellon Lectures, *The Quantification of Concern: Some Aspects of Social Accounting*. The dual emphases in Linowes' course appear to be social accounting in corporations and application of business management and control principles to public institutions.

Wichita State University. At WSU a social reporting model[2] is being used to provide a framework for estimating the full benefits and costs of a university, in the graduate accounting research seminar. The objectives are to (1) develop knowledge of and skill in research method through practice, (2) learn to confront and deal with a variety of "soft" measurements such as those encountered regularly by the practicing accountant, and (3) develop a perspective on social accounting. Emphasis in the research is on empirical data collection, innovative measurement approaches, and assignment of money values to non-monetary quantities. Materials used include Bauer & Fenn's *The Corporate Social Audit* (Russel Sage Foundation), Forcese & Richer's *Social Research Methods* (Prentice-Hall, Inc.), and government reports. A similar approach is used in a special studies course where an individual may undertake a social benefits costs evaluation of a business firm; presently one student is developing an evaluation of a local manufacturing firm.

The three approaches are quite different although there are similarities; this is to be expected at this stage in the development of social accounting. They are not offered as models of the "right" approach to courses in social accounting or of good pedagogy, but merely as examples of possible approaches.

Other Approaches

Obviously social accounting is a valid field for research in support of theses and course papers. But we should not overlook the need for continuing education programs—professional accountants are likely to desire an opportunity to learn of the potential and problems of this emerging field, especially when they receive inquiries from clients and management about it. In fact, the dynamic nature of social accounting with its potential for continuous change and development may require regular continuing education or management development seminars for many years.

The Short Run: Summary

The need for social accounting information, as well as progress in "real world" practices have been documented elsewhere (see list of bibliographies cited earlier); it seems clear to me that some accommodation is necessary in accounting education. Because of the dynamic nature of social accounting and the presently unstable "state of the art," I believe we should move firmly but deliberately; overreaction can be as costly to our students as no reaction. Thus I believe the best approach at present is to integrate a limited amount of material from social accounting into several undergraduate courses immediately, followed by gradual modification of such material and expansion, if this proves warranted.

Separate courses in social accounting can be justified but not, in my opinion, as requirements in the present undergraduate curriculum. Such courses do offer an opportunity, however, for research and experimentation which can extend the boundaries of social accounting. We should also consider offering seminars for practicing accountants to enable them to keep up to date on the latest concepts, advances, and applications of social accounting.

The Long Run: A Global Perspective

Long range predictions are dangerous and even ridiculous. After such a statement, we can invariably expect long range predictions. This paper will not break the pattern.

In a somewhat specific sense, the future will quite possibly bring attempts to assess entities for their external diseconomies and to reward them for external economies. For example, corporations may be assessed for air pollution and fined for racial discrimination, but rewarded for recycling programs; we can already find precedents. The logical conclusion of this approach would be an evaluation of the total impact—economic and "noneconomic"—of an entity on society. A positive net, or social surplus, would result in a governmental payment to the entity or possibly a credit balance in a central account (much like overpayment of income taxes). A negative net, or social deficit, would lead to an assessment or a reduction in a previous credit balance. This approach, which seems neither illogical nor unlikely when present trends are fully considered, would require measurement, reporting, and possibly independent attestation of all material social effects of an entity, including those not confirmed in market transactions. It would require rather massive additions of social accounting and measurement material to the accounting curriculum.

While this specific outcome is a possibility, it won't happen just as I've described it, simply because we are never very accurate in really long range predictions. But the lead time for accounting program changes is apparently long enough that we must at least attempt to predict the *direction* of change.3

When I think of social accounting in the context of the evolution of the whole of accounting,4 it seems to be a continuation of a trend toward extending the boundaries of accounting much as cost accounting, then management accounting, forecasting and budgeting, management advisory services, and program budgeting have pushed out those boundaries in the past. Why will the boundaries not stay put? I think it is because they have been artificially defined, or at least perceived, in the past.

But there must be some boundaries; accounting doesn't include the whole of existence. (Our problem here is roughly that of defining a system; we can always expand our definition repeatedly until we have included the universe and all that can be conceived—and possibly more.) Examination of numerous definitions of accounting as well as the variety of practices leads me to the conclusion that the only common concepts which are universally included are those of information and communication.

There appears to be a natural process in the world as we perceive it, centered around information and communication. This process is illustrated in Exhibit 2. Accounting's pervasive role in this process is easy to see; we are concerned with practically every step. But it is interesting to note the applicability of the process to other disciplines. History is involved with steps I-IV plus VIII, and possibly others in between. Medical diagnoses require I-III plus IX. Journalism is based on I-VIII (storage and retrieval occur as a story is researched and developed). Research methodology, law practice, library science, computer science, and photography are other fields in which the concern is with these steps in the process rather than the results of the process. (Management, production, philosophy, engineering, and political science are examples of disciplines which tend to focus on the action results rather than the information and communication process leading up to those results.) In other words, the process presented in Exhibit 2 circumscribes a large portion of human endeavor and study, presently compartmentalized into several different disciplines of which accounting is one.

Now, social accounting forces us to pay attention to questions like (moving from the bottom up in Exhibit 2):

To whom should we report?

What information do they need or desire?

EXHIBIT 2
Natural Process of Information and Communication

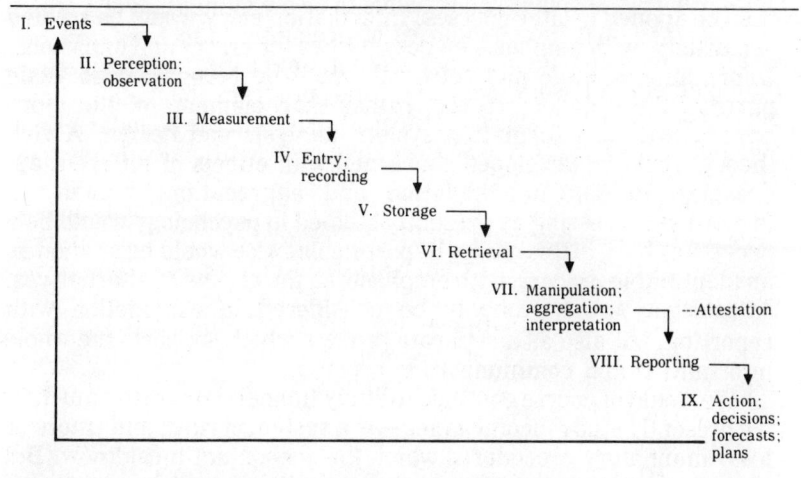

I. Events
→ II. Perception; observation
→ III. Measurement
→ IV. Entry; recording
→ V. Storage
→ VI. Retrieval
→ VII. Manipulation; aggregation; interpretation → ···Attestation
→ VIII. Reporting
→ IX. Action; decisions; forecasts; plans

In what form and what degree of aggregation do they want this information?

Do we have it in our information system at present?

Should we have it there?

How frequently should data be entered?

How do we measure the social phenomena and effects?

Are our perceptions biased or defective?

What events or phenomena are we interested in?

Of course these are essentially the questions we were interested in before we became interested in social accounting, but I don't know that we looked at them in the context of this global information and communication process.

From this analysis and reasoning, my conclusion is that our long run concern in accounting education should be to focus on the global information and communication process and its individual elements, rather than on the dimensions of accounting as presently accepted. Thus, we would study philosophy and psychology as these fields pertain to our perceptive abilities. Measurement would become a distinguishable part of the early accounting curriculum, constituting several credit hours, and the techniques studied would then be applied in later courses. Information entry would be studied separately, with emphasis on possibilities for errors and omissions. Information storage and retrieval would be recognized as basic parts of the broader process, rather than elements of the more narrow area of information system analysis and design. A rich theory would be developed concerned with effects of different approaches to data manipulation and aggregation; human information processing as presently studied in psychology would be a necessary base to this study. Reporting likewise would be studied as an identifiable *process,* with emphasis on the effects of alternatives. Attestation would probably be considered in conjunction with reporting, but also as a separate process which supports the whole information and communication process.

We would of course continue to study financial reporting much as we presently study income taxes—as a system of rules and (more or less) mandatory procedures which the accountant must know. But the basic core of the accounting curriculum would be structured around the steps in the process presented in Exhibit 2.

Well, would this really be accounting? No—not as accounting is defined and perceived today. But when we really get down to trying to define the boundaries of present day accounting, we come intriguingly close to this general process. For example:

Is "accounting" restricted to business entities? No.

Does "accounting" deal only with money quantities? No.

Does "accounting" require specific forms of data entry and storage, such as journals and ledgers? No.

Is there general agreement as to the events which can properly be recognized in "accounting"? No.

Is there any limit on the range of audiences for "accounting" reports? No.

As we continue this questioning process, we continue to strip away most of our perceived boundaries until we are left pretty much with the general information and communication process.[5]

Conclusions and Recommendations

Many companies are engaged in assessing their social performance and the effects of various social responsibility programs.

Some are reporting the results. New disclosure requirements with respect to environmental effects are being placed on companies and thus on auditors. Human resource accounting, especially for internal planning and decision purposes, is being adopted by a growing number of companies. Government agencies at all levels are engaged in efforts to better evaluate and account for social programs. And new social accounting proposals—for measurement, evaluation, and reporting approaches—spring forth with every new moon. It appears that the time has come to start paying some attention to social accounting in the accounting curriculum.

The recommendation in this paper is for firm but gradual implementation of social accounting material into present undergraduate courses, beginning at the introductory level. The nature and extent of such material can be modified as time passes, in response to changes in practice. Separate courses dealing with social accounting are tempting but ought to be viewed as a temporary compromise, except for professional development courses which will be required on a continuing basis.

In the long run, social accounting is viewed as a significant development in forcing accounting to shuck off its presently perceived boundaries, to ultimately become a discipline concerned with the broad and general process of information and communication. Such an evolution would require a complete restructuring of the accounting curriculum in the direction of dealing with elements of that general process.

In accordance with these conclusions, the following specific recommendations for the American Accounting Association are offered:

1. Encourage integration of social accounting material into existing courses.

2. Consider preparation of text, case, and other course material to facilitate this integration (commercial book publishers are constrained by the need to make a profit, and may be reluctant to provide these materials as soon as needed).

3. Develop a social accounting workshop for accounting educators at all levels.

4. Develop a professional development course in social accounting for practitioners, or encourage and assist the AICPA in developing such a course.

5. Appoint a committee to investigate and evaluate the curriculum, professional, and social implications of the evolution of the field of accounting into a global information and communication process.

Serious consideration of these recommendations should assure that the American Accounting Association and accounting educators are alert to and prepared for the impact of social accounting on accounting education.

FOOTNOTES

1. Taken from Thomas J. Burns, *Accounting Trends VII* (McGraw-Hill, 1973).

2. Ralph W. Estes, "A Comprehensive Corporate Social Reporting Model," paper presented at the Twentieth International Meeting of The Institute of Management Science, Tel Aviv, June 1973.

3. This lead time might be estimated generally as follows:

Perception of need for material change in curriculum	Cumulative Time
	0.0 years
Professional committee appointed to study	1.0
Committee issues report	2.0
Report published	2.8
First courses developed	3.0-4.0
General need perceived	5.0-9.0
Textbooks produced	6.0-10.0
Numerous institutions add courses	8.0-14.0
Major curriculum changes	10.0-18.0

This is even longer than it took to introduce the Vega!

4. At this point the paper leaves its solid empirical base of only 97 per cent opinion and becomes 100 per cent opinion. This may not be an uncommon percentage when we are predicting the future.

5. Few would accept a description of this general process as a definition of accounting today (but indeed, a few *would*). One of the obstacles, perhaps the major obstacle, is the word *accounting* itself. This word triggers an impression in our minds which describes the world of accounting *as it is now practiced*. Thus it is difficult to accept extension of that word's boundaries until accountants start to get involved in new developments like social accounting and push those boundaries back.

So perhaps we need a new word. A word to describe the global process of information and communication, and thus a word to define the broader discipline in which we are really involved and which we may be studying in twenty or so years. Perhaps we should purge *accounting*, with its artificial boundaries, from our vocabularies, as we have tried to purge such words as *reserve* and *surplus*.

Social Measurement in the Accounting Curriculum—Where and How?

A Critique
R. Lee Brummet

I think that Ralph Estes' paper provides very reasonable and appropriate suggestions for the introduction and integration of social accounting into undergraduate accounting curricula. He summarizes well in his introductory comments on The Short Run: Keeping Our Options Open in saying, "I believe our primary response should be to weave new material into present courses. In addition, separate courses or seminars might be instituted at more schools . . . encouragement should be given to the writing of theses and papers on social accounting within present programs. Continuing education seminars should be developed."

I see that Estes was asked to prepare a paper on social measurement and he chose to prepare a paper on social accounting. This gives me the opportunity to react with regard to definitions of the various areas that might be involved. I dislike definitions to the extent that they constrain and establish boundaries. Yet we need to have some understanding of the subjects with which we are dealing so I would like to react to the areas mentioned on the first page of Ralph's paper. Here Ralph has listed six possible areas of social accounting as well as mentioning national income accounting. His items (4) and (5) tend to say it all. He might have added the attest function as a separate item. While we might also consider national income accounting, I believe this subject is not really within the area of our concern here unless, in fact, he is thinking of social indicators. I suggest that national income accounting is the macro aspect of conventional enterprise accounting while social indicators is the macro aspect of enterprise social accounting.

While we might consider the propriety of including human resource accounting within the accounting curriculum I do not consider this to be a logical subset of the field of social accounting. It is true that certain socio-psychological kinds of measurement may apply in both of these areas, but the two subjects are in a sense contrary notions. I consider human resource accounting to be involved in the measurement and reporting of the significance of people to an organization whereas social accounting involves accounting for the significance of the organization to people.

An important general theme that should accompany extensions of our accounting material into the social field should relate to definitions of the entity and the public to which that entity is responsible. No longer is it adequate to consider entity boundaries as they relate only to financial transactions and to creditors and stockholders. Students should be encouraged to think of a much broader entity that involves externalities related to the firms' activities and all of the publics upon which the firm impacts.

While I might add another "X" or two in Exhibit 1, I think that this set-up is a good way of viewing the points within a typical curriculum where social measurements and social accounting should be involved.

While the objectives study group report provides some basis for a take-off into the area of social accounting, I am disappointed that it did not provide stronger support. The quotation from this report at least provides some legitimacy for the subject and is appropriately indicated in Ralph's paper.

As we consider the social accounting possibilities within the field of management accounting I think we should add to Ralph's suggestions the possibilities in the fields of budgeting and planning. As business managers consciously determine objectives of their organizations to relate to social well-being, accounting can be of assistance in the articulation of such goals as well as the measurement of performance in relationship to them. An additional possibility in this area relates to the impacts of budgets and financial plans upon employee satisfaction and well-being. This can give the subject of accounting and behavioral sciences a kind of new orientation.

Ralph refers to a "comprehensive reporting model" in his section on Modifying Present Courses. This is a very appealing notion, but, I am not optimistic that we will be able to integrate social measurement into such a model very soon. The important point is that we should proceed to do the best we can without forcing total integration. We should not delay our efforts until a totally integrated model becomes available.

Referring to the possible expanded role for the auditor and the attest function, I think social measurement provides a natural lead into the subject of performance or effectiveness auditing. This is a field that is bound to increase in its significance in practice as well as in our curriculum development.

Ralph has given us a glimpse at three examples of courses now being offered by Lee Seidler, David Linowes and himself. Of this group I tend to favor the approach taken by Ralph in his course because of its practical nature and because of its emphasis upon measurement as opposed to social philosophy.

We are likely to see substantial new materials available in the field of social accounting within the next few years. The Committee on Social Measurement of the American Institute of Certified Public Accountants is in the process of putting together a monograph on social measurement of some twelve or thirteen chapter length. It should be published within the next year. The National Association of Accountants is providing research funds for projects in the social accounting area that should provide useful information for classroom application. The American Accounting Association has had committees working in the area of social measurements over the last few years with several reports of the work of these committees in *The Accounting Review Committee Reports Supplement*. It is likely that this work will continue.

The second part of Ralph's two part paper is titled The Long Run: A Global Perspective. While this section is not an integral and necessary part of his recommendations I think that it is appropriate. The extension of accounting measurements into areas of social concern opens the door for a much broader look at the nature of the accounting field as a substantial part of the measurement and communication functions in society. While Ralph chooses to use the terms information and communication I think that we are not likely to differ in our views on this subject. We might of course use Ralph's Exhibit 2 as a setting for the entire accounting curriculum, but as Ralph understands, this will take a while. We should perhaps pursue extensions including that of social accounting a bit further before we turn the pyramid over completely and approach the subject of measurement and communication of which accounting may find a role as an important subset. I am in full agreement with Ralph's summary recommendations in the last two paragraphs of his paper.

Summation

The Steering Committee

The origins of the proposal for this symposium were in the deliberations of the 1971-72 Advisory Committee to the AAA Director of Education. Since that committee was intent on completing its recommendations for an Outstanding Accounting Educator Award and a Monograph on Accounting Education, a decision was made to carry the symposium idea over to the 1972-73 year.

Subsequently, the development of the symposium became the main thrust of the 1972-73 Advisory Committee's deliberations. By February of 1973 a preliminary proposal was developed. This proposal as well as some ideas flowing from the 1972-73 AAA Committee on Accounting Education formed the basis for a series of discussions between AAA Presidents Robert Sprouse (1972-73) and Robert Anthony (1973-74), 1974-75 President-Elect R. Lee Brummet, and William Gifford, Secretary of the Price Waterhouse Foundation which resulted in the $100,000 Price Waterhouse Foundation grant to AAA announced at the August 1973 AAA Annual Conference.

The Price Waterhouse Foundation grant was placed under the guidance of the AAA Standing Committee on Accounting Education chaired by Harold Q. Langenderfer, AAA Director of Education (1971-73). Shortly thereafter it was decided to implement the symposium plan as the first step in furthering the intended purposes of the grant. After consultation among Harold Q. Langenderfer, Doyle Z. Williams, current AAA Director of Education, and William L. Ferrara, a specific symposium format with suggested topics and speakers was developed and a steering committee was formalized to help implement the symposium plan.

In a short period of time all symposium participants were selected. The response of the participants was overwhelmingly enthusiastic especially in terms of the way they responded to invitations to participate and their meeting of deadlines for their papers and critiques.

Even casual perusal of the symposium program will attest to the fact that an outstanding group of educators, representative of the breadth of accounting education, was brought together for the symposium. In addition there were educators experienced in educational administration and representatives of a variety of relevant professional accounting activities and organizations. This combination of talents and backgrounds yielded the provocative interchange of ideas resulting in the following consensus recommendation:

> Appoint a select task force of approximately five to seven members who would initiate and supervise a study designed to determine, develop and test the content of the "accounting core" as discussed in the body of this report.

All remaining Price Waterhouse Foundation funds should be allocated to implementing this recommendation. A series of other recommendations or suggestions related to the above were also made. These will be considered in succeeding pages.

A review of the papers and critiques presented indicates without a doubt that the overwhelming majority of the participants took their assignments very seriously. Their papers, as was intended, identified a number of problem areas in the accounting curriculum. Since these papers were judged (by all symposium participants) to have great value to all interested in accounting education, Robert N. Anthony, 1973-74 President of the American Accounting Association, has approved making available at cost all papers and critiques to interested parties.

Creating a Task Force

Perhaps the best way to approach the task force's role is to recognize that a number of innovative approaches to teaching introductory accounting[1] as well as the various accounting specialties have come upon us in the past few years and we have not really spent much time and effort considering their impact on the accounting curriculum. It was the overwhelming majority opinion of the symposium participants that the greatest need and opportunity for curriculum research in accounting is in the area of the "accounting core," that is, the collection of courses, modules or study units that fits between the study of introductory accounting and the various accounting specialties as briefly outlined in Exhibit I. At first blush one might think only of "intermediate" accounting in this context; however, this is not appropriate unless we are thinking of an "intermediate" accounting which represents that collection of accounting subject matter which *every* accounting major should be required to take and be expected to understand.

Exhibit I

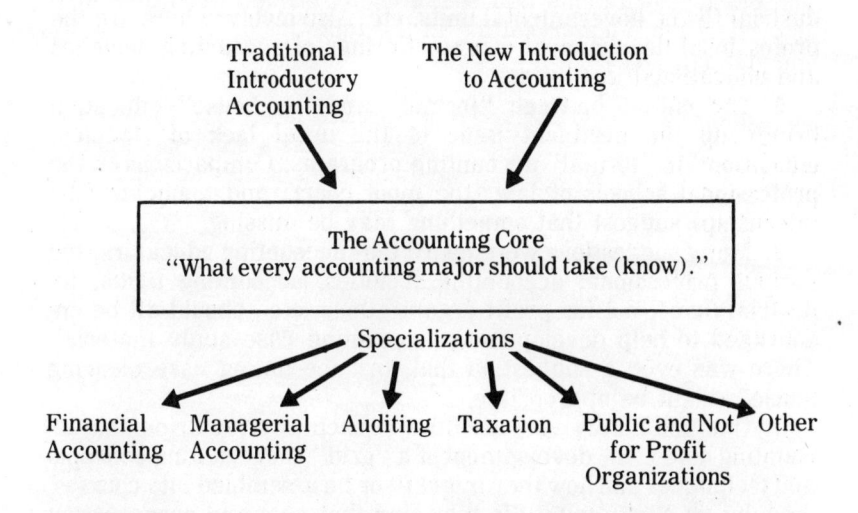

```
    Traditional          The New Introduction
    Introductory              to Accounting
    Accounting
            ↘                ↙
    ┌─────────────────────────────────────────┐
    │        The Accounting Core              │
    │ "What every accounting major should take (know)." │
    └─────────────────────────────────────────┘
                    Specializations
       ↙        ↙        ↓       ↓       ↘         ↘
  Financial  Managerial  Auditing  Taxation  Public and Not  Other
  Accounting Accounting                      for Profit
                                             Organizations
```

The determination of what should be included in the required core is no small task and neither is the development and testing of appropriate materials. But this should be the charge to the task force and their efforts should be facilitated through their ability to hire and supervise an appropriate combination of research and teaching talents.

Among the many issues and thoughts that the task force should consider as researchable ideas related to the definition and structure of an accounting core are the following which were suggested by symposium participants:

1. Integration with both the "traditional" introductory accounting and the "new" introductory accounting. With the "new" introduction, the function and social role of accounting is stressed as opposed to the preparation of accounting information.[2] Thus the new approach (to whatever extent it's ultimately adopted) anticipates that the accounting majors' studies of accounting essentially start rather than continue with the first course beyond introductory accounting.

2. Determination of that portion of each accounting specialization which should be considered part of the "core." The "core" should thus include some minimum coverage of the various accounting specialties.

3. A researchable issue may very well be the extent to which the "accounting core" does or does not fall short of meeting minimum

requirements for entry into the profession (broadly conceived).

4. The cut-off between formal collegiate degree oriented education and the "in house" education of accounting firms, industrial firms, governmental units, etc. Also involved here are the professional development course offerings of accounting societies and educational institutions.

5. The cut-off between "formal" and "in house" education brings up the pertinent issue of the usual lack of "clinical education" in "formal" accounting programs. Comparisons to the professional schools of law (the moot court) and medicine (the internship) suggest that something may be missing.

6. Many suggestions were heard that accounting educators, the various professional accounting societies, accounting firms, industrial firms, not for profit organizations, etc., should all be encouraged to help develop more accounting case study material. There was even a suggestion that an "accounting case clearing house" might be appropriate.

7. One potentially very useful approach to structuring the accounting core is the development of a "grid" of accounting concepts and techniques and how they might fit or be assembled into courses, modules or study units. We may find that past and even current practices in course structure are unnecessarily duplicative and not really relevant to the future.

The following suggestions were made to serve as guidelines in setting up and implementing the activities of the task force:

1. The researchers hired to determine and "flesh out" the accounting core should be expected to produce a research report which should be widely disseminated.

2. The "task force" should serve as an advisory board to the researchers, advising as to the research design, relevance of issues, validity of the conclusions reached and operational feasibility of the recommendations.

3. Upon completion and dissemination of the above research report, accounting educators (and institutions) should be invited to submit proposals for developing means of implementing the recommendations of the report. Implementation proposals might include developing multi-media modules as well as text and case materials.

4. The "task force" should probably serve as the group which decides which of the implementing proposals should be accepted and supported within the limits of remaining funds.

5. The "task force" could itself serve as an advisory board to each group of researchers chosen or it could set up separate advisory groups for each implementing proposal.

Summation

6. All materials developed should, insofar as possible, be widely disseminated and should be made readily available without any copyright constraints.

If the results of the efforts and resources expended by the task force are to have a significant impact, then follow through in the form of a series of seminars or workshops around the country may be essential.

FOOTNOTES

1. The Price Waterhouse Foundation sponsored *A New Introduction to Accounting* (1971) as well as the many *Introductory Financial Accounting* and *Introductory Managerial Accounting* textbooks of recent years are illustrative.

2. *A New Introduction to Accounting*, p. iii.